SOCIAL PSYCHOLOGY

302
THE
(Ref) CL

THEORY AND SOCIAL PSYCHOLOGY

EDITED BY ROGER SAPSFORD, ARTHUR STILL, DOROTHY MIELL, RICHARD STEVENS and MARGARET WETHERELL

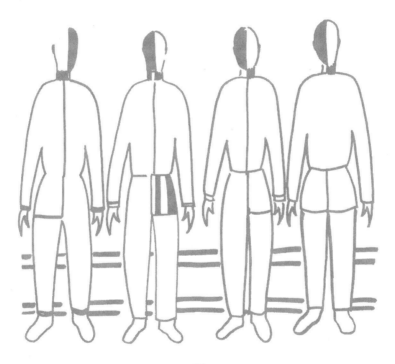

SAGE Publications
London • Thousand Oaks • New Delhi
In association with

The Open
University

Cover illustration: Kasimir Malevich, *Sportsmen*, c. 1928–32, oil on canvas, 142 x 164cm., State Russian Museum, St Petersburg.

The Open University, Walton Hall, Milton Keynes, MK7 6AA

SAGE Publications Ltd
6 Bonhill Street,
London, EC2A 4PU

SAGE Publications Inc
2455 Teller Road,
Newbury Park,
California, 91320

SAGE Publications India Pvt Ltd
32, M Block Market,
Greater Kailash – 1
New Delhi 110 048

British Library Cataloguing in Publication Data

A catalogue record for this book is available from the British Library.

ISBN 0 7619 5838 X
ISBN 0 7619 5839 8 (pbk)

Library of Congress catalog record available

Edited, designed and typeset by The Open University.
Printed in the United Kingdom by The Cromwell Press Ltd., Trowbridge, Wiltshire.

This text is based on one which forms part of an Open University course *D317 Social Psychology: Personal Lives, Social Worlds*. Details of this and other Open University courses can be obtained from the Course Reservations and Sales Centre, PO Box 724, The Open University, Milton Keynes, MK7 6ZS. For availability of other course components, contact Open University Worldwide, The Berrill Building, Walton Hall, Milton Keynes, MK7 6AA.

1.1

Contents

PART I

NATURE AND ORIGINS

Preface to Part I

This is not a textbook of social psychology as such; rather, it examines the foundations on which social psychology is built. Its main aim is to raise and discuss important issues which underlie the different endeavours which are included within the boundaries of the discipline. It presents some of the questions about the nature of the discipline which have emerged from the discipline's very existence – 'meta-issues' such as 'What is social psychology for?' and 'What kind of knowledge is possible in this area?'. Our aim has been to put the arguments clearly but in enough detail for the reader to be able to form a view (necessary for any student or practitioner) of what the discipline is about and how it is to be characterized.

The book is designed to stand alone, but it may also be read with profit in conjunction with textbooks of social psychology, in which case it will amplify and provide a more theoretical base for the substantive theory and research which they describe. Its original version was published in 1996 as part of an Open University course on social psychology, and this new version is still particularly suitable as a companion to the three published books which form the bulk of this course: *Understanding the Self* (edited by Richard Stevens), *Social Interaction and Personal Relationships* (edited by Dorothy Miell and Rudi Dallos) and *Identities, Groups and Social Issues* (edited by Margaret Wetherell). Where readers of this book need information about substantive issues in social psychology, we have often suggested one or more of these three books as a good source, because they were all put together at the same time and inspired by the same general 'vision' of what the discipline is and could be.

A major problem for all of us in coming to grips with current social psychology is that there is so much of it and such great diversity of approach. Human behaviour, action, experience and social relations are conceived from a vast array of more or less independent and sometimes incompatible perspectives. A 'perspective', in the sense in which we are using it in this book, is a distinct vision of how human behaviour and experience is to be explained: it sets out the kinds of data which are to be relevant and the kinds of explanation which are to be seen as satisfactory. Thus biological social psychologists and social constructionists seem to inhabit different social worlds (compare the chapters by Toates and Wetherell in Stevens, 1996), and the systems perspective on group functioning (described, for example, by Rudi Dallos in Chapter 3 of Miell and Dallos, 1996) is equally distant from both.

A perspective is like a consistent and extended piece of science fiction. The author of a certain kind of science fiction asks 'What would it be like if... ?' – for example, what would be the consequences of some people living for ever, or of the invention of a cheap and sustainable power source? In something of the same way, the social psychologist asks 'How much can I explain if I assume that...?' Behaviourists, for example, ask 'How much can I explain by assuming that all behaviour and experience is ultimately controlled by environmental stimuli?' (to which the answer is that a surprising amount can be explained in this way – but not everything, most of us would say, and only under restrictive assumptions about what counts as an explanation). The social constructionist would ask 'How much can be explained by positing beliefs, and the self that believes them, as products of cultural and historical trends?' – an issue with which we are still grappling as a discipline.

The problem of defining social psychology is made more complex by the fact that its boundaries and its contents show considerable local variation. There are, for example, broad national traditions. The development of the discipline in Britain and the United States tends to have been influenced strongly by the notion of psychology as science. It is less concerned with the broader society and more concerned to demonstrate kinship with psychology as a whole. In France social psychology has been more philosophical and more influenced by sociology (though there is also a flourishing French experimental tradition). In the USA some of what we consider social psychology would be taught within sociology departments rather than psychology departments; conversely, some of what we would consider sociology in Britain would be taught in the USA as social psychology.

It is not always obvious, even, what social psychology is *not*, and this ambivalence is reflected in this book. It is not simply general psychology, the study of the structure and function of the human mind, but it is sometimes presented as a specialized branch of this; some branches of social psychology show an obvious affinity with the general discipline, while others seem quite distinct from it. It is not sociology – the study of social structures and social relations – but the distinction has always been clearer in Britain than in France (where classical sociological theory has had some influence on social psychology) or in the USA (where some of what is done by sociologists of the symbolic interactionist school shows strong affinities with some branches of social psychology). It is not psychotherapy, though it is often closely related to psychotherapy and influenced by it (see the chapter on 'Resisting social psychology' at the end of this volume). It is also not philosophy, but it faces many of the same questions as are faced by the 'philosophers of mind' and often requires a degree of philosophical competence beyond what is required of non-social disciplines. Although it is an 'academic' discipline, it has never for long inhabited an ivory tower of pure theory; its roots are in its widespread application to social problems and its contribution to social organisation (see Chapter 10, 'Using social psychology').

The first chapter of this book begins the task of grappling with diversity within the discipline, and with what makes social psychology a distinct area of study, by clustering the separate perspectives into three 'voices' which express different visions of what the scope and aims of the discipline should be and what methods and concepts are acceptable within it – three ways of conceiving of social psychology as a coherent field of study, determining what its 'problems' are and deciding ways of solving them. The three authors have written about 'scientific' social psychology, humanistic/experiential social psychology and critical social psychology, giving (necessarily) their own ways of looking at them but mostly expressing views which are reasonably typical of their perspective.

The second chapter is a history of social psychology, written to bring out the essential dichotomy which lies at social psychology's roots. Histories are accounts, of course – they cannot cover everything that could be said but select material to make a point about the present state of things. The chapter introduces a difference which will assume greater importance in the next part of the book, between 'cognitive' accounts of how we understand the world and 'embodiment' accounts of how we live as part of it – between psychology as the study of mind and psychology as the study of relationship (including the relationship of biological entities within the body and the species) and social location. This account places social psychology at the focus of one of our culture's great bifurcations – between individualistic explanation based on the assumption of essentially self-contained selves and social (or societal) explanation in terms of interrelated and historically produced systems of meaning and belief.

A point which emerges clearly in both chapters is that any conflict between perspectives is not just a matter of disagreement about how best to understand the human condition, important as understanding may be. The way in which we understand our lives and how we act as a result of this understanding have important practical consequences; disputes between psychologists are about ethics and politics as well as about knowledge. Overall the book has four main themes, all of which are addressed to some extent in every chapter.

1   The diversity of social psychology and how to come to terms with it.

2   The nature of knowledge: what kind of a discipline social psychology is, what legitimates its claims and how its conclusions are argued from its evidence.

3   Culture and values: the way in which social psychology expresses or resists the dominant beliefs of our culture. This expresses itself as a question about factual propositions – models of the nature of the person and of social relations and the social order. These factual propositions are value-linked, however: they call into question what kind of a thing the human being shall be and how social relations shall be ordered.

4 Politics and practice: how social psychology is applied and what impact it has on our ways of thinking and behaving – which is a political question.

References

Miell, D. and Dallos, R. (eds) (1996) *Social Interaction and Personal Relationships*, London, Sage.

Stevens, R. (ed.) (1996) *Understanding the Self*, London, Sage.

Wetherell, M. (ed.) (1996) *Identity, Groups and Social Issues*, London, Sage.

CHAPTER 1
DEFINING SOCIAL PSYCHOLOGY

By Margaret Wetherell with Patrick McGhee and Richard Stevens

1 Introduction

Most social psychology textbooks begin with a definition of their field. In thinking about these definitions, and the task of defining social psychology, I was reminded of this discussion between Humpty Dumpty and Alice in the children's classic *Alice Through the Looking Glass*:

> 'When *I* use a word', Humpty Dumpty said in rather a scornful tone, 'it means just what I choose it to mean – neither more nor less.'
>
> 'The question is', said Alice, 'whether you *can* make words mean different things.'
>
> 'The question is', said Humpty Dumpty, 'which is to be the master – that's all.'
>
> *(Lewis Carroll, reprinted 1962, p. 75)*

There is certainly no one final answer to the question 'what is social psychology?' The term has diverse meanings and there are struggles of the Humpty Dumpty kind over who is to be master – about whose definition is correct. But there is also a long history to discussions about the nature of social psychology which structure questions of definition. There are established canons of knowledge which constrain what we can make the words mean. In this chapter I want to look at some of the debates underlying different understandings of social psychology. These debates produce the wide range of approaches, definitions and perspectives found in the discipline but they also mark out some of the common ground for social psychologists' discussions with each other and with researchers from other disciplines.

2 Diversity in social psychology

As is noted in the Preface to this part of the book, one of the reasons for the diversity in definitions of social psychology is the existence of broad national traditions of scholarship, along with the splitting of social psychology between sociology and psychology departments. Social psychology as practised in Santa Barbara, California is different in many (but not all) respects from the social psychology found in Paris, in Barcelona, in Milton Keynes or in London. Similarly, it makes a big difference if social psychologists share their work space with social theorists, with cognitive neuro-psychologists or with psychoanalysts working in a clinical setting. Daily conversations about knotty problems of social stratification and social organization encourage a different view of the fundamental problems of social psychology, compared to conversations about hormones and neural nets, or mental health and child abuse.

These variations are not just institutional, however, they also reflect core disagreements about the nature of knowledge, understandings of the individual, and views on the role of science (disagreements about *epistemology*). So, even within one university department, there can be diverse views on what is truly social psychological research.

At this point, you should read the different characterizations of social psychology contained in Boxes 1.1, 1.2 and 1.3. These are polemical pieces written by three experienced social psychologists. Each author was asked to write from a particular perspective in response to the question 'What *should* social psychology be like?' You can see the answers as three extended, but preliminary, visions of social psychology.

In the first statement, in Box 1.1, Patrick McGhee argues for a strongly scientific approach and for an experimental social psychology which he describes as the dominant approach in social psychology at the moment. The second statement, in Box 1.2, comes from a humanistically and experientially-oriented social psychologist, Richard Stevens. The debate between experimental social psychologists stressing control and objectivity and experiential social psychologists stressing subjectivity, meaning and people's introspections has a long history in western intellectual thought, which Chapter 2 on the historical origins of social psychology will discuss.

In the final statement in Box 1.3 I try to develop a vision of a 'critical social psychology' which draws on currents and themes sometimes described as 'social constructionist'. This position piece develops the kind of social psychology found in pockets of Europe, the UK, the USA (often in communication studies departments) and other places. In the past, and still today, this approach has been associated more with the development of social psychology in sociology departments than psychology departments.

Inevitably, the position statements set out in the three boxes are simplifications of complex perspectives, designed to emphasize points of contrast rather than concordance. They should be read as *personal* accounts which draw on the views of wider constituencies in social psychology but which make no claim to represent accurately the range of views in these wider communities.

ACTIVITY 1.1   As you read, make notes on how each writer:

1   defines the scientific basis of social psychology

2   lays out the topics and focus of social psychology.

The Preface to Part I of this book, argues that many social psychologists could unite around the view that, whatever else it is, social psychology is *not* philosophy. If social psychology is a science, therefore, as the contrast term to philosophy, what kind of science do you think it should be?

BOX 1.1   Experimental social psychology

Patrick McGhee

Experimental social psychology is the dominant form of social psychology in North America and Europe (including the UK). Whether this dominance is desirable, secure or important is another matter, but dominant it is. The perspective of experimental social psychology is that the most scientifically efficient and intellectually rigorous method for understanding human social behaviour involves assuming that:

- social behaviour is objectively describable and measurable;

- social behaviour does not just happen spontaneously, randomly, chaotically or mysteriously but is caused by a range of factors internal and external to individuals;

- relationships between these factors and behaviour are regular (i.e. lawful) in a way which generally holds true for most people, most of the time.

It is further assumed that these relationships are only to be discovered through carefully controlled empirical investigations, preferably *experiments*. These 'laws' (though few experimental social psychologists would actually use the term in any unqualified way) are of the form 'Everything else being equal, increases in variable x (e.g. frustration) will lead to increases in variable y (e.g. aggressiveness)'.

Experimental social psychologists, however, do not believe that their scientific method is the *only* legitimate method, or that *all* social psychological questions can be answered by this method, or that human beings are *just* like machines, or that total objectivity is *ever* possible, or that people *always* tell the truth in questionnaires, or that structural and historical forces do *not* shape and constrain our social behaviour, or that their work is *totally* free from personal biases, or that it is *only* a matter of time before all the puzzles of our social being will be solved through experimental methods. The most compelling value of experimental social psychologists is that the scientific approach is *pragmatically* the best way of making definite progress in the study of social behaviour.

Through objective methods a consensus can be arrived at about what the discipline knows about some particular issue. All the better if that consensus is a temporary one shattered by a crucial experiment which shows the earlier consensus to have been only partially right – or even totally wrong. At least there is a sense of coherent progression. In some (but not all) non-experimental forms of psychological enquiry, the danger is that no one really knows where the debate is at – a thousand voices articulate their own description of reality, with acceptance often being determined by fashion and the judgements of academic gurus. There is no progress without *some* common agreement on methods and evaluative criteria. Without controlled empirical studies, clear theories, specific testable hypotheses and laws, it is very difficult to enter into any intelligent dialogue about, say, depression and aggression. Non-experimental social psychologists can write very persuasively about subjective experiences, cultural trends and authenticity, and we will often feel they ring true for us, that they resonate with our deepest sense of meaningfulness, purpose and identity. The problem is that, from the point of view of the experimental psychologist, these subjective interpretations of personal, public or cultural experiences are just too unreliable, too ambiguous and too untestable to use as the foundations for the systematic study of human social behaviour.

The core question for experimental social psychology is: how can we develop general laws about human social behaviour that will develop our knowledge and be of practical value for those working in applied areas? Most of the developments that are likely to occur in the future in experimental social psychology will reflect the increasing sophistication and decreasing cost of powerful information technology. Psychologists have always been keen to use new technology to obtain novel measures of behaviour. We know how people make inferences from small amounts of specific information, but how do people integrate information from the real external world that is often complex, contradictory and vague, and act on it? How can we increase the accuracy of our predictions about vulnerability to depression and stress-related disorders? We know how and why people watch different television programmes and what they feel and remember about them, but how are people adapting to information networks as replacements for traditional social networks? How do individuals' mental (cognitive) representations of other people change? We know how the social context can influence how people interpret arousal and other bodily sensations but how does social behaviour affect physiological/neurological events, and vice versa? We know the impact of group membership on self-esteem and identity is very strong, but how does awareness of membership of social groups affect our emotions and personal relationships? How do people process information (milli)second by (milli)second in complex social episodes? These are the questions for the future.

BOX I.2   Humanistic and experiential social psychology

Richard Stevens

The concern of an experiential, humanistic social psychology is to ground the study of personal and social life in the actualities of lived experience. Our personal worlds, as we experience them, should be our starting point and the point to which we constantly return to check out the understanding we are developing. If that sounds obvious to you, it has not been the way that psychology has typically worked.

One of the paradoxes of studying social psychology is that the discipline can often seem to move away from psychological realities. There are good reasons for this, of course. One is methodological. The use of scientific methods, such as experimentation, means that only certain kinds of problems can be investigated and that they have to be looked at in a special way. The behaviours concerned have to be isolated and expressed in some measurable way and as testable hypotheses. What comes out is the provisional and, usually, probabilistic establishment of a causal link or effect. The problem, however, is that such results are usually far removed from people as we know them. While this method works well for investigating the natural world of gravitational fields and mechanical causality, it has limited value in helping us to understand people and ourselves better. Though there are notable exceptions, adopting the necessary requirements of an experimental approach to social psychology can all too often result in a focus on the peripheral and trivial. Worse than this, it can be alienating in that it encourages us to think of people as objects and to replace useful wisdom with esoteric jargon.

The other main approach in social psychology, influenced by theoretical sociology and discussed in Box 1.3, is to theorize about the way society constructs our psychological being. The problem here is a different one: it is that we find intangible abstractions and analyses which are difficult to evaluate and to relate to the world and ourselves as we experience them.

So how does experiential humanistic social psychology approach its subject matter: what does it do? Its starting point is not assumptions about what methods to employ but about the nature of the lived reality of experience, which, it argues, is quite different from the material world.

- This approach regards people's *experience* and the *meanings* they attribute to their actions and that of others as the core subject matter of social psychology. Behaviour always has to be interpreted to be made meaningful. So the idea of behaviour which is objectively observable and analysable is regarded as a myth. Psychological theories and research are useful only in so far as they help us to understand better our experience of being and living in the world.

- An experiential approach assumes that lived experience involves a greater or lesser degree of *active construction*. Although many factors influence and help to make us what we are, we are not simply the determined products of the forces that act upon us. A particular feature about the experience of being a person is that we are always in the process of becoming. We are never fixed or finalized: there is always the possibility of change, and we ourselves are the *agents* of change for ourselves, others and the world around us. This raises questions about the relevance of causal analysis and the assumption that people are explicable simply in deterministic terms. From the experiential, humanist standpoint, social psychology is regarded more as a 'moral science' in that it is concerned as much with what we *may become* – our potential – as it is with explaining what we *are*. An important function is to take account of and, if possible, to stimulate people's awareness of the factors affecting them and their scope for autonomous action.

- The experience of being has complex roots. Experiential social psychology acknowledges that we are embodied beings: biological factors and unconscious influences both play a role in determining our feelings and actions. Our relationships with others and the culture in which we are immersed also affect both what we are and what we can become. We need to look at, and try to become aware of, the interplay of these varied influences in our reflexive experience of ourselves. In this way we may gain some capacity to transcend their influence. This places social psychology at the intersection between several disciplines. We can learn from biology and the social sciences but, as psychologists, we must always return to ground the insights they give us in the actualities of our experience.

- Experiential social psychology acknowledges and respects individual uniqueness; no two of us are quite the same. Paradoxically, there is also a focus on fundamental aspects of being a person, such as our capacity for choice and our awareness of mortality – what are often called the *existential* issues of life. The focus is on the common experiences of humanity – of pain, desire, frustration and joy – that make us human and override surface differences such as race and class.

The core of experiential social psychology is to develop a discipline which will help us to make sense of our conscious experience of personal being and relationships and provide a basis for enhancing the ways in which we experience and live our lives. One important issue here is the self-fulfilling nature of social psychological approaches. If people become aware not only of the influence of different factors on their lives but also of their potential to exercise choice, they are more likely to be empowered to participate in creating what they are to become.

The kind of research and activities in which experiential social psychology engages includes developing techniques such as repertory grids or phenomenological analyses of the content of people's experience, collecting accounts of different kinds of situation such as the experiences of being near death or in 'flow'. It is concerned to find ways to stimulate people's awareness of themselves and their potential and techniques for enhancing the exercise of autonomy and coping with the existential issues they confront. Its topics include philosophies of living, new ways of relating to others, strategies for improving psychological well-being, changing beliefs and managing emotions, and the development of wisdom and psychological health.

BOX 1.3   Critical social psychology

Margaret Wetherell

I want to argue for a 'critical social psychology' which takes the term 'social' very seriously indeed. We are not isolated individuals but social beings. Our dreams, hopes, fears and expectations may be the products of solitary reflection but they also tell us a great deal about the ways in which we are inserted into society. Social psychology should be a social science, not an imitation natural science. We belong with disciplines such as sociology, politics and cultural studies rather than with physics, chemistry and astronomy. Our methods, research aims and theories should reflect the *particular* nature of social action, difficult though this is. We should work with and study the ambiguities, fluidity and openness of social life rather than try to repress these in a fruitless chase for experimental control and scientific respectability.

'The social context' is a vague term and sometimes, particularly in laboratory experiments, it is taken to mean just the presence of an audience or one or more bystanders in the person's environment. It should mean much more than this, in my view. Social influences are pervasive and inescapable. The social context is structured by power inequalities; it is an *organized* way of life which includes the material environment, technology and modes of economic production as well as language, meanings, ideologies and culture. Social psychologists should study not just the immediate effects of one person upon another, but relationships built up over time, family life, our broader communities, reference groups and the collective history of our society. The canvas should be broad, not narrow, and we need to keep more than half an eye open to developments in the rest of the social sciences.

Social psychologists should be studying topics such as identity and the development of a sense of self in this social matrix. We should be looking at representations, stereotypes and cultural images and the way these act back and define people. Our research should have an immediate social relevance. We should be looking at gender, ethnicity and class and the way the structuring and organization of society (including conflicts between groups) directly impact on people's experiences, thoughts and feelings. Social relationships are complex and multi-layered. The lines of influence from one person to another are intertwined and difficult to disentangle. The controlled experiment has never been adequate to this task. The patterns involved are much more complex than the linear laws of experimental social psychology suggest.

Social psychology should try to develop methods which can take account of mutual chains of cause and effect, recursive loops, chaotic systems, variability and inconsistency and the constantly changing nature of social interaction. These methods will be based on the painstaking analysis of materials gained from observation (including participant observation), interviews and records of naturally occurring events. The emphasis should be on scholarship and on the development of theories and concepts – developing good descriptions and explanations of what is happening to people in social life which can be evaluated and compared in terms of their pragmatic value in helping us understand our forms of life and helping us to change these. As one experimental social psychologist, Kurt Lewin, acknowledged, there is nothing more practical than a good theory.

Through the exploration of social and cultural influences on the human psyche, critical social psychologists have come to question the wisdom of much mainstream experimental work and the emphases of experiential and humanistic social psychologists. Memory, language, experience and introspection do not occur in a social vacuum. These aspects of our psychological life can only be understood in the light of their social and collective basis and their role in social interaction. Critical social psychologists are *not* arguing that people are pawns of their social situation and totally determined by social forces. On the contrary, we suggest that people are active and make choices. However, these choices and this autonomy always need to be set in context. Human choices are structured and guided by the social materials that are available. There is little point from this perspective in trying to identify existential issues seen as timeless, universal and unchanging. People are differently positioned in society. Concepts of the independent, detached and autonomous agent found in liberal political theory and in experiential psychology have an uneasy relation, for example, to many women's lived experiences, and to the experiences of many people who are not members of the professional middle classes.

The term 'critical' suggests that social psychology should not stand on the sidelines of society. Research is a value-laden activity, from the choice of questions to investigate through to the interpretation of results. Social psychology should not just be a *moral* science; it should also be a *political* science. Research is rarely neutral. We should not be afraid to be critical and see our work as part of a process of social change. Social psychological findings are not laws set in stone or facts with only one meaning. The significance of research has to be decided by discussion, dialogue and debate and we should see ourselves as contributing to these kinds of negotiations, which are at the core of the democratic process.

Reading these position statements gives some sense of the Pandora's Box which makes up social psychology. As the box is opened a chorus of squabbling voices emerges, and weird new words ('empirical', 'recursive', 'reflective', 'existential') echo around the room. One response to this diversity might be to wonder why these people don't get their act together. Do physicists and chemists have the same trouble deciding what physics and chemistry are about? Perhaps they do, and, if they don't communicate in this way, perhaps they should; for I would argue that this plurality of positions is a sign of a vibrant and open science. Some things are settled, but much is up for grabs. There is nothing moribund here and these basic disputes about the very nature of the discipline have had a bracing effect on research activity.

The three 'voices' here do not by any means exhaust the diversity of current social psychology. Stevens (1996), for example, identifies five 'perspectives' within the discipline ('biological', 'experimentalist', 'experiential', 'social constructionist' and 'psychodynamic'), and even this leaves other identifiably different perspectives out of account (for example, the 'systemic' perspective discussed by Dallos in Miell and Dallos, 1996, and cross-cutting perspectives such as feminist social psychology). Perspectives sometimes illuminate each other's findings, but more often they battle for 'the right to explain' and for control of the agenda – not just out of assertiveness, but because important ethical and political consequences could follow from our explanations of what it is to be both human and social.

Our aim is that this volume should provide you with the skills to enter the fray on your own behalf, confidently and assertively arguing for your own resolutions of these issues, or for different kinds of integrations of material. By the end of the book you should be in a position to write your own vision of social psychology, or argue in your own words for one of the visions described in the boxes above. To aid this process, in the rest of this chapter I want to introduce in more detail *two* of the main issues which divide social psychologists and which underpin the different definitions of social psychology found in Boxes 1.1 to 1.3 and in textbooks.

3 The scientific basis of social psychology

In Box 1.1 above, Patrick McGhee calls for an objective science of social psychology. Richard Stevens in Box 1.2 refers to social psychology as a moral science, while my statement in Box 1.3 seems to suggest that social psychology should be a critical or politically informed social science. These demands reveal different views about the neutrality of science and the special nature of its methods. The different anxieties of the writers are also revealing. I worry that social psychology will not be social enough. Both Patrick McGhee and Richard Stevens are concerned that the field will become dominated by vague generalizations and abstractions. For Richard Stevens, this danger arises whenever social psychologists stray too far from the bedrock of personal experience. For Patrick McGhee, the concern is that, without the application of rigorous scientific criteria, fashion will become the only arbiter of knowledge. The nature of science, what it is and how it works, will be discussed in detail in Chapters 8 and 9 in Part 2 of this volume. For now, I want to note how these contrasting views have impinged on definitions of social psychology.

Some social psychologists see a strong distinction between social psychology and common sense. In this view, some of the conclusions which social psychologists reach may be the same as the views of the woman or man in the street, but the use of scientific methods guarantees the objectivity and truth of social psychologists' claims. Scientific method is seen as a bulwark, too, when social psychological findings depart from what everybody 'knows' already. This school of thought would make a strong distinction between social psychology and disciplines in the humanities such as literary criticism or art history. The definitions of social psychology which result from this understanding are likely to stress not just its systematic basis (literary criticism is also systematic) but also the role of certain procedures such as theory testing by means of experiments, replication and processes of verification based on comparisons of claims with observable evidence. In this view, knowledge claims made without these steps would not be social psychology.

This definition of social psychology as *the scientific study of human social behaviour* can be contrasted with other possible definitions. These might refer similarly to the importance of being systematic but will define 'systematic' in terms of scholarship and the quality of the analysis. Are the social psychologists' conclusions coherent, logical, plausible, useful and valid? Both critical social psychologists, working from a social constructionist perspective, and experiential social psychologists are less concerned about comparisons with observable evidence. They argue that such approaches unacceptably narrow down the range of questions which can be investigated. Furthermore, the 'facts' are never just there; they are always produced in some context. Observations always need to be interpreted. You will remember Patrick McGhee's response to these points on behalf of experimental social psychologists. He argues that without a grounding in what is observable and measurable we can not proceed or know that we have progressed. In a real sense, then, the debate between different visions of social psychology is about what constitutes objective criteria. What is necessary proof, and what is sufficient evidence for claims?

The words 'behaviour' and 'action' also often feature in standard definitions of social psychology along with 'scientific' and/or 'systematic'. A standard definition of social psychology might refer, for instance, to the systematic study of social action or to the scientific study of social behaviour. Superficially, behaviour and action seem to be the same thing. But, as the position statements in Boxes 1.1, 1.2 and 1.3 begin to suggest, the choice of one or other term in a definition of social psychology is a deliberate one and keys into the debate about science and objectivity. The term *behaviour* as opposed to the term *action* signals something that is observable. From an experimental social psychological point of view, as we have seen, it is important to be able to translate the phenomena being studied (perhaps people's mental images and feelings) into behaviour which can be measured and observed. People might be asked, for instance, to tick boxes on a questionnaire to indicate their attitudes on a controversial social issue. In this case, something unobservable, a thought, a private opinion, is being transformed into something which can be counted and compared.

The more global term *action* suggests that what is important is not necessarily what is observable but the *complex* of intentions, feelings and interpretations which produce events in social life. The term *action* draws our attention to the aspects of psychological life which Richard Stevens stresses – the role of meanings and people's personal constructions of events. Again, this discussion will continue in Part 2 of this volume in Chapter 6 which looks at different views in social psychology on the role and nature of meaning. For the moment you might like to consider whether your definition of social psychology would refer to the study of behaviour or whether you would want to include terms such as 'thoughts', 'experiences' or 'interpretations'. If you do decide to include 'unobservables', then how would you respond to Patrick McGhee's point that social psychology becomes little more than speculation about the minds of others if those private events are not translated into measurable and observable public events?

4 The individual and the social

The dichotomy of the individual and the social is often described as the core issue of social psychology. Textbook definitions frequently refer, for instance, to social psychology as 'the study of the individual in a social context'. Such definitions immediately raise questions about the nature of the individual and the nature of the social context. But they also raise questions about whether social psychology is properly part of general psychology or a sub-area of sociology. As Arthur Still notes in Chapter 2 of this volume, an important contrast is emerging here, between *psychological social psychology* and *sociological social psychology*.

I argued in my position statement in Box 1.3 that people are not isolated individuals locked in a spiral of solitary rumination and introspection, although in extreme circumstances it may feel like that. I suggested that people are social beings and so the nature of our dreams, hopes and fears will be moulded and influenced by our social context. I also claimed that one of the problems with the experimental method in social psychology is that it cannot capture the social context in all its manifestations. Often, in social psychological experiments, the social context boils down to the presence of one other person, and the complex interactions of people in groups and collectivities over time are neglected.

In response, Patrick McGhee, in Box 1.1, notes that experimental social psychology is not so inflexible. It does acknowledge the influence of large-scale social forces on people's lives and experimentalists do turn to other methods such as surveys, questionnaires and observation, when appropriate, to measure the effects of these. Some of the most influential social psychology to emerge from the UK in recent years has come from experimental investigations of social groups and social identity (although this has not focused on changes in group process over time) while in France, the UK and Europe another important recent theme in experimental work has been the study of social representations (see the chapter by Potter in Wetherell, 1996). Similarly, Richard Stevens, in Box 1.2, argues that an experiential or humanistic approach recognizes social influences on individual lives but he is concerned about the over-deterministic nature of social theories which rob individuals of their agency.

The debate, in other words, is not about the importance or the existence of the social context. It is about how influential social forces are, and what remains to the individual. From these decisions flow other points and claims about how best to study social life. To help follow the debate about the individual and the social, I would like now to trace out what is typically assumed when social psychology is seen as a branch of general psychology (*psychological social psychology*) and when it is seen as either an autonomous discipline in its own right or as part of the social sciences (*sociological social psychology*).

When social psychology is seen as a branch of general psychology, the social context tends to be regarded as an additional variable which modifies individual psychology but is not formative or constitutive in itself. In other words, it is often assumed that it is sufficient to discover the nature of the individual through looking, for example, at the study of learning in the physical environment, at how people's memory for objects and words works, through studying how the brain operates in both normal and deviant cases, through the study of visual perception, and the investigation of motivation and behaviour, say, in cases of thirst or hunger. These topics make up general psychology and if you have read introductory textbooks or books on cognitive psychology you will be familiar with this style of work. Social psychology then becomes the study of how these basic processes established by psychologists, such as the categorization and recognition of objects, are modified in a social context to become, for instance, the categorization and recognition of other people and social situations.

Thus, for long periods, the study of social psychology was divided up into the study of social perception, social cognition, social motivation, social development, and so on. The reasoning here is that social perception (the study of the process of forming judgements of others), for example, is a sub-field of the study of perception more generally. This approach to the field, which encourages the definition of social psychology as 'the study of the individual in the social context' often implies that the nature of the individual is presumed to be established and seen as pre-existent and social life becomes a 'context' in which these basic individual processes are acted out.

Typically, sociological social psychologists have begun at the other pole – with the nature of the social context. If social life follows a particular pattern, then how does this construct the person? What kinds of people and forms of identity do different social and cultural contexts and the combined flow of biological and social evolution allow and create? In this approach, society and cultural life are assumed to be pre-existent while people are seen as flexible and malleable, their psychology reflecting and being built from their communications and relationships with others. If your background is in social policy or sociology, this approach will be more familiar to you. (If you are not at all familiar with sociological social psychology you might like to look at Chapter 5 of Stevens, 1996, and the discussion there of two central figures within sociological social psychology – the American social philosopher George Herbert Mead and the Russian developmental psychologist Lev Vygotsky.)

As this debate comes into prominence, it is possible to begin to see the shape some of the discussions between social psychologists of varying persuasions might assume. The psychological social psychologist, for instance, might ask if the sociological social psychologist is really denying a universal human nature or that human minds work in much the same way across history and culture. The sociological social psychologist might retort 'How can you establish the basic psychology of the individual (motivation, desire, the formation of beliefs and opinions) without considering the formative nature of social life?' This debate, of course, is only possible because of the importance the individual–social dichotomy has assumed in Euro-American thought in general terms. Again this is an issue to which we shall return many times, and in Chapter 4 in Part 2 of this volume there will be a discussion of the notion of domains of analysis. Does it solve this debate to divide up the phenomena which need to be explained into individual variables, interpersonal variables and societal aspects with their own concepts and theories?

5 Conclusion

Although this is a chapter about definition, I have not tried to offer any one description of social psychology. Indeed, to do so would be misleading. Rather, the focus has been on the diverse nature of social psychology and on introducing, as a basis for further discussion, the kinds of conversations social psychologists have with each other when faced with the question 'what is social psychology?' Chapter 2 goes on to examine the history of these and other conversations between social psychologists, tracing back the origins of the ways in which the person and social life are currently conceptualized. Part 2 of this volume will then revisit aspects of the key debates raised here, such as views on the nature of science and criteria for judgement, as well as asking how to structure the diversity and multiplicity emerging in these initial definitions of social psychology. Part 3 will show how these debates have featured in attempts to apply social psychological knowledge.

References

Miell, D. and Dallos, R. (eds) (1996) *Social Interaction and Personal Relationships*, London, Sage.

Stevens, R. (ed.) (1996) *Understanding the Self*, London, Sage.

Wetherell, M. (ed.) (1996) *Identities, Groups and Social Issues*, London, Sage.

Wetherell, M. and Stevens, R. (1996) 'The self in the modern world: drawing together the threads' in Stevens R. (ed.)

CHAPTER 2
HISTORICAL ORIGINS OF SOCIAL PSYCHOLOGY

By Arthur Still

1 This volume and the two social psychologies

Social psychology has two histories in English-speaking countries. Sometimes it has formed part of university sociology departments, sometimes it has been part of psychology departments, and these two traditions have remained. They are known as sociological social psychology (SSP) and psychological social psychology (PSP) respectively. They have their own journals and different textbooks, and analysis of citations in articles and books shows that SSP and PSP writers refer to different sets of authors. Generally SSP writers refer to other SSP writers, and vice versa, which suggests two distinct disciplines (Collier et al., 1991; Good, 1980, 1993).

Roughly speaking, experimental, cognitive psychology (e.g. Lalljee, 1996) belongs to PSP, while social constructionism (e.g. Wetherell and Maybin, 1996) belongs to SSP. But recently in Britain social constructionist approaches have thrived in a few PSP departments and ideas are flowing more freely between the disciplines than ever before. Psychoanalysis plays an important part in SSP, but is usually ignored in PSP, though that was not true earlier in the century (Collier et al., 1991, p. 5). Humanistic psychology (see Stevens, 1996) has drawn widely on a number of disciplines as a 'third force' in opposition to experimental and psychoanalytic approaches and has established itself in both SSP and PSP in North America.

2 The origins of narrative and subjectivity: St Augustine

Consider for a moment how we make sense of people, events and situations by 'telling stories' about them. Think, for example, of Alex, described in Stevens (1996a, p. 2). He is fighting cancer, his wife has left him, and he is out of work. How does he reflect on his experience of being a person? Does he look away from his world of shadows and sadness, and convince himself that he has never been so happy, that he has found a new diet and yoga that will shrivel his cancer away, that his wife will return and that he will find fulfilment in a new career? Or does he find only despair and self-pity in this unfair curtailment of a meagre life? Or perhaps, as the author suggests, he feels this but also finds solace in God and the promise of a future life to compensate for his present misery. In these ways Alex might try to make sense of his predicament by fitting it into a narrative which has a past, a present and a future.

This beginning from an individual viewpoint and then making sense of it as narrative is largely a Western practice, both as history and as autobiography. It is at the centre of the Judaeo-Christian tradition, whose bible is a history of a people which culminates, for Christians, in the life of Christ. It was also well developed in Classical Rome as *narratio*, the rhetorical skill of relating what happened in order to sway an audience. In the fourth century AD these two traditions came together in St Augustine of Hippo, a teacher of rhetoric who was converted to Christianity. His best known book was his *Confessions*, in which he told his own story to trace the journey of his soul towards God. This autobiography was not just the story of a life, an outer journey, it was also an inner journey, with subjectivity as its starting point. It tells of the struggle between reason, leading the individual soul to God, and fleshly desire, which leads the soul away from God. It depended on belief in the uniqueness and indivisibility of the individual soul, and its capacity for transcending mundane life and stretching towards immortality. Augustine not only expressed this struggle in his autobiography, he also established the Christian philosophy of a soul that is immortal, and therefore pure and unchanging, free, unique and indivisible. Yet this soul was enclosed within a mortal body, and somehow able to apply itself to the impure and changing world in which human beings live. Starting with Augustine, Christian scholastic philosophers tried to reconcile these irreconcilables for a thousand years and created an intellectual culture which is still with us.

Our psychology has grown out of that culture and is unique to it. We speak of Buddhist or Hindu psychology, but these Eastern psychologies are soteriological, concerned with achieving enlightenment rather than with knowledge. There is a Christian soteriology, but psychology did not develop from this. Instead it arose from a pervasive desire to find meaning in personal existence by ordering the world intellectually. Additionally, it has been constrained by a view of the mind and body and their interrelation which was absorbed into Christianity from Greek philosophy and has no parallel in Eastern thought. This view splits the mind into *anima* and *animus*. These were made famous by Jung as female and male archetypes, which he drew from his study of hermetic writings, especially on alchemy. The split was less esoteric than Jung implies, and it is not a 'differentiation of the intellect that began in the Christian Middle Ages' (Jung, 1968, p. 68), for it was well established as a distinction in Latin speech by the time of Christ and appears in Augustine's writings.

3 The origins of 'Psychology': Animus and Anima

The word 'psychology' first occurred in the sixteenth century, and the first book with the title 'Psychology' was published in 1590 by a Protestant theologian, Rudolph Goclenius (1547–1628). It was about the *animus*, the immortal, intellective soul, responsible for bringing eternal truths to bear upon mundane affairs. In the scholastic philosophy of the preceding four hundred years, and in the Latin language for much longer, the *animus* was contrasted with the *anima*, the embodied soul, which, as the body's organizing principle, could not outlive the body. Aristotelean Catholic philosophers, following St Thomas Aquinas, had tended to concentrate their account of human beings around the *anima*. If the human essence was contained in an embodied soul, it made it easier to understand how it could change with development through life, be subject to shifting emotions, and be so firmly rooted in the physical world.

An important product of this Catholic philosophy was Michel de Montaigne (1533–1592), whose essays explored further the possibilities of subjectivity opened up by Augustine. But unlike Augustine's single-minded focus on his struggle against worldly desire, Montaigne was more tolerant of human weakness, less insistent on grasping at Universal Truth. He was a Renaissance writer, a humanist who was familiar with the works of classical philosophy and literature that had become newly accessible in the sixteenth century, and he was alert to the tales brought back by explorers. He noted that different civilizations held vastly different conclusions about religion, morality and the world, which undermined the claims of a God-given universal reason. He was thus a sceptic, but not about religion. Since the nineteenth century debates about evolution, it is too easy to think of religion as forever in opposition to science, and of scepticism as an essentially scientific attitude. But in the sixteenth and seventeenth centuries the rhetoric of scepticism was part of religious debate, often used to undermine faith in reason, and to restore faith in traditional religion. Scientific discoveries and knowledge of other civilizations were potential threats to religious tradition, and one defence against this was scepticism about any claims to absolute knowledge based on reason, not just claims about the immortality of the soul. This form of scepticism opened the way, not necessarily to atheism but to fideism, that is, to justification by faith rather than by reason. Catholics used the relativity of worldly knowledge to argue for faith in the traditional wisdom of the church and to question the power of reason.

Such reason, inherent in the transcendent *animus*, had traditionally been used to elevate humans above nature. However, Montaigne quotes a wealth of anecdotes in his essays to demonstrate the intelligence and moral sense of animals and the stupidity of people, so blurring their separation. This is the beginning of *anima* psychology, whose twin pillars are that there is no clear dividing line between animals and humans, and that knowledge and reason are culturally relative. It is a psychology of relativism, a potential threat to the power of claimants to absolute, universal knowledge, not only that of the Christian church, but also of science.

Unhappy with the dangers in such Catholic worldliness, with its tendency to confuse the embodied *anima* with the pure, immortal, unique and indivisible *animus*, Protestant theologians like Rudolph Goclenius reasserted the traditional separation by focusing on the *animus* itself and shelving the problem of the soul's embodiment. This intellectual focus was called 'Psychologia', and thus, at its birth and its first naming, '"Psychology" discriminated the discourse on anima from that on animus' (Vidal, 1993). It did so by focusing on an entity closer to the eternal truths of logic and mathematics than to the shifting cycles of love and hate, birth and death, ingestion and excretion. This is *animus* psychology. It marks the start of modern psychology, that has been a product of the continuing tension between these two versions of the Christian soul, between *animus* and *anima* psychology. The names were dropped as Latin was forgotten, but the dialectic continued – with the aim no longer of reconciling philosophical tradition with Christianity, but as the sources of rival accounts of the mind.

4 The Society of Jesus, Descartes and the origins of 'consciousness'

The stern Protestant philosophers of the Reformation may have upstaged the Aristoteleans, with their concern to understand God's creation in all its earthliness and their relative neglect of the immortal soul and the eternal verities, but not for long. The Counter-Reformation, led by Ignatius Loyola (1491–1556) and the Jesuit order he founded, was well underway, and soon restored the balance. Loyola's *Spiritual Exercises*, written around 1523, showed how to detach oneself from the world and recover the immortal soul through meditations during a lengthy retreat. Loyola had been a soldier and his book was written with the precision and exactness of a military manual. His methodical approach, tempered with Christian gentleness, was expressed in one of the most effective educational systems the world has seen.

For a time its finest school was at La Flèche, near Paris, lavishly founded in 1603 by Henri IV. One of its pupils in 1606 was René Descartes (1596–1650) whose *Meditations on First Philosophy* is a founding document of modern thought, including psychology, with a structure that parallels a Jesuit meditation. Descartes begins by describing a retreat into complete subjectivity, where nothing about the world is taken for granted, and then tries to establish, from subjectivity, the basis for our knowledge of outside reality. His result describes how the immortal soul (the *animus*), the source of universal reason, can be attached to, yet remain distinct from, a purely mechanical body. Reason is universal because it deals with logic and mathematics, and it can establish knowledge through the application of a method, that of clear and distinct ideas. This method, spelt out in Descartes' *Regulae*, has become an accepted recipe for acquiring empirical knowledge: proceed step by step; each step being clear and distinct and leading on to the next. Applying it, Descartes began the modern study of how the individual mind applies reason or experience to the deliverance of the senses, especially vision, to gain knowledge about the world in which it is embodied. This capacity for applying reason to obtain knowledge was, Descartes believed, God-given and innate.

In many respects this study of the mind remained focused on the *animus* and its origin in the complexities of Christian philosophy were forgotten. It was an investigation of knowledge rather than of emotions and actions, which had been the province of the now neglected *anima*. Like the *animus*, Descartes' mind or soul was unique, indivisible and independent of the body in its essence, though temporarily attached to it. These requirements were captured in the word 'consciousness'. Literally meaning 'knowing together', this is how it was first used, in the seventeenth century, as mutual knowledge within a group of people. Later John Locke (1632–1704) used it to refer to the 'knowing together' that occurred, he believed, in the human mind: 'Consciousness is the perception of what passes in a Man's own mind' (John Locke, 1975/1689, p. 115) and 'Nothing but consciousness can unite remote Existences into the same Person, the Identity of Substance will not do it' (p. 344). Thus consciousness holds together past and present and the different sources of sensory input in a unique, indivisible and detached self.

5 'The Way of Ideas' and the rise of scientific psychology

Locke was the first *British Empiricist*. He followed Descartes' lead along what its critics have dubbed 'The Way of Ideas'; later this became *Associationism* – the study of how ideas combine in the mind. Like Descartes, Locke believed that our experience is of the ideas which are representations of the world, not of the world directly; but Locke differed from Descartes in believing that our ability to form representations is based on prior experience rather than being innate. Associationism included the French followers of Locke in the eighteenth and nineteenth centuries and was the equivalent of what we might now call an international scientific community. The most prominent member was a Scot, David Hume (1711–1776) who labelled his work 'experimental psychology'. It was not what we now know by this name, yet it was based on careful observation and invited agreement or disagreement. It was disciplined writing for a community of practitioners, even though they developed no clear-cut or repeatable methods for making observations. In their work, the mind was studied as though it were a mirror of nature, striving for clarity and distinctness. Distinct physical objects were mirrored by ideas, and causality in the world was mirrored by the association of ideas, but there was a reliance on experience rather than reason for giving a coherent reflection. It thus inclined towards the scepticism about reason that we saw in Montaigne. David Hume seems to have belonged to this tradition (Fogelin, 1983). He concluded that philosophy could not give a coherent account of how the mind knows the world, and supposed that our confidence in its solidity and predictability was no more than habit and convention. Reason was relegated to being a 'slave of the passions' rather than a mirror of truth. So, if it had been accepted, Hume's theory would have undermined the *animus* altogether and heralded a return to the *anima*.

But it was not accepted and Hume was much abused for his scepticism. Immanuel Kant (1724–1804) acknowledged the force of the arguments but could not accept that science and knowledge were based on habit and convention. He argued persuasively that the mind is so structured that our experience is bound to be as it is, confined in space and time within a world of distinct objects, of causality, and of other basic categories. For Kant, knowledge was based on an innate principle of rationality, either God-given or evolved. He believed empirical psychology to be impossible, since examination would involve stepping outside our mental structures. Instead of observation he used a *transcendental* argument – given that experience is structured in the way it is, this is how the mind must be.

6 Experiment in psychology

Kant revived the flagging *animus* and initiated the search for mental structures that is still with us today. But his impact was on theory rather than on method, since most psychologists ignored his strictures against observation, and continued to follow the empirical methods of the Associationists. During the nineteenth century, the experimental methods which had proved so successful in the natural sciences were imported into psychology. The study of reflexes in animals and humans was well established by the start of the century, and later a psychological analogue was developed, correlating sensory stimulation with verbal report. This was called 'psychophysics' and its basic methods were formulated by Fechner in 1860. The first laboratory was opened by Wundt in Leipzig in 1879, and by the end of the nineteenth century experiments were applied to memory, animal learning and to acquired skills such as typewriting.

Early experiments included what is often cited as the first social psychology experiment, by Triplett (1898). Two notable social developments had occurred towards the end of the nineteenth century – the invention of the bicycle and a growth in the popularity of competitive sport. These merged in cycle racing, and Triplett noticed as a psychological curiosity what most observers take for granted as obvious: that a cyclist in competition will achieve faster times than when alone. He set up experimental analogues of this situation, using schoolchildren winding fishing reels, jumping and counting, and found marked improvement when in the social, competitive presence of others. Like many subsequent experiments in social psychology, Triplett's experiments were more remarkable for the ingenuity of setting up an experimental analogue of a real life phenomenon than for surprising results. This search for explanation through experimental analysis had proved successful in other laboratory sciences, like physiology, physics and chemistry – which had all been influential as sources of psychological method and theory. It was still the study of individuals, with competition treated as an independent variable, like noise or fatigue. As such it set a precedent that continues to be followed by many social psychologists.

Triplett's experiments have traditionally been treated as the starting point of experimental social psychology, but this is inaccurate. By treating psychology experimentation as a social encounter, Danziger (1990) has shown that the modern laboratory experiment evolved from a number of different sources. There was the laboratory experiment in the style of Wundt, which often involved multiple observations by a single expert colleague, who was trained in introspection and was, typically, the senior member of the team. Later came the now familiar group experiment, the North American model, suited to modern university life with its pools of captive subjects. Triplett's was an early example of this genre.

But another kind of experiment derived from the medical clinic, where experimental methods on single patients were used to study hypnosis. Here the experimenter was sharply distinct from the 'subject' (a word originating from clinical tradition). During the 1880s, Alfred Binet and others used experiments to investigate dissociative phenomena under hypnosis and in hysteria. Later Binet experimented to demonstrate the power of suggestion, both on hysterics and within groups of children. These experiments, distinctly on a topic in social psychology, were published by 1895 (Wolf, 1973). Unlike Triplett's experiments they were on social interaction itself, rather than on the effect of social presence as an independent variable. The early experiments of Piaget and Vygotsky on child development (see Wetherell and Maybin, 1996) were similar in style to those of the French clinical tradition. Both relied on an accumulation of individual cases, rather than averaging results over a number of subjects.

During the twentieth century, the experimental tradition based on the American model came to dominate psychology departments. At the same time, social psychology tended to be treated as an extension of individual psychology. It was defined either as a new subject matter, with the methods of individual experimental psychology being applied to social issues, or was defined as an additional variable – complex and important but not likely to add fundamental new principles to the problem of *how* an individual adapts to his or her environment, by, for example, modifying his or her behaviour or by forming appropriate mental representations of the outside world. Attempts to treat social psychology as a distinct discipline with its own characteristic methods and theories had an important impact, as we shall see, but have repeatedly been absorbed by the prevailing movement towards experimental and laboratory thinking in psychology departments.

7 The crisis of consciousness in the nineteenth century

By the end of the nineteenth century the status of consciousness as a distinct coherent realm – a unique, indivisible and detached *animus*, as seemed to be demanded if it was to be amenable to scientific study – came under attack from several directions. Within experimental psychology itself, questions were being raised about the completeness of conscious experience. Külpe and his students at Würzburg found that thinking could not be reduced to a series of steps (what Descartes had called clear and distinct ideas) but proceeded in a less orderly manner and sometimes made successful jumps that were inexplicable within the processes of consciousness itself. Others, notably Titchener in the USA, refused to accept the Würzburg results, which they put down to faulty technique.

This unseemly debate opened the way to an important shift of emphasis. Instead of the experimenter's data being the conscious processes, they became the verbal reports or other signals that *indicated* conscious processes. This let in behaviour in general as potential data, including the behaviour of animals, and made possible the emergence of behaviourism (Watson, 1913). Observable behaviour rather than private thoughts became the object of study, but this did not always mean a shift from *animus* to *anima* psychology. Just as the processes of the *animus* have necessarily been abstractions from natural settings, so laboratory psychologists continued to study abstract learning and perceptual processes in animal and human subjects, developing models of internal processes that are independent of any embodiment. Modern cognitive psychologists have continued in this tradition, drawing on the language of computing to develop powerful new theories. PSP has shared in these changes, first drawing on behaviourism, then on cognitive psychology for its experimental studies of social behaviour. In both cases it has tended to remain individualist, with social psychology throwing up important and complex problems for an individual psychology, first of behaviour then of the mind, rather than requiring its own principles and methods.

Critique of the animus

The most damaging critique of consciousness in the nineteenth century came from the *anima* tradition in psychology. Descartes' theory of the mind had always had its critics, most forcefully writers sympathetic to historical knowledge and poetry rather than science. Vico (1668–1744) argued that the kind of method suited to the natural sciences and geometry may not fit the hurly-burly of practical affairs or history. Rousseau's *Emile* (1762) is a celebration of the educational merits of direct contact with nature rather than through systems of knowledge inscribed in books. Other critics included what we now think of as Romantic thinkers, such as Herder, Hamann and Coleridge. John Keats had probably never read Descartes but his concept of negative capability sums up the opposition to Descartes' belief in certain, abstract knowledge articulated through a chain of clear and distinct ideas:

> ... it struck me what quality went to form a Man of Achievement especially in Literature and which Shakespeare possessed so enormously – I mean Negative Capability, that is when man is capable of being in uncertainties, Mysteries, doubts, without any irritable reaching after fact and reason.
>
> *(Keats, 1954, p. 53. The letter was written in 1817)*

But it would be a mistake to look at that period through eyes that are familiar with the gap between the arts and the sciences that has become codified in the structures of our universities. Goethe (1749–1832), perhaps the most outstanding intellectual figure of his time, was less concerned with establishing the credentials of a literary or historical sensibility alongside scientific method than with bridging the widening gap between them. His own scientific writings were an attempt to replace the minute analysis of atomism, encouraged by Descartes' method, with a concern for form over detail. In that spirit, his novel *Elective Affinities* applied a non-reductive chemistry of attraction and repulsion to human erotic attachment. It was part of an attempt to rescue chemistry from mechanistic thinking. The outcome has been the opposite of what he intended – chemistry has remained mechanistic, and has drawn psychology with it. James Mill's (1773–1836) atomistic 'chemistry of the mind' has had a more lasting impact on psychology than Goethe's theory of sexual chemistry.

Yet Romantic criticism of the *animus* certainly did leave its mark. By the end of the nineteenth century the twin pillars of the *anima* tradition (see section 3), celebrated by Montaigne, were firmly grounded. Charles Darwin had established a clear and convincing argument against any sharp division between animals and human beings, and knowledge of other cultures led to their acceptance alongside Christian civilization. The claims of universal reason had been thoroughly undermined and it was time to look again at what could be salvaged from the traditional theory of consciousness that had started with Descartes. In addition to the focus on experimental psychology referred to above, three different resolutions were offered to this crisis of consciousness:

1 phenomenology (William James and Edmund Husserl)

2 the unconscious (William James and Sigmund Freud)

3 cultural consciousness and the primacy of the social (Wundt and Dilthey; Marx and Durkheim).

Each has provided, in different measure, the material drawn upon by SSP.

1 Phenomenology

Although William James and Edmund Husserl returned to Descartes' starting point in subjectivity, the outcome was very different – both tried to shed the preconceptions that they believed had distorted the thinking of 'The Way of Ideas'.

In his *Principles of Psychology* (1890) William James (1842–1910) criticized what he called the 'psychologist's fallacy', which is 'the confusion of his own standpoint with that of the mental fact about which he is making his report'. In describing our thoughts about an object we are apt to be misled by what we know about an object. Thus because we know the world to be made up of distinct objects, we tend to believe that our thoughts are made up of distinct ideas that correspond to the objects. Putting aside the fallacy, James found that there are thought objects, certainly, but these are immersed in a stream of thought which is neither generally clear nor distinct. We select from the stream and may be able to give a well articulated narrative of what we experience, but this is 'knowledge-about' not direct 'knowledge of acquaintance'. Thus scientific knowledge is 'knowledge-about' which must be established not by any psychological state of clear and distinct ideas in the detached *animus*, as Descartes believed, but by active selection and through verbal articulation. Similarly 'the Self' is not some inner reality expressed in action, but is largely established socially, and, therefore, through social interaction.

The outcomes of James's investigations were the focus of later pragmatists, notably John Dewey (1859–1952) and George Herbert Mead (1863–1931), both prominent in the SSP tradition. According to pragmatism, knowledge and the self are grounded in social activity rather than internal cognitive processes. Thus to understand abstract knowledge we need to understand social and other everyday practices that establish knowledge. As in Wittgenstein (see Chapter 6 in this volume), meaning is not in the head, but part of a form of life.

Edmund Husserl (1859–1948), the founder of phenomenology, went 'back to the things themselves'. He argued for a fresh start, taking nothing for granted (akin to James's earlier 'psychologist's fallacy') in order to discover how we know truth and reality. He described the psychological structures necessary for knowledge of various kinds to occur – not reducing knowledge to psychology (that would be psychologism, which Husserl abhorred) but showing how it is constituted. At first he assumed that a transcendental ego, like the *animus,* was the basis for constituting reality, but in his later work, influenced by his pupil Martin Heidegger, he accepted that we are, from the start, grounded in a 'life-world' which cannot itself be constituted out of subjectivity. It was this last phase that was seized upon by Merleau-Ponty, Schutz, and other phenomenologists who have been influential in SSP.

2 The unconscious

In *Principles of Psychology*, William James considered and rejected ten arguments in favour of retaining the already popular notion of the unconscious in psychology. The advantage of introducing it as a resolution of the crisis of consciousness was that it preserved the mind as an entity distinct from the body and retained it as a realm open to study by an autonomous science of psychology. Such a realm requires causality to hold, or to be subject to, the rules of reason. James himself was happy to give up the autonomy of a psychology of consciousness, with physiology (as in his account of the stream of consciousness) or extra-individual factors, including social ones, making sense of the gaps, irrationalities and vagueness. James wrote *Principles of Psychology* at a time when there was great interest in the splitting of consciousness associated with hysteria and hypnosis, especially in France. Binet's research was in this tradition and was described at length in the *Principles*. James himself did experiments on automatic writing, in which some subjects were able to carry out a normal conversation, unaware that they were also writing down answers to questions whispered by the experimenter. This dissociation did not suggest unconscious processes to James, but a dysfunction of attention.

Freud also was much impressed by the phenomena of hypnosis and hysteria, but they led him towards a very different psychology. He preserved mental causality by introducing the unconscious, so that the mind acts as a coherent system, without James's recourse to physiological or social factors to fill the gaps. The unconscious can be used as the basis for an autonomous science, like archaeology, in which fragments of the historical record have to be filled in by interpretation. The two most important aspects of this theory for the history of social psychology have been the following.

1   The process of socialization – resolving conflicts between instincts and the demands of social reality; individual personality is a product of the way the individual resolves the conflicts. This aspect of the theory was drawn on extensively by PSP psychologists during the first half of the twentieth century.

2   The possibility of understanding ideology and self-deception through psychoanalysis. Just as the sadistic schoolmaster can hide his true desires from himself in his self-righteous morality, so a whole culture can be constructed around such useful self-deceptions.

3 Cultural consciousness and the primacy of the social

Wilhelm Wundt, although one of the founders of experimental psychology, laid down clear limits about what can be achieved by the scientific observation of consciousness. In this he was followed at the end of the nineteenth century by a group of neo-Kantians (Wilhelm Dilthey, 1833–1911; Wilhelm Windelband, 1848–1915 and Heinrich Rickert, 1863–1936). As Kantians they accepted that the mind is structured to yield up knowledge from the senses, but refused to limit this advantage to scientific knowledge. They extended the possibilities offered by the mind to historical knowledge, implying that both methods and thinking are fundamentally different in the two cases. They distinguished between *Geisteswissenschaft* – human science leading to idiographic understanding (*Verstehen*) of individuals, and *Naturwissenschaft* – natural science leading to nomothetic understanding, or general laws. These distinctions have become thoroughly assimilated into North American psychology, and appear regularly in textbooks, especially in SSP.

Dilthey, whose first book was a biography of Schleiermacher, the founder of hermeneutics (the art or science of interpretation), went on to develop a philosophy or psychology of cultural knowledge based on interpretation through empathy. He argued against an experimental psychology of the complex workings of the mind, and favoured an analytical psychology: '... the systems of culture, commerce, law, religion, art and scholarship and the outer organization of society in family, community, church and state originated from the living context of the human mind and, ultimately, can only be understood through it' (Dilthey, 1976, p. 90). 'Living context' suggests that the interpretation is not a static process by a detached mind struggling with data. Instead 'The germinal cell of the historical world is the experience in which the subject discovers himself [sic] in a dynamic relationship with his environment. The environment acts on the subject and is acted upon by him' (p. 203). Dilthey was thus a mutualist rather than a cognitivist and found in the *hermeneutic circle* an account of the relationship between subject and object similar to that of Giddens (see Chapter 6 of this volume). Here it is applied to textual interpretation:

> Here we encounter the general difficulty of all interpretation. The whole of a work must be understood from individual words and their combination, but full understanding of an individual part presupposes understanding of the whole. This circle is repeated in the relation of an individual work to the mentality and development of its author, and it recurs again in the relation of such an individual work to its literary genre ... [Schleiermacher] started with a survey of the structure, comparable to a superficial reading, tentatively grasped the whole context, illuminated the difficulties and halted thoughtfully at all those passages which afforded insight into the composition. Only then did interpretation proper begin. Theoretically we are here at the limits of all

interpretation; it can only fulfil its task to a degree; so all understanding always remains relative and can never be completed.

(Dilthey, 1976, p. 259)

George Herbert Mead (1863–1931) was a student of Dilthey and a friend of William James, and he described the development of the self as though it were a 'hermeneutic circle' – the self is constituted through the Social, which is itself constituted by selves. (See Wetherell and Maybin, 1996, for more on Mead and his work.) This followed Cooley's (1902) concept of the 'looking-glass self'. Cooley used the term 'looking-glass' because, he argued, awareness of self does not come in isolation but through interaction with others.

Several other nineteenth-century thinkers did full justice to social factors and to the circular relation between subject and object, but few spelled it out as clearly as Dilthey in his account of Schleirmacher's method. The mutually constitutive structure underlying the hermeneutic circle goes back to Hegel's account of knowledge at the start of the century, and was used by Marx in his historical theory of society. Consistent with this, 'Consciousness is ... from the very beginning, a social product' (Marx, p. 86), a slogan which has formed the basis of Marxist social psychologies in the twentieth century.

John Dewey used a similar mutually constitutive relation in discussing stimulus and response in his paper on the reflex arc in 1896. Dewey had read both Hegel and James very closely, and he describes a stream of be-haviour in which stimulus and response are not independently defined entities, as they were and have continued to be in laboratory psychology, but are mutually constitutive. Stimulus alters response, which alters stimulus, etc. – not back and forth like a ping-pong ball, but in a con-tinuous flow. The stimulus–response connection of the laboratory set-up is an abstraction from this flow and apt to be too artificial to further psychological knowledge. Dewey himself set up an infant school in Chicago (where he worked closely with Mead) for experimental investi-gations of child-centred learning, in which the individual is seen as being formed in mutual interaction with its social and physical environ-ment. This was closed down in 1904 during Dewey's absence on sabbati-cal leave, a victim of intellectual rivalries and economic pressures. Dewey, Mead and other pragmatists continued to insist on the constitut-ive role of the social in the development of the individual and of knowl-edge, but never returned to empirical investigation after this brief attempt. But their ideas were taken up by the Chicago school of soci-ology, which led to symbolic interactionism (see Wetherell and Maybin, 1996) and, less directly, to the work of Goffman (see Radley, 1996).

In France, sociologists led by Emile Durkheim (1858–1917) looked for a different primacy of the social. Psychologists in the British empiricist tra-dition had argued (like Mrs Thatcher many years later) that society is no more than the totality of individuals, who combine together in order to further their individual ends. Durkheim believed that although the social order is based on individuals and the division of labour, it can be treated as an independent entity which determines individual actions. In his book, *Suicide,* he argued that the suicide rate varies with the kind of society forming the individual, and he developed the concept of *collective representation* as a socially-based explanation of individual action, equivalent to the determining ideas of the empiricists. This is the direct ancestor of Moscovici's *social representations* (see Potter, 1996).

8 PSP in the twentieth century

PSP textbooks of general psychology and histories of psychology (Murphy and Kovach, 1972; Leahey, 1994) reflect the priority given to individual psychology. They offer a chapter on a mainly experimental social psychology, usually late in the book after individual biology, learning and perception have been dealt with. But even this was only after 1930. In the most influential of the histories, Boring's *History of Experimental Psychology*, written in 1929, there is no more than a brief section on McDougall's *Social Psychology* of 1908, and an acknowledgement that Wundt, the founder of the first experimental psychology laboratory in 1879, was equally interested in social psychology. Wundt contrasted 'experimental psychology' with *Geschichte*, the natural history of human beings studied in a comparative, non-experimental, cross-cultural approach.

William McDougall (1871–1938) was an extremely prolific English psychologist, who had carried out cross-cultural as well as experimental research and became Professor at Harvard in 1921. His *Introduction to Social Psychology* (first edition 1908) was about social instincts, derived directly from Darwin and, increasingly through its numerous subsequent editions, from Freud. It also owed much to social Darwinism, a philosophy based on Herbert Spencer rather than Darwin, whose Spencerian slogan, 'survival of the fittest', was popular with apologists for capitalism in the late nineteenth century. But even by 1908 such simple and self-serving applications of biology to social relations were discredited. And when Boring's book was published, instinct theory had been thoroughly undermined (Allport, 1924; Collier et al., 1991). Explanations of aggression in terms of an aggressive instinct, for instance, easily become circular and empty, unless the instinct can be identified and isolated, and traced through development. But McDougall's book was certainly very popular and went into many editions. Boring refers to it as 'extremely influential', but in reality it had little long-term effect on psychology. Perhaps, however, its vogue with a non-academic audience foreshadowed a similar popular success for sociobiology fifty years later. But, unlike McDougall's evolutionary social psychology, sociobiology is based firmly on biological theory and seems likely to prove more enduring (see Toates, 1996).

Another of McDougall's many books was *The Group Mind* (1921) which drew on the French tradition of theorizing on crowds and society (Le Bon, 1977/1885) and this too was the target of effective criticism on the grounds of vagueness and lack of definition. What triumphed in place of

McDougall's declining influence was the prospect of applying individual experimental psychology to social issues (Allport, 1924; Dunlap, 1925). Many writers in the 1920s and 1930s urged the application of psychology to the problems of society. In 1936, during the economic depression and the looming threat of fascism, the Society for the Psychological Study of Social Issues (SPSSI) was formed. One prominent member was J.F. Brown, who tried to bring together field theory and psychoanalysis with a Marxist recognition of the formative influence of society on the individual. His book *Psychology and the Social Order* (1936) was widely read, and is still worth reading, but it was the more general principles of individualism and experiment that dominated social psychology. This continued until the 1960s when cognitive psychology replaced behaviourism as the dominant theory. The period from 1920 to 1955 was the heyday of behaviourism, and behaviourism certainly had an impact on social psychology, especially during the later part of this period. Miller and Dollard (1941), and Bandura (1973) described theories of imitation and aggression which have been the starting point for most subsequent debate on these topics. Skinner's radical behaviourism (1953) provided part of the framework for George Homans' social theory, which in turn led to social exchange theory (see Miell and Croghan, 1996). This is a case of cross-fertilization between PSP and SSP, since Skinner was a psychologist, Homans was a sociologist, and research on social exchange theory took place largely in psychology departments.

The familiar experiments of Sherif, Asch and Milgram (see Radley, 1996; Brown, 1996) did not really break away from this tradition of individualism and experimentation, even though their experiments (like Binet's) involved genuine social interaction, rather than mere social presence or absence, as in Triplett's classic experiment. The tradition even survived as it assimilated the influx of refugees from Germany and Austria in the 1940s, notably Kurt Lewin, Fritz Heider and T.W. Adorno. German social psychology had been much more rooted in social and psychological theory than the more practically-oriented North American variety (see Chapter 10 in this volume). Marx, Freud and Husserl were familiar background figures, and German *Gestalt* psychology, descended from Husserl and Külpe, with its belief in wholes that are more than the sum of their parts, favoured group roles, not just individuals. Lewin developed a theory of field forces, which viewed activity as a function of the social setting as a whole, rather than as filtered through individual minds. This was applied to his empirical work on leadership and group choice (see Brown, 1996), but he is probably better remembered now for the experiments themselves and the practical issues raised by them, than for his field theory. He needed to earn a living and so did Adorno, whose work on the 'authoritarian' personality (see Thomas, 1996; Wetherell, 1996) was a compromise between his interest in Marxist critiques of capitalism and the practical demands of research funding bodies in the USA. Understandably, the theoretical background of these German psychologists became watered down in the face of economic necessity and the pervasive individualist and experimental bias of North American psychology. Problems in society became translated, through research, into problems in the head. Leon Festinger was one of Lewin's students, and was the most cited social psychologist during the 1970s and 1980s (Collier et al., 1991). He is known especially for his experimental demonstrations of 'cognitive dissonance', that is, tensions between forces which are in the mind of the individual rather than existing in the situation that includes the individual.

There was a similar movement towards individualism in the assimilation of Fritz Heider into North American social psychology. One of Heider's gifts to psychology was his writing of an autobiography (1983) in which he records, in some detail, the experiences and the thinking that went into the production of his comparatively limited output. His best known and most influential work, *The Psychology of Interpersonal Relations* (1958), followed years of careful observation of himself and others, not casually but with the conscious aim of distilling the essence of social situations. This is similar in spirit to Husserl's phenomenology, but Heider related it to the more immediate influence of Lewin's work on the relationship between observation and theory. In thinking about anger, for instance, he made notes on his own anger and that of others, attending especially to the social settings, and writing short stories (or 'sketches') to explore and clarify his observations, before representing the relationships in the two dimensional geometrical form familiar to readers of Lewin and of *The Psychology of Interpersonal Relations*. Heider recognized that when abstracted in this way something may be lost. What is missing is the mutual flow recognised by Dewey in 1896 and by Dilthey in the hermeneutic circle. Heider did not mention these but described the same structure in a quotation from Merleau-Ponty, a phenomenologist in the same *anima* tradition. What is gained is the possibility of experimental investigation using the stimulus response structures of the laboratory that had been criticized by Dewey in 1896. These possibilities were duly realized in the abundant research in the 1960s and 1970s on balance theory and attribution theory (see Lalljee, 1996; Dallos, 1996). On a broader time scale, there is a similar shift from the work on attitudes of Thomas and Znaniecki (see Potter, 1996) and in the French tradition (Tarde, 1903). Allport, in a 1935 review article which celebrated work on attitudes, credited Thomas and Znaniecki with distinguishing external social values from internal attitudes (Collier et al., 1991), thus, in effect, enabling psychologists to focus on the individual aspect. But this scarcely accords with the social focus of the original research.

9 SSP in the twentieth century

From our point of view, the two central figures of the SSP tradition have been Talcott Parsons (1902–1979) and George Herbert Mead, whose place in the Chicago School of sociology has already been discussed. From 1944 Parsons was the director of the Department of Social Relations at Harvard. This department brought together workers from anthropology, and PSP, as well as sociology and SSP. They published the fruits of their collaboration in *Towards a General Theory of Action* (Parsons and Shils, 1951). In Parsons' theory of action, the actor was considered as acting freely on the basis of a set of internalized guides – rules, roles, norms – a theory investigated most thoroughly in studies of doctor–patient relations. The doctor and patient were treated as a system, each acting out their parts according to their respective roles. It was a rational theory, an *animus* theory, in which agents freely chose to do what was in their own interests. Cognitive social psychology continues to work in this vein, but within Harvard's Department of Social Relations, research in the 1950s began to move away from Parsons' rationalism in a switch to the *anima* tradition.

Phenomenologists, as we have seen, had gone beyond a rational foundation for action, and had discovered a basis for action that is both deep and superficial, based on the pre-reflective and the 'life-world'. It is deep because, wrapped up in thoughts driven by the anxiety of reason, we fail to notice its massive pervasiveness; yet it is superficial just because it is pervasive and ever-presently before our eyes (and ears and touch). Harold Garfinkel and other *ethnomethodologists* were very familiar with phenomenology, especially that of Alfred Schutz and Aron Gurwitsch (see Chapter 6 in this volume) and they believed that Parsons' account of knowledge omitted the pre-reflective entirely, and therefore missed precisely what is most important in understanding action in human beings when they are not mechanically following rules (Heritage, 1984).

Using detailed descriptions of the minutiae of social interaction, which came to be known as 'conversation analysis', ethnomethodologists made their point in a wide variety of situations, such as in jury deliberations, inappropriately asking a stranger to give up a seat in the subway, and many others. Typically they illustrate what happens when the pre-reflective is disrupted, for instance following sex change. It is not a matter of acquiring rules for a new role, but of *becoming* a new body, where, because movement is added, the body is not the static thing of anatomy but is essentially in dynamic interaction. In this research, the biological and the social factors become indistinguishable. David Sudnow (1978) prefaces his account of learning to become a jazz pianist with a quotation from Husserl's most original student Martin Heidegger:

> The hand reaches and extends, receives and welcomes and not just things: the hand extends itself, and receives its own welcome in the hands of others. The hand holds. The hand carries. The hand designs and signs ... Every motion of the hand in every one of its works carries itself through the element of thinking, every bearing of the hand bears itself in that element.
>
> *(Heidegger, quoted in Sudnow, 1978)*

Thus the hand, like the body itself, is a social object and a social construction.

10 The 1960s and after: a crisis in PSP

During the 1960s academic knowledge came under attack (see Chapter 11 in this volume). There were many reasons for this, but a prolific focus was the anti-psychiatry movement. In 1957 R.D. Laing published *The Divided Self*, which invites us to enter the world of the insane and to recognize that their utterances are a cry of sanity in an insane world; a cry whose true meaning is suppressed by psychiatry. More soberly, Michel Foucault's *Madness and Civilization* appeared in a series edited by Laing in 1967. This was much shorter than the original French version, and it was easier to extract a simple radical message from beneath the subtleties of Foucault's historical thought. This message was that the traditional account of psychiatric history, of progress from cruel suppression to gentle concern, should be reversed. Foucault's story was of social tolerance in the Middle Ages, moving to increased policing of aberrant behaviour in the interests of government control over all aspects of human life. In 1961, Szasz published *The Myth of Mental Illness*, which described the label 'illness' as a device for shutting away troublesome individuals without the bother of a trial. And in the same year Goffman's *Asylums* appeared. This was a product of the Chicago School that had begun with Mead and Dewey, and it shows how the person who comes to be labelled 'insane' moves from the life of a citizen to that of the inmate of a 'total institution' through a process akin to socialization. It is not that the person is first diagnosed and hospitalized, and then has to be socialized. Instead, madness is a potential label linked with a massive complex of activities involving family, police and psychiatrists, as well as the 'victim' who, willy-nilly, collaborates in the incarceration – just as the child collaborates in the often painful process of becoming an adult, and of seeing the world and him – or herself from an adult point of view.

The radical message from these very different books was captured in David Cooper's introduction to Foucault's (1967) *Madness and Civilization*: 'Madness in our age has become some sort of lost truth'. This was a 'truth' that was hostile to control by oppressive governments, but could be found in the drug LSD, in sexual freedom, and in the celebration of 'flower power' against the seemingly insane butchery of the Vietnam war. Striving for more control over their time and their curriculum, students occupied university offices, first in France, then in North America, Germany and Britain. Radical psychologists insisted loudly on the importance of relevance and political awareness in research.

Social psychology was especially vulnerable during this period. It was already undergoing a period of self-questioning. Theory had outstripped practice and observation, so that a culture of experimentation had grown up that was split off from the realities in which it had been born. It was a distinct form of life with its own language, practices, humour, initiations and rituals. In many ways it was analogous to the crisis of consciousness experienced towards the end of the nineteenth century. As in James's 'psychologist's fallacy', psychologists had become used to describing the mind in terms drawn from their theories; these concepts had become refined through experiment and seemed increasingly remote from social realities. Faced with this, and the political challenges described above, some social psychologists looked for a new start. A few in Britain in the 1970s turned away from North America and towards Europe (Israel and Tajfel, 1972) or towards history and philosophy (Harré and Secord, 1973) to legitimate their practice of social psychology.

11   Conclusion

A final word about the nature of the theme loosely holding together this chapter, that of the tension between *animus* and *anima*. It is a theme among other possible themes, but this does not mean that all such themes are equal. It was not chosen arbitrarily, but because it structures the historical record in a way that makes sense historically as a causal story of influence and creativity. In some respects it is like a scientific hypothesis, couched in psychological terms grounded in a peculiar linguistic practice (the distinction between *animus* and *anima*) that was prevalent at the start of our era. It is designed to replace an older hypothesis, that modern psychology began with Descartes in his mind/body dualism when he set apart a realm of mind for separate study, and a more recent one that 'psychology' refers to an academic discipline which began in the mid-nineteenth century (Smith, 1988). There is much truth in these, but they fail to do justice to the part played by the alternative tradition referred to as anima psychology, or to the extraordinary persistence of the tension between the traditions.

References

Allport, F.H. (1924) *Social Psychology*, Boston, Houghton Mifflin.

Allport, G.W. (1935) 'Attitudes' in Murchison, C. (ed.) *A Handbook of Social Psychology*, Worcester, MA, Clark University Press.

Bandura, A. (1973) *Aggression: A Social Learning Analysis*, Englewood Cliffs, NJ, Prentice Hall.

Boring, E.G. (1929) *History of Experimental Psychology*, New York, Century.

Brown, H. (1996) 'Themes in experimental research on groups from the 1930s to the 1990s' in Wetherell, M. (ed.) (1996) *Identities, Groups and Social Issues*, London, Sage.

Brown, J.F. (1936) *Psychology and the Social Order: An Introduction to the Dynamic Study of Social Fields*, New York, McGraw Hill.

Collier, G., Minton, H.L. and Reynolds, G. (1991) *Currents of Thought in American Social Psychology*, Oxford, Oxford University Press.

Cooley, C.H. (1902) *Human Nature and the Social Order*, New York, Scribners.

Dallos, R. (1996) 'Creating relationships' in Miell, D. and Dallos, R. (eds).

Danziger, K. (1990) *Constructing the Subject Historical Origins of Psychological Research*, Cambridge, Cambridge University Press.

de Montaigne, M. (1993) *The Complete Essays*, Harmondsworth, Penguin.

Descartes, R. (1641) *Meditationes de Prima Philosophiae (Meditations on First Philosophy)*. An English translation can be found in Cottingham, J., Stoothoff, R. and Murdoch, D. (1985) *The Philosophical Writings of Descartes*, vol.2, Cambridge, Cambridge University Press.

Descartes, R. (1701) *Regulae ad Directionem Ingenii (Rules for the Direction of the Mind)*. An English translation can be found in Cottingham, J., Stoothoff, R. and Murdoch, D. (1984) *The Philosophical Writings of Descartes*, vol 1, Cambridge, Cambridge University Press.

Dilthey, W. (1976) *Selected Writings* (ed. H.P. Rickman), Cambridge, Cambridge University Press.

Dunlap, K. (1925) *Social Psychology*, Baltimore, Williams and Wilkins.

Durkheim, E. (1952) *Suicide*, London, Routledge and Kegan Paul.

Fogelin, R.J. (1983) 'The tendency of Hume's skepticism' in Burnyeat, M.F. (ed.) *The Skeptical Tradition*, Berkeley and Los Angeles, University of California Press.

Foucault, M. (1967) *Madness and Civilization: a History of Insanity in the Age of Reason*, London, Tavistock.

Goclenius, R. (1594) *Psychologia: Hoc Est, De Hominis Perfectione, Animo, et Inprimis Ortu Hujus*, Marburg, Paul Egenolph.

Goethe, J. (1971) *Elective Affinities*, Harmondsworth, Penguin. (First published 1809.)

Goffman, I. (1968) *Asylums: Essays on the Social Situation of Mental Patients and Other Inmates*, Harmondsworth, Penguin. (First published 1961.)

Good, J.M.M. (1993) 'Quests for interdisciplinarity: the rhetorical constitution of social psychology' in Roberts, R.H. and Good, J.M.M. (eds) *The Recovery of Rhetoric*, London, Bristol Classical Press.

Good, J.M.M. (1980) 'Sociology and psychology – promise unfulfilled?' in Abrams, P. and Lethwaite, P. (eds) *Development and Diversity: British Sociology 1950–1980*, London, British Sociological Association.

Harré, R. and Secord, P.F. (1972) *The Explanation of Social Behaviour*, Oxford, Basil Blackwell.

Heider, F. (1958) *The Psychology of Interpersonal Relations*, New York, Wiley.

Heider, F. (1983) *The Life of a Psychologist: An Autobiography*, Lawrence, University of Kansas Press.

Heritage, J. (1984) *Garfinkel and Ethnomethodology*, Cambridge, Polity Press.

Homans, G.C. (1961) *Social Behavior: Its Elementary Forms*, New York, Harcourt Brace Jovanovich.

Israel, J. and Tajfel, H. (1972) *The Context of Social Psychology*, London, Academic Press.

James, W. (1890) *The Principles of Psychology*, New York, Holt.

Jung, C.G. (1968) *Psychology and Alchemy* (2nd edn), London, Routledge and Kegan Paul.

Keats, J. (1954) *Letters of John Keats*, Oxford, Oxford University Press.

Lalljee, M. (1996) 'The interpreting self: a experimentalist perspective' in Stevens, R. (ed).

Laing, R.D. (1960) *The Divided Self: An Existential Study of Sanity and Madness*, London, Tavistock.

Leahey, T.H. (1994) *A History of Modern Psychology*, Englewood Cliffs, NJ, Prentice Hall.

Le Bon, G. (1977) *The Crowd*, Harmondsworth, Penguin.

Locke, J. (1975) *An Essay Concerning Human Understanding*, Oxford, Oxford University Press.

Loyola, I. (1950) *The Spiritual Exercises,* London, Mowbray. (First published 1635.)

Merleau-Ponty, M. (1962) *Phenomenology of Perception*, London, Routledge and Kegan Paul.

McDougall, W. (1908) *An Introduction to Social Psychology*, London, Methuen.

McDougall, W. (1921) *The Group Mind: a Sketch of the Principles of Collective Psychology with Some Attempt to Apply Them to the Interpretation of National Life and Character*, Cambridge, Cambridge University Press.

Miell, D. and Croghan, R. (1996) 'Examining the wider context of social relationships' in Miell, D. and Dallos, R. (eds).

Miell, D. and Dallos, R. (eds) (1996) *Social Interaction and Personal Relationships*, London, Sage.

Miller, N.E. and Dollard, J. (1941) *Social Learning and Imitation*, New Haven, Yale University Press.

Murphy, G. and Korach, J.C. (1972) *Historical Introduction to Modern Psychology* (6th edn), London, Routledge and Kegan Paul.

Parsons, T. and Shils, E.A. (eds) (1951) *Towards a General Theory of Action*, Cambridge, MA, Harvard University Press.

Potter, J. (1996) 'Attitudes, social representations and discursive psychology' in Wetherell, M. (ed.) (1996) *Identities, Groups and Social Issues*, London, Sage.

Radley, A. (1996) 'Relationships in detail: the study of social interaction' in Miell, D. and Dallos, R. (eds).

Schutz, A. (1964) *Collected Papers*, vol.2, The Hague, Martinus Nijhoff.

Skinner, B.F. (1953) *Science and Human Behavior*, New York, The Free Press.

Smith, R. (1988) 'Does the history of psychology have a subject?', *History of Human Sciences*, vol. 1, pp.147–77.

Stevens, R. (ed.) (1996) *Understanding the Self*, London, Sage.

Stevens, R. (1996a) 'The reflexive self: an experiential perspective' in Stevens, R. (ed.).

Stevens, R. (1996b) 'Introduction: making sense of the person in a social world' in Stevens, R. (ed.).

Sudnow, D. (1978) *Ways of the Hand*, London, Routledge and Kegan Paul.

Szasz, T.Z. (1972) *The Myth of Mental Illness*, London, Paladin. (First published 1961.)

Tarde, G. (1903) *Laws of Imitation*, New York, Holt.

Thomas, K. (1996a) 'The defensive self: a psychodynamic perspective' in Stevens, R. (ed.).

Toates, F. (1996) 'The embodied self: a biological perspective' in Stevens, R. (ed.).

Triplett, N. (1898) 'The dynomagenic factors in pacemaking and competition', *American Journal of Psychology*, vol. 9, pp.507–33.

Vidal, F. (1993) 'Psychology in the 18th century: a view from encyclopaedias', *History of the Human Sciences*, vol. 6, pp.89–119.

Watson, J.B. (1913) 'Psychology as the behaviorist sees it', *Psychological Review*, vol. 20, pp.158–77.

Wetherell, M. and Maybin, J. (1996) 'The distributed self: a social constructionist perspective' in Stevens, R. (ed.).

Wolf, T. (1973) *Alfred Binet*, Chicago, University of Chicago Press.

PART 2

MAKING SENSE OF DIVERSITY

Preface to Part 2

As you will have gathered, there is no overall consensus on the perspective(s) that social psychology should take or the methods it should adopt. The second part of the book offers a variety of structuring principles for trying to come to grips with diversity within social psychology and making some sense of it. It is possible to acknowledge that there are multiple perspectives, concepts, theories and areas of research within the discipline and treat them as independent areas of study which have little impact on each other – a sort of 'peaceful co-existence'. It is possible to look for some kind of synthesis – a true 'multiple perspectives approach' – and to use what you regard as the strengths of each to cover what you see as the weaknesses of the others. It is possible also to regard different perspectives as competitors, striving to be accepted as *the* explanation of behaviour and experience, and to deny the possibility of synthesis or peaceful co-existence. To find our route through these possibilities we need maps; the chapters in this section are attempts to map and simplify diversity. They do not provide firm answers to how you should come to terms with the richness of the discipline, but they put forward structuring principles which the authors have found useful.

The first four chapters offer classification schemes – ways of grouping theories and perspectives that the authors have found to yield some degree of understanding. The chapters tackle the problem of integration or non-integration systematically and give you tools with which to classify and compare perspectives. They may be taken as suggesting that this or that way of categorizing perspectives and theories picks out what is important about them and their differences.

Chapter 3 suggests ten dimensions on which perspectives may be located. The dimensions enable us to relate the perspectives to each other, underline their differences and, perhaps, help us to decide between them. The next three papers offer ways of classifying perspectives according to underlying differences of approach. In other words, they offer ways of forcing some structure onto what, at first sight, may appear to be an incoherent diversity of perspectives. They offer different ways of saying that this piece of work is like that one but is unlike the other, compatible with this one but at odds with that one. Chapter 4 looks at 'domains of analysis' – from the societal to the intrapersonal – and focuses on the kinds of data which perspectives and their proponents consider important. Chapter 5 suggests that perspectives may be classified according to the different epistemologies which underlie them. Such differences emerge, it is argued, because different epistemologies are appropriate for the different bases of human action with which each perspective is concerned; for a full understanding of social behaviour we need to interrelate these. The chapter illustrates one way in which we could make integrative sense of the different perspectives by classifying them according to their evolutionary and historical development as a basis for action. You may wish to contrast this form of integration with the quite different schema put forward in Chapter 6.

Chapter 6 offers a two-part classification which cuts across perspectives to some extent. 'Cognitive' perspectives, which posit a perceiver who receives sensory messages and interprets them (probably in the light of a store of 'knowledge', variously conceived, about the social world), are contrasted with a 'social environment' approach in which this information is conceived as inhering in the environment rather than being brought separately to bear on it. This chapter highlights how different perspectives can agree that human beings live in a world of meaning, but how 'meaning' itself can offer different things to different perspectives.

The next two chapters continue to impose structure on diversity by looking in more detail at epistemology – what we mean by 'truth' and how the validity of perspectives, theories and research conclusions is to be judged. Chapter 7 is about the basis of truth; the provable and perceivable existence of a 'real' world independent of the perceiver and the possibility that the best we can say is that something is true *because it is agreed to be true*. The debate sounds abstruse but is of fundamental importance. Extreme realism posits an unproblematically existent world and a social psychology where all the problems are problems of measurement, while extreme relativism legitimates the notion that what is true for me may not be true for you, and neither position is tenable; this being so, it is important to find a solid place between which to rest our arguments. Chapter 8 picks up from earlier chapters the question of 'social psychology as science' and looks at what we can validly say about science as a whole and how well social psychology can be seen as conforming to it. In the process, myths about the nature of science which have been imported into the discussion of social science by the social scientists themselves are dispelled. Finally, Chapter 9 reminds us that social psychology *is* a science in the sense that its claims to truth are based on research evidence. The chapter explores the criteria which have to be met in order that the arguments in research reports are reasonably plausible.

It is important to recognise that the mechanisms we offer for dealing with social psychology's diversity are themselves very diverse, and there is a danger that the reader will become lost among them. As a structuring principle which works for some people, you might want to identify two kinds of approach in the book so far - two 'strands' which show some degree of internal consistency. On the one hand, there is a more 'traditional' strand which tends to take the existence of social psychology and its research for granted as given and to confine debates to what may be said about them and done within them. This strand of thought is represented in the book by Chapters 1, 3, 4, 5 and 9. The different voices within social psychology (Chapter 1) lead to a diversity which can be handled through classification (Chapters 3 and 4) and perhaps hierarchical ordering (Chapter 5, as an example of one such order); constraints are also imposed by the research basis of the discipline and how such research is conceived and interpreted (Chapter 9). On the other hand, Chapters 2, 6 and 8 constitute a different strand, which treats social psychology much more as a tension between warring intellectual traditions. This involves questioning the 'cognitive' orientation which is central to what we learn as 'science' and common in current thinking about people and societies. These chapters raise fundamental philosophical questions about these traditional ways of thinking and suggest different ways of characterizing the conceptual world. Chapter 7 is central to both strands, questioning the real existence of selves and psychologies as something other than the product of historical construction and underlining some fundamental differences between discursive psychology and other perspectives. Finally, Chapter 9 reminds us that all perspectives within social psychology stand or fall, ultimately, by their ability to create and make credible sense of empirical evidence.

CHAPTER 3

DIMENSIONS FOR DISTINGUISHING BETWEEN THEORIES IN SOCIAL PSYCHOLOGY

by Richard Stevens

Introduction

One of the problems facing anyone attempting to study social behaviour and experience is the multiplicity of approaches and theories that can be found in social psychology. The impact of this can be overwhelming and confusing. The purpose of this chapter is to provide you with a conceptual framework to help you cope with the plethora of theories you will encounter. You can use this framework to set in context, and to contrast and compare, different perspectives and theories at various points in the book. It consists of a list of ten ways or 'dimensions' in which perspectives and theories in social psychology may differ. By assessing them in terms of these ten dimensions you will be able to compare, in a systematic way, their different qualities and usefulness.

Do remember that any system of this kind is itself inevitably a conceptualization. So do not regard it as absolute: it is, to some extent, an arbitrary list and it would certainly be possible to think up a somewhat different system. Furthermore, it is not always easy to determine precisely the position of every theory in relation to each dimension. But I hope that you will find the system a useful means of integrating and contrasting the various approaches to be found in social psychology.

Perspectives and theories in social psychology come in different varieties and the boundaries between them are not always clear, so a word about what is meant by these terms may be useful to start with. A *perspective* refers to a broad conceptual and methodological approach. *Theories* are more limited in scope. They are likely to be centred on the work of a particular psychologist trying to make sense of a particular aspect of human behaviour or experience (e.g. personal construct theory). However, the term might also be used to denote a way of approaching a particular topic (e.g. discourse theory in contrast to social representations theory – see Potter, 1996).

Table 3.1 summarizes the ten dimensions that this chapter proposes. Further discussion of each dimension is given in the rest of the chapter.

Table 3.1 Ten dimensions for contrasting and comparing different perspectives and theories in social psychology

1   Basic assumptions

2   Concepts

3   Emphasis on description or explanation

4   Kinds of explanation

5   Emphasis on differentiation or testability

6   Methodological base

7   Focus and range of convenience

8   'Inside' or 'outside' perspective

9   Level of analysis

10   Formality of exposition

1 Basic assumptions

Underpinning any perspective or theory is a set of assumptions, i.e. ways of approaching and looking at the subject matter which the theorist takes for granted. As these are usually implied rather than clearly asserted, it is not always easy to uncover them. This is particularly true for the theorist him or herself and people working in that perspective, for the assumptions are usually very much a part of their way of thinking about things. I remember that one of the exciting features for me when I came to work at the Open University was working with the inter-disciplinary group which produced the social science foundation course. This was my first opportunity to work with academics from other disciplines (such as political science, economics and sociology) rather than just with other psychologists. I found myself having to explain and re-flect on all sorts of assumptions of which previously I, like most other psychologists, had never been aware, let alone questioned.

Underpinning each of the perspectives and theories of social psychology there are different *kinds* of assumptions. One, for example, is about the best *method* to use. As an illustration, take the approach of experimental psychology: this assumes that the only way to make progress in psychology is to use the methods of natural science. As precise observation and measurement are viewed as being essential to natural science methodology, experimental social psychologists (at least the traditional ones) consider that the qualitative study of subjective experience lies outside the scope of a scientific psychology. In direct contrast, other schools of thought in social psychology (examples include psychodynamic, experiential and social constructionist approaches) would argue that this is to put the cart before the horse. Subjective experience and the meanings which people attribute to themselves and their world are social psychology's core subject matter. We have to find ways which allow us to study these effectively, whether or not this fits with the traditional requirements of the methods of the natural sciences. Not surprisingly, these contrasting assumptions generate very different kinds of research concerned with very different questions.

Another assumption adopted from physical science which underlies most experimental approaches in psychology is that the best way to study social behaviour is to break it down into manageable parts for investigation. In contrast to this are approaches such as systems theory (see, for example, Dallos, 1996) which assumes that you can understand an individual's behaviour only by seeing it in the context of patterns of interactions with others. In other words, you need to study the whole system rather than the separate parts. The first theory in academic psychology to assert explicitly such a 'holistic' approach (treating the whole or pattern rather than the separated parts) was Gestalt psychology, which was originally formulated by three German psychologists (Wertheimer, Koffka and Kohler) in the 1920s. (*Gestalt* is the German word for form, shape or configuration.) The basic premise of Gestalt psychology is that the whole is different from the sum of its parts. To demonstrate this principle, Wolfgang Kohler used to play a melody backwards on the piano to his students. As he pointed out, even though all the components were the same, the Gestalt (or form) was very different. From this it follows that you should not assume that, because you understand the components, you understand the whole. The nature of a part also will depend on its context. You will find both *reductionist* (i.e. reducing to component parts) and *holistic* approaches in social psychology. In the study of group processes, for instance, Bales' method of Interaction Process Analysis (see Bales, 1950) classifies communication in groups into components such as questions and attempted answers. In contrast, the psychodynamic analysis of groups (see Morgan and Thomas, 1996) focuses on the pattern and flow of underlying group feelings.

Gestalt theory stimulated much of the early work on group processes and dynamics (e.g. by Asch, Sherif and Lewin) which are discussed by, for example, Brown, 1996. It also influenced the experiential perspective (see Stevens, 1996b); this assumes not only that studying the way individuals perceive themselves and their world is of central importance for social psychology but also that it is necessary to study this pattern as a whole.

Another point of difference between theories is *which factors are assumed to be most significant in determining behaviour.* Social constructionists (see Wetherell and Maybin, 1996), for instance, regard the processes of social interaction and communication as being fundamental to what we are as persons. To understand a person it is essential to understand the cultural context in which he or she lives. By contrast, the sociobiologist (see Toates, 1996) understands human social behaviour by considering it first in the context of evolutionary development and biological processes.

Most psychodynamic theories adopt an intermediate position here and regard the determinants of human behaviour as arising from the interplay of biological and social factors, especially during childhood. They assume the need to take into account the biological nature of human beings and also how this changes over time as a result of the emotional impact of relationships the child is in. One contribution which psychodynamic theories have made is to develop concepts (e.g. Freud's defence mechanisms) which help us to unravel the complexities of this interaction process.

One way of looking at the set of assumptions held by a theorist is as a reflection of a particular *model of the person*. In the theory in question, are people thought of as self-governing machines defined in terms of inputs and outputs, as biological organisms in a complex two-way relationship with their surroundings, or as sophisticated information processors like a computer? Are they seen as reflexive beings capable of choice and will, or as essentially constructed by their culture, or as people whose actions are essentially determined by unconscious feelings which are outside their control? It is worth looking at such underlying models and considering what they imply about the nature of people and society.

These are samples of some of the assumptions which may underlie a theory or perspective. They are not always easy to determine for, as we noted, theorists do not usually make them explicit, nor indeed may they themselves be always aware of them. Nevertheless, such assumptions play a major role in determining the kind of problem explored, the strategy of research adopted, the interpretation of results obtained and the content of a theory.

2 Concepts

ACTIVITY 3.1

Look through the following lists of concepts. If you can, identify the theory or general perspective from which each is taken.

A   neurotransmitter, peripheral activation, reproductive advantage, split brain, adaptation, blindsight, gene

B   emergent, relational, contextual, discourse, mutual, indexical

C   internalization, phantasy, transference, defensive identification, signal anxiety, splitting, libido

D   authenticity, autonomy, phenomenology, finiteness, reflexiveness, flow, existential issue

E   permeability, constructive alternativism, element, commonality, corollary, core construct, grid

Answers are given at the end of the chapter.

Juxtaposing the perspectives in this way may serve to draw your attention to the fact that, although psychological theories are usually expressed in a form of English prose, in effect they utilize very different concept 'languages'. The concepts in each list are used by that particular perspective but rarely, if ever, by any other.

One important difference between theories, then, is the nature and range of concepts they use. Sometimes theorists invent new terms especially to denote the significant concepts of their theories (e.g. libido, blindsight, existential issue). More often, they use words selected as approximations from everyday language and given a meaning of their own in the context of the theory (e.g. adaptation, flow, permeability, discourse).

The use of different sets of concepts in different theories means there are formidable problems in contrasting the propositions of one theory against those of another. It is often not easy to tell whether they are in direct opposition, are saying the same thing in different words, are complementary or bear no relationship to each other. Problems arise also in that the same word may be given a rather different meaning in the context of different theories. As an example, 'instinct' in ethology (a branch of biology involving the study of animals in their natural habitats) refers to a specific inherited behaviour pattern. In standard translations of psychoanalytic theory, however, it designates a more general instinctual drive which may manifest itself in a variety of ways.

The concepts employed in different theories vary in explicitness (as do the theoretical statements themselves) from those given highly precise definitions (e.g. reproductive advantage) to those which are used variably and whose precise meaning can only really be determined by the context in which they appear (e.g. internalization).

3 Emphasis on description or explanation

Theories are usually concerned with *explaining* or helping us to understand why something comes about. By originating concepts and ways of looking at the phenomena in question, they can also serve as a means of *describing* too. It is not always easy to separate out the two functions. The concepts used for a description may in themselves imply explanatory propositions. For example, if I say a piece of toast is burnt I am describing what it looks like (i.e. black and crumbly). I am also explaining how it came to be that way (i.e. by over-application of heat). To attribute to a person an 'anal personality' is not just a description of potential aspects of their personality (obsessive, scrupulous, miserly, creative, etc.), it also implies a theoretical explanation (psycho-analytic) of how they came to be like that (over-emphasis on toilet training in early life).

Although descriptions and explanations are often intrinsically interwoven, it is worth distinguishing between them as our third dimension along which theories differ, for the emphasis on description and explanation varies from theory to theory. While almost every theory provides both, its descriptive and explanatory powers may not necessarily be equivalent. Thus a theory may be concerned with demonstrating *why* a particular behaviour occurs, but may not provide concepts which allow one to *describe* the behaviour in question any better than in everyday terms. In the area of research into relationships, you will find that much of the experimental work is focused on how a particular variable predicts or relates to others: for example, some experiments have looked at the relationship between measures of physical attractiveness and of liking (Walster et al., 1966). In contrast, the work of Goffman (e.g. 1959) serves both descriptive and explanatory functions. The concepts he has developed (e.g. role, impression management, maintaining face, etc.) serve to describe social interactions but at the same time can be used to understand why they take the form that they do.

4 Kinds of explanation

A fourth way in which theories differ is in the *kinds* of explanation they propose. When we explain something, we demonstrate how it has come about. Explanations depend on the assumption that events, including behaviours and experiences, are interrelated and ordered in a consistent way. To explain why this behaviour, rather than any other, has occurred is to reveal the conditions without which that event would not have taken place in quite that particular way.

Most psychological theories assume some kind of determinism (i.e. that there will be antecedent or related events or experiences without which the behaviour in question would not have occurred). But they differ substantially in the kinds of answer they give to the question of why a particular behaviour or phenomenon has occurred.

Hypothetical constructs

One point of difference between theories is the degree to which they rely on hypothetical constructs. A hypothetical construct is something which is essentially inferred but which is, nevertheless, assumed to be the source of the behaviour or characteristics in question. It is not, then, something you can actively observe or locate in itself. (A hypothetical construct is, in a sense, the opposite of an operational concept, which is essentially specifiable in terms of observable operations or events.) Important examples of hypothetical constructs in psychology include personality, instinct, attitude, social representations and intelligence. None of these can actually be seen or observed; they are inferred from actions or words. Nevertheless, as concepts, they can be of value. They may enable us to tie together and to make sense of otherwise unrelated actions and statements. They may help us to predict what a person may do or say in the future. A danger here, however, is tautology. This is exemplified by the use of the hypothetical construct 'instinct' in some theories in early social psychology. Thus aggressiveness was explained as due to the instinct of pugnacity, mothering behaviour as due to the maternal instinct. These are, of course, no explanations at all, if, as was the case, the existence of the instincts was entirely inferred from the behaviours they purported to explain.

Use of models

Some explanations depend on the use of *models*. A 'model' is an analogy, metaphor or representation used to help make sense of the pattern of phenomena observed. So, for example, the analogy of improvisation or performing a play has been used by Goffman to conceptualize the way people interact with each other, and a family may be depicted visually by systemic theorists as a system of feedback loops. Models are often devised on the basis of other processes whose operation is known. Thus models of thinking and skill performance have been developed on the basis of the design of computer operations.

Kinds of determinant

Another point of variation between different theoretical explanations is in the *kinds of determinant* which they emphasize. This is not just a question of prior assumptions about which general aspects of behaviour should be focused on (for examples of these see the discussion of *basic assumptions* in Section 1 above) but is a matter of the specific explanations which theories come up with. Such differences can be illustrated by contrasting the sorts of statements that different perspectives might typically produce to explain a hypothetical event, say the actions of a boy who repeatedly misbehaves in class.

The *psychoanalyst* might search for the unconscious meaning that this behaviour has for the child. Is it, for example, a manifestation of a need for attention? If so, what factors in the past history of the child created such a need? Perhaps it represents an attempt to compensate for affection he craved as an infant and was denied? Alternatively, perhaps the child's conflict with a male teacher represents the re-playing of an unresolved, residual hostility experienced earlier in relation to his father and now 'displaced' onto the teacher.

The *experiential* or *phenomenological psychologist* would search for reasons in the conscious experience of the boy. How does he perceive the classroom situation? Is he bored? Is it irrelevant to his needs? Does he see himself, each time he challenges the authority of the teacher and the school, as the hero defying the mighty? David against Goliath? Robin Hood against the Sheriff of Nottingham?

A *biologically-based theorist* might look for an inherited need for a high level of stimulation. If stillness, quietness and activities of a non-exciting nature are expected in the classroom situation, this need for stimulation can express itself only in talking, fidgeting and playing pranks – activities construed by the teacher as misbehaviour.

A *social constructionist* might see the situation in terms of the nature of the institution of schooling. What expectations are constructed by the social practices and discourses this involves? Does the child not understand these, or has he been socialised in a different set of beliefs and expectations by, perhaps, his home context? What are the power dynamics here? Who is controlling whom and how?

Other kinds of perspective could also be brought to bear. The *behaviourist* or *learning theorist*, for example, would look for factors such as the approval and admiration of other children which might be reinforcing the misbehaviour. A *systemic approach* might involve plotting the child's position in the systems of classroom and family relationships.

The danger of such brief accounts of a hypothetical situation is that they can tend to sound a bit like parodies, but I hope these illustrations give some idea of the range of explanations which different perspectives can produce. Because they invoke different terms, such explanations may appear quite distinct. However, it is worth noting that on closer examination some differences between explanations prove to be more apparent than real. For instance, in spite of the very different concepts they employ, the biological and psychodynamic approaches are both likely to look for the source of the misbehaviour in the gratification it provides for the child (whether this be arousal or attention experienced as symbolic affection). And, though they will differ in the way that this is conceptualized, most perspectives would also consider that past learning experiences are likely to play an important role.

One not uncommon failing of some proponents of particular theories in psychology (and in the social sciences generally) is to exaggerate the explanatory power of the theory they endorse. Behaviour and experience are inevitably the outcome of many factors. While a theory may provide an accurate account of one or two influencing factors, narrow over-emphasis on these may preclude taking into account other factors which are equally influential. Suppose, for example, we accept our biologically-based theorist's assertion that the child's restlessness is a function of his temperament. This is still not sufficient to account for his misbehaviour. The latter arises out of the interaction between a child who gets bored easily and a situation which demands that he sits still and does not behave in the way that he wants to. In a different context, a different class even, for example one that provided sufficient stimulation so that the child would not get bored, this temperamental predisposition might not result in misbehaviour or conflict at all. The point here is that, in this example, the behaviour is a function of the interaction between the biology and the social setting of the person. Each has to be seen in relation to the other. Interrelated explanations may, therefore, seem desirable. However, because the concepts and propositions of each theory from which the explanations are drawn form a system, this is not usually possible by merely 'adding' them together. Any real integration will almost surely require development of new and higher-order concepts and principles. (For further consideration of this issue, see Chapters 4 and 5 of this volume.)

5 Emphasis on differentiation or testability

For our fifth dimension I want to introduce the notions of *differentiation* and *testability*.

Differentiation

By differentiation I mean the power of a theory to encompass the detail, subtleties and nuances of human behaviour and experience. Clearly, descriptions can vary according to their degree of differentiation. Take the example of a man and woman quarrelling. An observer from another planet may be able to report only 'two living organisms in proximity to each other'. For 'it' (the alien from another planet) may not have concepts available to it which enable it to pick up and communicate attributes such as sex and emotions such as anger. With a little more familiarity with the human species, our 'green being from Planet X' may learn the concepts 'male' and 'female' and so be capable of greater differentiation of the events it observes.

Human beings observing our quarrelling pair will be capable of much more differentiated descriptions. Even if they do not know the language the couple use, they will probably be able to tell that the couple are angry. If they do understand it, they can describe what the quarrel is about and probably whether it is 'for real', in play or merely a theatrical performance. Observers with special sensitivity and experience (a perceptive novelist or psychotherapist, say) may pick up more subtle cues which would elude the more prosaic and, with their help, construct an even more highly differentiated description of the scene. Dispersed among the angry words and gestures they might note the occasional fleeting look and reaching hand. They would scan the choice of words and perhaps observe the softness that colours the end of an embittered phrase, the eagerness that just occasionally lights up the woman's face. She is jealous, yes, but her jealousy brings with it not pain but a curious joy and excitement. In spite of her bitter words, her feelings are still of love not hate. Such an observer might also note the care with which the man picks his words and fends off abuse; the cautious, flattened tone suggests perhaps guilt, perhaps anxiety that this time he has gone too far.

Descriptions, then, form a continuum of differentiation from simple to more complex. To describe any objects, behaviours or events means placing them in a 'network of inference concerning their other observable properties and effects' (Bruner, 1957): it involves going beyond the information given. Looking back at our descriptions, it might seem that the more differentiated they are, the more they tend to involve inference and to go beyond the information given. Concepts like 'organism' and 'proximity' are closely tied to observables. The concepts in the more differentiated descriptions – 'quarrel', 'lover', 'jealously', 'guilt', etc. – require a considerable degree of inference.

Validity

Other things being equal, we might assume that a theory with a greater power of differentiation is better in that it can give us more information about what is going on. But (and it is a sizeable 'but') the question arises of accuracy. However differentiated the description, it is of little use to the seeker of understanding unless it is more or less *valid*, i.e. unless it corresponds in some way to a 'reality' which we assume to exist independently of the observer. The difficulty here is that we do not have access to an 'objective reality' against which we might assess its validity. As is pointed out in Chapter 6 of this volume, many, if not most, social psychologists believe that the only awareness of psychological realities we have is that which we, with the help of our culture and our sensory and cognitive capacities, construct. So what does the accuracy or validity of a description refer to? And how can we assess it?

In everyday life one way is by *consensus*. We invite other people to try out our description and see whether it makes sense for them. This does pose problems though, for their constructions of what they see may be as subject to limitations and bias as our own. History is full of examples of consensus on theories which turned out to be false (for instance, that the earth is flat).

A more powerful method is *predictive consistency*. No description can be made without the use of concepts of some kind. The meaning and implications of such concepts can be analysed. Further observation of what is implied by the analysis may then be made. The behaviour observed may be that which occurs spontaneously or, as in the case of experiment, it may be deliberately contrived. The consistency between the observations anticipated on the basis of the description and those actually observed can then be assessed.

To illustrate this point, let us return to our earlier example of the quarrelling couple. Our sophisticated observers, as you will remember, described the woman as 'jealous'. Such a concept implies not only behaviour of a certain kind but a state of mind. As such, it goes beyond the information given. It is a probabilistic inference based on observation of styles of behaving (tone of voice, facial expression, particular utterances, etc.) which are usually indicative of jealousy. But suppose the woman was not really a jealous lover but an actress playing a part. The observers' attribution of 'jealous lover' is then inaccurate, for feelings of 'jealousy' are not actually present and the description, therefore, lacks predictive validity. If we are given further information – suppose, say, we watch the rest of the woman's performance and ask her what she is actually feeling, or we find out more about the context in which the interaction is taking place (a theatre) – we will find such information is inconsistent with the description given.

Testability

There are different ways in which we can test for consistency, and they differ in terms of their precision and rigour. In everyday life and in much of social psychology too, we check the consistency of a statement against other relevant knowledge and experience we have acquired. It makes sense to us or it does not. Sometimes we may purposely look around for evidence which either confirms or negates what has been said. An account is likely to be accepted as valid if it is plausible, fits our expectations and seems consistent with what we know.

The methods of science and philosophy are concerned with finding more rigorous means of validation. In the first place, the original statement must be rendered as precisely as possible so its key implications can be seen. A philosopher will carefully analyse logical relations with other concepts. A scientist will seek to observe, find or set up situations which yield the appropriate information to enable us to test their implications effectively. The most rigorous test is when the description enables us to make precise predictions which are then borne out by our observations. This is the reason for science's heavy dependence on experimentation and operational concepts (i.e. those that are definable in terms of observable operations or events). In a good experiment, appropriate situations can be set up, the influence of variables extraneous to the hypothesis can be avoided or controlled and the outcome can be recorded precisely and matched against predictions made.

We can test the validity of a proposition in different ways of varying rigour, then, and the testability of any description or theory is thus a matter of degree. However, although we may not be able to submit a proposition expressed in concepts of a non-operational type to a *precise* experimental test, we can still make some evaluation of its consistency with the other events it purports to relate to. We cannot *know* whether or not a man genuinely feels no anger or whether he is, in contrast, repressing his angry feelings, but we can assess the degree to which each interpretation is supported by other observations.

Testability versus differentiation

One of the major paradoxes of social psychology is the tendency for testability and differentiation to be inversely related. Richness appears to be in inverse relation to reliability and the possibility of validation – in other words, more meaningfully differentiated descriptions about social behaviour tend to be less likely to be potentially testable in a rigorous way. We can choose to demand highly testable measures and lose meaning and subtlety of description, or opt for meaning and subtlety and run the risk of a less valid account, or, of course, we may select some mixture of the two. It is possible to describe a simple behavioural movement in operational terms, and a description or proposition expressed as a series of linked concepts of this type may be fairly readily tested for accuracy or validity. However, a description confined to behavioural movements precludes experience, ideas, concepts and language and hence verbal communication – most of what is interesting, relevant and significant about people. To go beyond simple observation of behavioural movement involves the use of hypothetical constructs. Propositions of this kind are far more difficult to test. To conceptualize the most subtle and complex areas of action and experience may require constructs definable only in terms of other concepts and thus not even directly relatable to observable behaviour. For example, the psychoanalytic concept of *latent* characteristics (e.g. latent aggression, latent homosexuality) can be defined only by reference to other hypothetical concepts such as *repression*. (Repression denotes a situation where, because it arouses anxiety or conflict, a feeling or desire is not allowed into consciousness. Nevertheless, it may still remain operative at an unconscious level.) 'Latent aggression' is where aggressive feelings are hidden or masked as a result of repression. Although they may not be expressed in directly aggressive acts, such feelings may still affect behaviour and experience, but in different ways. Thus it is not always easy or even possible to infer latent aggression directly from behaviour. Yet in spite of such limitations it has been found to be a useful category by psychoanalysts and many psychologists and distinguishes one particular psychological pattern from others. Without a concept of this kind, differentiation would be reduced. Validity in social psychology has, therefore, to take the form not just of testable consistency but also of plausibility or even usefulness.

One way in which approaches and theories used in social psychology vary is in the emphasis they place on testability as opposed to differentiation. So, for example, social constructionist, psychodynamic and experiential perspectives use concepts which are capable of encompassing the complexity and subtlety of social behaviour and experience and which thus facilitate highly differentiated accounts. However, they are difficult to test in any rigorous way. In contrast, most experimental work uses operational concepts which can be put to experimental test but which often end up by being somewhat limited in their power to capture the subtleties of human relationships.

This is one reason why it is not really possible simply to compare one theory with another and say which is the *better*. They are likely to have virtues and utilities of different kinds. While one may allow more efficient hypothesis testing, another may offer scope for richer and more differentiated description.

It should not be assumed that the more experimentally testable theories are necessarily more valuable, though many psychologists do make this equation. Such an evaluation is not as 'objective' as is often implied but, like any other evaluation, is rooted in assumptions adopted by the evaluator. As testability is the fundamental criterion of value for experimentalists, it is not surprising that they cast a jaundiced eye on a theory which falls short of this, regardless of its differentiating power. But evaluation depends on your goal. If your aim is to understand complex human social behaviour or to offer people help in changing their lives, a theory with a higher power of differentiation but less rigorous empirical support may often prove more useful than one with greater experimental support but with propositions of limited applicability.

Some psychologists who emphasize that psychology is a young science retain a naïve optimism that, at some point in an indefinite future, differentiation and rigorous testability will go hand in hand. What they seem to ignore is that the most significant attributes of personal lives and social worlds are constituted by concepts, ideas, thoughts, values and feelings, and that these are constructed, can only be interpreted and are, therefore, in constant flux. They can only be expressed as symbols (e.g. language) which, by their very nature, permit no precise definition or quantification of the phenomena they denote, still less of the complex interactions operative between them (see Chapter 5 of this volume).

6 Methodological base

One of the interesting features of social psychology is the variety of sources and contexts from which theories and data emerge. Many kinds of people have an interest in exploring social behaviour and experience. In addition to academic investigators concerned with understanding for its own sake, there are clinicians concerned with helping patients or clients, psychologists concerned with the procedures and problems of education and those facilitating personal growth and awareness; also occupational psychologists whose task it is to increase the effectiveness and satisfaction of people in their working environments. Each of these specialist areas has generated tools and methods appropriate to its task.

The nature and role of methods used in the study of social behaviour and experience will be discussed in more detail in Chapter 9 of this volume. They are introduced briefly here because the methods used play a very substantial part in determining the nature of theory. This can be illustrated by a comparison between psychoanalysis and experimental social psychology. Psychoanalytic theory evolved through clinical work (on the couch, you might say!) The psychoanalyst's primary interest is to understand the patient, not to evaluate his or her own ideas. The psychoanalytic methods instrumental in the development of psychoanalytic theory are *elicitation* techniques designed to give the psychoanalyst access to unconscious material not readily available to the normal observer or to the person undergoing psychoanalysis. Examples are free association and dream analysis. Little or no use is made of methods for the rigorous testing of hypotheses. In contrast, attribution theories (see Lalljee, 1966) have been developed by academic psychologists working in university laboratories. The goal is knowledge, whether or not this is immediately applicable to the complexities of everyday life. The methods used are primarily directed at evaluating hypotheses. The effects of such differences in methodological base show in the nature of the content of a theory. Psychoanalysis offers concepts which allow richly differentiated descriptions of a complex and subtle kind but which are hypothetical and involve propositions which are often untestable in any rigorous way. Experimental social psychology offers propositions with far more limited scope for differentiated description but ones which are expressed in a testable form.

In comparing different approaches to social psychology, it is worth looking out for examples of the link between methods and theory and the dependence of both on the context in which the theorist works.

7 Focus and range of convenience

The expression 'range of convenience' was first used in George Kelly's theory of personal constructs (Kelly, 1955) to indicate the breadth and scope of the constructs a person uses to make sense of the world. I have borrowed the phrase here to denote the vast differences between theories in the range of phenomena to which they are intended to apply and are capable of accounting for. Theories in social psychology range from mini-versions which are hardly more than single hypotheses applicable to one aspect of social behaviour, to grand theories capable of accounting for (or so their proponents claim) virtually the entire repertoire of human behaviour and/or experience. An example of a theory with a restricted range would be attribution theory. This is largely about whether people explain behaviour in terms of personal or situational attributions and, therefore, has a relatively limited focus. Psychoanalysis and social constructionism, on the other hand, are two examples of the 'grand' or perspective type of approach and offer principles applicable to human behaviour of almost any kind.

A problematic feature of social psychology is the lack of an agreed and coherent superordinate theory. Many theories with very different characteristics and ranges of convenience co-exist and do not necessarily fit easily with one another, giving social psychology a fragmentary feel (see Chapter 5 of this volume for discussion of this issue and a proposed solution).

8 'Inside' or 'outside' perspective

A significant difference between theories of social behaviour is whether explanations are couched from the standpoint of the behaving person (i.e. an 'inside' or 'first person' perspective) or from the standpoint of an observer (i.e. an 'outside' or 'third person' perspective).

Of the four detailed explanations of the child's misbehaviour given on pages 51–2 of this chapter (i.e. psychoanalytic, phenomenological or social constructionist) only one is primarily an analysis of the 'inside' type. Look back at them quickly and note which this is.

The answer is given at the end of the chapter.

ACTIVITY 3.2

I choose to use the rather cryptic dichotomy *inside/outside* to denote this difference because the immediate alternatives which come to mind – *subjective/objective* and *experience/behaviour* – both have connotations which I do not wish to imply. An 'outside' view is not more objective in the sense of being more valid or real than an 'inside' perspective. Nor are explanations of an outside kind confined to behavioural studies. Explanations in terms of physiological processes and some psychodynamic explanations are also of an outside kind in that they adopt the viewpoint of an outside observer.

Because of the methodological difficulties confronting the 'inside' approach (see Stevens, 1996b) academic psychology has tended, until relatively recently, to emphasize the 'outside' approach. One problem is getting access to the subjective experience of someone else. You can only infer what another person is experiencing from his or her words and actions and on the basis of knowledge of the context and awareness of one's own experience. It is not always easy to communicate the quality of personal experience, let alone ensure that someone else appreciates what you mean. Nevertheless, as everyday conversation, poetry and literature testify, it can be achieved. Many meanings are shared: indeed, social constructionists would argue that meanings actually emerge from our communications and interactions with each other. (This, of course, makes the distinction between 'outside' and 'inside' problematic, which is why many social constructionists would be chary of using it.)

Traditionally, the two positions have developed independently of each other, and those who adopt one approach usually regard the other with some scepticism. It might be argued, however, that the two viewpoints complement each other and that each adds understanding which is capable of enriching the contribution of the other.

9 Levels or domains of analysis

It is possible to conceptualize and analyse humankind at different, though related, levels. Imagine for a moment the view glimpsed by an observer in a plane. At this level all that may be seen are the artefacts of humans – houses, streets, roads, railways, canals and the chequered pattern of fields. Or think of an archaeologist's view of a civilization from long ago, pieced together from the fragmented traces left behind. Or think of China, Russia, America or any society outside your own. The view of humanity from any of these perspectives is one in general.

Humans are not individuals but component parts of an inordinately larger fabric – society. From such a perspective, people are conceptualized as units of an organized whole: units controlled by and given meaning essentially by their place in the larger framework – environment, communication and power structures, status hierarchies, work areas, resources, etc. At a lower level of analysis, people can be conceptualized as members of various groups and subcultures – family, gang, work-group, play-group, school, factory and office – each with its own structure, interactions, roles and associated behaviours. Humankind is more tangible now; groups, if they are small enough, can be perceived as entities. But still the meaning of 'person' is a part and function of a larger, organized whole. At yet a lower level, we can study people as specific experiencing and behaving individuals. The analysis of people can be pitched at levels more molecular still. We can attempt to reduce an individual's functioning to physiological operations and couch our description and explanation in terms of neural, muscular or even biochemical processes.

What has been described is a hierarchy, but it should not be assumed that the levels are interchangeable or 'reducible', i.e. that explanations at any one level can be translated without loss to another. Each has attributes and meaning of its own. As the Gestalt postulate has it, each whole is different from the mere sum of its parts. But we must add the rider that, for some purposes, each part can often be understood more effectively when analysed and separated from the whole. So to understand people fully, we need somehow, in some way, ideally at least, to pitch our understanding at each level in turn, and to interrelate each with the other. Traditionally, each level has been the province of one or other discipline, ranging in order down our hierarchy from anthropology and sociology, psychology, anatomy and physiology, to neuro-anatomy and biochemistry. Some disciplines (physiological psychology for example) attempt to bridge two or more levels. Social psychology is one of these. You will find in it analyses pitched not only at the level of individual behaviour and experience, but in terms of interactive relationships and group processes and of society.

As the question of levels or domains of analysis is an important issue for social psychology, it is discussed in more detail in the next chapter of this volume.

10 Formality of exposition

This dimension of variation between theories has been implied, if not expressed, in the earlier discussion of concepts and kinds of explanation. Theories vary greatly in the explicitness or formality with which they set out their propositions. Some theories attempt to define concepts carefully and systematically and make their principles clear. Others develop them in a more haphazard fashion, often embedding them in a discussion of experimental findings, case studies or general issues. It is probably true to say that there is a tendency for the more molecular and 'outside' theories, because they are more likely to be able to specify concepts operationally, to be expressed in more formal terms. But an experiential approach or analysis at higher levels does not preclude the possibility of formal propositions. Kelly's personal construct theory is a good example (see Stevens, 1996b). The theory is set out in the form of a series of corollaries (i.e. derived propositions) which stem from, and elaborate on, a fundamental postulate which expresses the basic principle of the theory. The great advantage of stating a theory in this formal way is that it increases the possibility of supporting it with an effective research programme.

Summary

I have suggested that ten ways in which perspectives and theories may be distinguished are in terms of their:
1   basic assumptions
2   concepts
3   emphasis on description or explanation
4   kinds of explanation
5   emphasis on differentiation or testability
6   methodological base
7   focus and range of convenience
8   'inside' or 'outside' perspective
9   level of analysis
10 formality of exposition.

It is worth noting that these dimensions of difference vary in significance. I would suggest that the first six are particularly useful.

It will be apparent from the preceding discussion that the dimensions are interrelated. For example, a theory whose basic assumption is that the methods of natural science provide the only valid approach (dimension 1) is likely to try to use concepts which are operationally defined (dimension 2). It will also adopt an 'outside' perspective (dimension 8), and is quite likely to use experiments (dimension 6) and to emphasize testability (dimension 5).

An example of the dimensions in use

As a demonstration, each of the dimensions in turn will be applied to psychoanalysis. This is not intended as a definitive or complete analysis and you may come up with somewhat different ideas if you try, but at least it should serve as a way of starting you off in using the dimensions in practice.

Psychoanalysis

1   *Some assumptions*

(i)   Clinical methods (such as talking with clients, applying dream analysis or using free association to elicit the meaning of the experience) are the best way of studying the subject matter of psychology.

(ii)   Important influences on behaviour are:

- biology (drives, pleasure principle)

- socialization and the conflicts it may produce (repression, sublimation etc.)

- early childhood experience is crucial.

(iii)   It is important to take into account unconscious motivation.

2   *Concepts* – libido, id, ego, superego, internalization, repression, etc.

3   The theory provides the means for *both describing and explaining* behaviour. Descriptive concepts (e.g. projection, reaction formation) tend to be strongly tied to explanatory assumptions.

4   *Kinds of explanation* – explanation is in terms of drives and biologically programmed development and the conflicts produced between these and internalizations from the experiences of people and events, particularly in childhood. Explanations are sought in the *meanings* (particularly unconscious ones) which events and behaviour have for the person concerned. Much use is made of non-operationalizable hypothetical constructs.

5   Has great *differentiating* power but is weaker on *testability*.

6   Its *methodological* base is clinical. Hypotheses are derived (and tested) partly at least by talking with clients and analysing dreams, associations etc.

7   The *focus* is on emotional experience and behaviour but the *range* of the theory is very wide indeed. It can be applied to the behaviour and experience of individuals as well as groups and also to the phenomena of culture (e.g. mythology and art).

8   It takes *both an inside and an outside perspective*. It is concerned with the analysis of behaviour and experience from the external perspective of the analyst but as it is also concerned with meanings, it requires viewing the situation from the perspective of the subject as well.

9   *Level of analysis* – it usually operates very much at the level of the experience of the individual though it has been applied to analysis at a group level.

10   It was not originally set out as a set of *formal propositions* but research concerned with testing the validity of psychodynamic ideas demonstrates that much of it is relatively easily convertible to propositional form.

Answers to activities

Activity 3.1

The lists of concepts were drawn from the following perspectives/theories:

A   Biological perspective

B   Social constructionist perspective

C   Psychodynamic perspective

D   Experiential perspective

E   Personal construct theory

Activity 3.2

Only the experiential/phenomenological account works primarily and essentially from the 'inside' perspective of the child's experience.

The biological explanation is couched in terms of physiological processes (inherited need for stimulation); the social constructionist account works from an analysis of social practices and discourses; the psychoanalytic one looks at the past history of the child and its influence on unconscious feelings. All these are thus largely third person 'outside' accounts. (The same is true for the behavioural and systemic approaches, which are also mentioned.)

References

Bales, R.F. (1950) 'The analysis of small group interaction', *American Sociological Review*, vol. 15, pp.257–64.

Brown, H. (1996) 'Themes in experimental research on groups from the 1930s to the 1990s' in Wetherell, M. (ed.).

Bruner, J. (1957) 'On perceptual readiness', *Psychological Review*.

Dallos, R. (1996) 'Creating relationships' in Miell, D. and Dallos, R. (eds) *Social Interaction and Personal Relationships*, London, Sage.

Goffman, E. (1959) *The Presentation of Self in Everyday Life*, New York, Anchor/Doubleday.

Kelly, G. (1955) *The Psychology of Personal Constructs*, New York, Norton.

Lalljee, M. (1996) 'The interpreting self: an experimentalist perspective' in Stevens, R. (ed.).

Morgan, H. and Thomas, K. (1996) 'A psychodynamic perspective on group processes' in Wetherell, M. (ed.).

Potter, J. (1996) 'Attitudes, social representations and discursive psychology' in Wetherell, M. (ed.).

Radley, A. (1996) 'Relationships in detail: the study of social interaction' in Miell, D. and Dallos, R. (eds) *Social Interaction and Personal Relationships*, London: Sage.

Stevens, R. (ed.) (1996a) *Understanding the Self*, London, Sage.

Stevens, R. (1996b) 'The reflexive self: an experiential perspective' in Stevens, R. (ed.).

Toates, F. (1996) 'The embodied self: a biological perspective' in Stevens, R. (ed.).

Walster, E., Aronson, V., Abrams, D. and Rottman, L. (1996) 'Importance of physical attractiveness in dating behavior', Journal of Personality and Social Psychology, vol. 4, pp. 508–16.

Wetherell, M. (ed.) (1996) *Identities, Groups and Social Issues*, London, Sage.

Wetherell, M. and Maybin, J. (1996) 'The distributed self: a social constructionist perspective' in Stevens, R. (ed.).

CHAPTER 4
DOMAINS OF ANALYSIS

by Roger Sapsford

1 Introduction

One way of beginning to come to grips with the diversity of possible perspectives in social psychology is to classify them according to where they
locate their explanations and the conceptual framework within which
explanations are cast. A common metaphor to describe this is 'levels' of
analysis, drawing on notions of geological strata (for example layers of
different kinds of rock making up a mountain, one above another and
distinguishable from each other even if a bit blurred at the edges). There
are problems with this as a metaphor, however; it suggests relationships
between levels which do not necessarily hold. Levels are 'higher' or
'lower', and can be identified as 'foundation', 'basis', 'superstructure',
'pinnacle', none of which is necessarily appropriate for discussing different ways of doing social psychology. This chapter therefore uses instead
a metaphor from political geography, the notion of 'domains'.

A political 'domain' is a coherent area under a common government or
hegemony. (Note the parallel use of 'kingdom' and 'realm' in, for
example, biology.) Domains may be adjacent, but none is identifiable as
'above' or 'below', so we are not tempted to regard one domain as in
some way primary just because of the nature of the metaphor. The over-
tones of hegemony ('sovereignty' or 'rule') are also useful: a domain of
analysis is defined by a common 'knowledge', an agreement as to the objects of analysis – societies, or social institutions, or groups and social
systems, or interpersonal relationships, or persons, or the constituents of
persons – and thus one 'position' about the *kind* of questions to be asked
and the *kind* of thing that will count as an answer tends to govern the
debate. In a sense a domain of analysis is like the government of a political domain in that it claims sovereignty over the territory it calls its
own, in terms of the discourse that it accepts as valid. To be avoided,
however, is the metaphor's suggestion of rigid distinctions between domains; political domains have clear and definite boundaries but, as we
shall see, domains of analysis tend to blur into each other and it is not
always possible to assign a theory or a piece of research uniquely to a
single domain.

To suggest that a fixed number of domains can be identified would be
highly artificial, but for the purpose of this argument I shall use a four-
part schema: *societal* explanations, *group* explanations, *personal/
interpersonal* explanations, and *intrapersonal* explanations. This
oversimplifies, but in the interests of clarity. The list is not exhaustive,

but it covers the areas in which social psychology is most engaged and makes useful distinctions within them. (If I had been making a similar list for biology, I should probably have collapsed the first two categories into one; biology is not much concerned with these. On the other hand, I should have elaborated '*intra*personal' into a larger number of domains; explanations in terms of innate behaviour patterns, for example, do not comfortably share a domain with explanations in terms of the migration of molecules across cell membranes.)

2 Four 'domains'

2.1 Societal analysis

The first domain to be discussed is the *societal*, traditionally the home ground of sociologists, economists and political scientists, though social psychology finds itself taking increasing account of it. This comprises analyses in terms of 'the wider society' or 'social relations', where 're-lations' is taken to mean not relationships between individuals but the relations of whole groups or classes to other groups or classes (mostly power relationships) as mediated and defined by social structures and the economic system inherent in a given society. Explanations in this do-main tend towards sociological determinism; for the individual or the group to make significant changes to structures or ideologies is seen as something very difficult.

As an example of analysis in this domain, we may see the nuclear family in *structural* terms as an institution which largely determines what behav-iour is possible for women, in combination with the institutional forms which paid work takes in our society. Women are constrained, on the whole, to 'run the home' and care for children, irrespective of whether family finances in fact also constrain them to seek paid work. These 're-sponsibilities' to the family make it less easy for women than for men to follow a career and in many cases largely determine the kind of work they are free to take. The labour market is structured according to the view that women have families rather than careers (despite the fact that most women show a life-long commitment to participating in paid em-ployment – see Martin and Roberts, 1984). There is a great deal of part-time work for women, and beyond this there is still some tendency, not wholly overcome by Equal Opportunities legislation, for discrimination against women in jobs which offer extensive training, on the grounds that women would leave too soon after being trained. Thus the fact that *some* women leave the labour market to have babies (but generally return to it when the children are part-grown) structures employment oppor-tunities for *all* women.

Culturally this situation is maintained in large part by the fact that all parties substantially accept it. It is 'normal', 'accepted', 'taken for granted' that men go out to work while women look after the home and children, or that home and children are a woman's responsibility even if she does go out to work. Where this does not in fact occur, the expectation is still there, as something against which a defence has to be formulated. The modern nuclear family stereotype, of man going out to work and woman staying at home to 'fulfil her nature' by having and rearing children, is so well entrenched in our society that we take it for granted, but it has a relatively recent historical origin and is by no means self-evidently necessary (see Donzelot, 1979). These cultural expectations (ideologies) form another level of constraint, on experience as well as behaviour. They also have an impact in their turn on the structures of employment: women are seen as having certain kinds of ability, those connected with family life, and so tend to find themselves segregated in occupations predominantly staffed by women, such as nursing, care work, personal service work, typing/secretarial work and primary (but to a much lesser extent secondary) teaching. Feminists would say it is no coincidence that these are occupations which are relatively badly paid and of relatively low prestige. It is also noticeable that the managers and supervisors in these occupations are disproportionately male (Abbott and Wallace, 1996).

So societal explanations *are* about people and their interactions; they are about how people think, experience each other and the social world and act within it. What characterizes them is (1) that they are always fundamentally social in their nature, but (2) that they do not necessarily focus on the interactions or experiences of *particular* individuals, and (3) that what they take for granted is a social world which is not the property or the creation of any individual or group of individuals. The social world of societal explanations is already in existence before any given individual comes into it, it presents only limited 'spaces' or 'roles' for the person to adopt, and in many versions it is seen as constituting individuals rather than *vice versa*.

2.2 The domain of the group

In some respects the behaviour of people in groups can be handled within the societal domain: organizations and large groups can profitably be treated as 'subcultures' and analysed in very similar terms to those used in societal explanations. There is also, however, research on *groups* as distinct from the wider society. Much social psychological research, for example, has demonstrated how the physical structure, communication structure and power hierarchies of groups can affect the kinds of processes that occur within them and the behaviour and experience of participants (see Brown, 1996, for examples). Groups generate their own 'emotional climate', their own needs and sometimes their own collective pathology (see Morgan and Thomas, 1996). In other words, such research takes the standpoint that groups have their own dynamics and 'laws', to be studied and understood in a different way both from the dynamics of immediate one-on-one relationships and the wider structures and ideologies of cultures and societies. Much of this work has aspired to 'psychology as science'.

The group domain is concerned with what people create between them – though not primarily with what the participating *individuals* do and think; the focus is either on the system of which the individuals are a part or the meanings they create between them. Thus the family may be seen as a dynamic system with identifiable and predictable features which are not properties of the individuals concerned and cannot be explained purely in terms of individuals; the system has emergent properties which do not exist and cannot be explained except *inter*personally. This is also true when attention is focused on the system of meanings which people create between them; although it is possible to concentrate on the meanings held and expressed by the individuals involved – what each participant does and understands – a different kind of sense can be made if we focus on overall 'group constructs' as things in themselves. (For a discussion of shared construct systems see Dallos, 1991.) Analysis of family dynamics is one place where this level of explanation has been particularly developed in the last thirty or forty years.

2.3 The interpersonal/personal domain

The next domain to be considered is that of personal action and interpersonal interaction. The two could be separated, but I have put them together here because most of what I want to say holds for both. The key feature of this domain is that it treats the person as a whole – living in interaction and relationship with other people, but analytically separate from them – rather than looking on the one hand at the person's position in a group or social order or on the other at the constituents of the person. Explanations in this domain tend on the whole to be cast in terms of 'reasons' and 'actions' rather than 'causes' and 'behaviours'.

The distinction between 'group' and 'interpersonal' domains is sometimes a fine one, but it can be useful to make it. To analyse families as systems, to look at properties of the system as a whole rather than the actions and reactions of individuals within it, is to set the description within the group domain. However, very similar descriptions could be set within an interpersonal domain, looking at the interactions between family members – 'he does this, and then she does that, and the reaction of the children leads them to...' Here what is being described is not the group as a group, but the interplay of actions and reactions within it – 'moves in the game' and 'parts in the play' are metaphors that have often been used. Where a writer is looking at the pattern of 'moves' or 'actions' as actions of individuals rather than parts of an overall system, problems are differently constituted and different kinds of solutions may be proposed. Analysing a family within the group domain, for example, it is natural to attribute any problems to the family as a whole; analysing it in the interpersonal domain, it is equally natural to explore whether one 'player' is distorting or destroying the pattern of communication. (The distinction between these two levels is often confusing because the same writers will adopt both positions at different times within the same book or article.)

Family dynamics and interactions is a field where explanations located in this domain are well developed – looking at the special salience within this small and intensely interacting group of people's ability to reward or punish each other, confer or withhold validation and in general 'manage' their own selves and the selves of others. Another area, as we would expect, is the study of attraction and friendship (see Dallos 1996a, 1996b for discussions of both of these areas). Another is the psychological study of child development. There has been a long tradition in Western thought of assuming that 'private existence' is a property of individuals from birth – which leads to a very 'rational' and 'adult' picture of how children experience the world. One way out of this 'adultmorphism' is to drop the process of inference to inner states and focus on what the child actually *does* and *says* in a social context, relocating 'the action' from inside the child's head to inside developing social relations and competencies. (See, for example, Kaye, 1982; Morag Donaldson, 1986; Margaret Donaldson, 1992. See also the contrast in Wetherell and Maybin (1996) between Mead's essentially interactional account of socialization and Vygotsky's more 'socialized' account, as exemplifying (despite similarities) the difference between the interpersonal and the societal domains.)

The key feature here, which unites accounts of interpersonal relationship with accounts of 'active' socialization and some aspects of humanistic/ experiential psychology, is that 'the person' is treated as the basic unit of analysis. What we are looking at is what 'the person' thinks, believes, feels, decides and does. The focus is on 'the players' rather than 'the game as a whole', if you like. George Kelly's approach to personality is an example of an explanation in this domain – the person as scientist, testing a model of the social world through behaviour and modifying it to make better sense. The distinctive feature of this kind of explanation is the way in which it presupposes the idea of the individual or person as something distinct from the social world, treats the person more or less holistically and is concerned with how individuals think and feel and what they believe. Explanations in the personal domain are rarely individualistic in the sense of ignoring social interaction, and mostly make great play with the idea that we are shaped by our interactions with others. All, however, are centred in the concept of the integrated and to some extent self-determining individual, analytically distinct from others even if most worthy of study when in interaction with others. This picture comes closest to how we normally talk about ourselves and others in the ordinary language of 'common sense'.

As I have stressed throughout this chapter, the boundaries of domains are blurred, not sharp. On one side this domain blurs into that of the group; on the other it blurs into the *intra*personal domain, concerned with the constituents of the person rather than the person as a whole.

The fuzzy edge with the intrapersonal domain comes somewhere round the concepts of attitude and belief. I have classified classical attitude research, below, as belonging to the *intrapersonal* domain because it conceptualizes attitudes or beliefs as something located *in* people but analytically separable from them. The distinction between this and a more humanistic treatment of beliefs is a fine one, but it seems to me to make sense to distinguish between 'having a belief' (and research on how beliefs are formed in people) and 'believing something' (and research on why people believe what they do).

2.4 Intrapersonal perspectives

We have many *intrapersonal* theories in social and individual psychology whose primary focus is on what goes on *inside* the individual – explanations in terms of internal dynamics or structures. George Kelly, mentioned above, might also be considered in this domain, as a part of his theory concerns the structure of personal understanding – the contents of a given person's 'bank of constructs'. Most Freudian and other analytic perspectives fit here, being explicitly concerned with internal dynamics. Biological explanations clearly belong in this domain. So too do personality theories which conceptualize the person as being constituted by components – extraversion, stability, anxiety, Machiavellianism, or whatever – and classical attitude theories which portray 'attitudes' as something stably located in individuals. Cognitive and experimental psychology also belongs here.

Again the boundaries are blurred, and it is not always easy to distinguish this domain of analysis from the personal or even the interpersonal domain. Psychodynamics, which I have presented here as based ultimately in the intrapersonal domain, can equally be concerned with the interaction between patient and therapist and the decisions and actions which the latter needs to take – typical personal/interpersonal theorizing (see Thomas, 1996). However, what is distinctly psychodynamic about the Thomas chapter is that it is based ultimately on a picture of the self as made up of fragments which are linked by active internal processes – a fundamentally intrapersonal basis for explanation. Kelly, on the other hand, can be presented as an intrapersonal theorist – his psychology is about the 'contents of the mind' – but the focus of his work is the *actions* people take to test and change their views of the world, so I am inclined to classify much of his work as located in the personal/interpersonal domain.

3 Using the concept of domains

Within a domain, different perspectives may be complementary, or contradictory, or capable of combination but only by doing violence to one or both. For example, Freud's and Piaget's approaches to socialization are complementary; they share the view that the young child is mentally and emotionally something fundamentally different from the adult, and Piaget's account of cognitive development fits neatly within Freud's picture of the development of emotions and motivation. Psychodynamics and the experimental psychology of groups can co-exist; each can be useful, and they generally deal with phenomena in quite different domains so that there is little or no overlap. 'Societal' work on the dominance of discourses in the constitution of the self can co-exist with psychodynamics, but by making use of it and assigning it a subordinate position; psychodynamics then becomes an explanation of the mechanisms whereby ideologies, for example, are reproduced from generation to generation (see Jacoby, 1975).

Stop and think for a few minutes about how you would handle differences in perspectives where the perspectives are *not* located in the same domain.   ACTIVITY 4.1

Comparing perspectives *between* domains, three broad strategies have been employed.

1   You may declare a given domain to be the primary one, the one in which explanations have ultimately to be cast, and regard the others as temporary working systems viable only because the 'real' answers are not yet known. This has been the strategy of some physiological psychologists, who would say that all behaviour has ultimately to have a biological basis and explanation; it was the position of Freud in his earlier writing. This kind of reductionist strategy has also been typical of some sociologists, who assert that social structures and social relations provide the only ultimately satisfactory explanations, though other forms of analysis may have some practical utility.

2   You may regard explanations from different domains as simply incommensurable – not comparable because cast in totally irreconcilable languages and conceptual systems. This has been the strategy of very many social psychologists who have been content to regard the societal domain as the purview of sociologists, to treat social structures and relations as, for their purposes, a relatively constant and stable background environment, and to concentrate their attention on other explanatory domains.

3   Finally, you may look for complementarity between theories from different domains, as when functionalist sociology borrows a form of psychoanalytic theory to explain how social structures impact on the behaviour and personality of individuals (see Parsons and Bales, 1956) – the sociology explains how social institutions function in the societal domain, and the psychology offers an intrapersonal account of motivation and of the mechanisms by which values and norms are constructed and transmitted.

The foregoing suggests, however, that theories, or even perspectives, map neatly onto domains of analysis, and this is not always the case.

1 Some lines of theory may contribute to a variety of domains but in themselves be grounded in a single one.

Can you think of a good example of this?

The most obvious example of this, for me, is the psychodynamic perspective, which can be 'intrapersonal', and/or concerned with relational group processes. Indeed, psychoanalysis and related lines of theory have contributed to analyses which are clearly concerned with societal problems – uses of Freud to explain how ideologies are reproduced between generations in terms of relations to the means of production (for example Jacoby, 1975) or in terms of patriarchal relations (for example Chodorow, 1978). In all these uses, however, psychoanalysis remains quite clearly based in the intrapersonal domain – concerned with dynamic internal processes of conflict and contradiction *within* the supposedly integrated person. What it does is to show how problems set in different domains can be illuminated by an account which is grounded in one domain. Psychodynamics can handle questions set in the personal or interpersonal domains, and even render accounts which appear to belong in those domains (see Thomas, 1996). It can even make a fair attempt to handle phenomena set in the group domain (see Morgan and Thomas 1996). However, the perspective is grounded ultimately in accounts of processes which are internal to the self, and therefore in the intrapersonal domain. (Indeed, some might argue that when it begins to travel away from this ground in considering group phenomena – in the work of Bion, for example – it loses what makes it distinctly psychodynamic.)

2 The work of some theorists has been taken over and used in different domains by different 'users'. George Kelly, for example, is a paradigmatic 'level of the person' theorist, concerned with the strategies people use to find their way through the social world. As we have seen, however, he can be annexed by intrapersonal attitude theorists on the one hand – because his theory is essentially cognitive, and cognitions have to be 'located' somewhere – and also by 'systems' theorists concerned to examine shared construing in the 'group domain'.

3 Finally, some perspectives are naturally located in more than one domain.

Again, can you think of a good example?

One example would be the kind of discourse analysis which is concerned with collective and historically and structurally influenced representations of the nature of social life. This describes the constraints on thinking, experience and action which are the result of our society's history and the way it organizes itself structurally. At the same time, *because* it is about constraints on thinking, it is equally clearly located in the personal or the intrapersonal domain (depending on the degree of determinism in the account – more deterministic accounts have models of the world caused *within* people, and less deterministic ones have people learning them from their environment).

In summary, then, the principle of 'domains of analysis' helps us to sort out certain kinds of confusion – where a question naturally posed in one domain is being answered *inappropriately* in another, as, for instance, where questions about the social and structural constitution of gender roles are answered with reference to biological differences. It also enables us to note that a given perspective can be used *appropriately* to cast light on phenomena naturally framed within a different domain – as where psychoanalysis is used to cast light on relationships or socially transmitted values. Some perspectives are reductionist in the sense that they tend to constrain the scope of explanation to a single domain, seen as primary – the biological perspective is often used in this way – while others have a natural 'home' in more than one domain and are designed to tackle problems natural to more than one – the most obvious example being social constructionism, which is concerned both with the structures and history of societies and with their impact on the experiences of people within them. The principle of domains of analysis cannot provide simple 'decision-rules' for preferring one perspective to another, but it can help to clarify the territory which is under dispute, where conflict between perspectives occurs.

References

Abbott, P.A. and Wallace, C. (1996) *An Introduction to Sociology: Feminist Perspectives* (2nd edn), London, Routledge.

Brown, H. (1996) 'Themes in experimental research on groups from the 1930s to the 1990s' in Wetherell, M. (ed.) *Identities, Groups and Social Issues*, London, Sage.

Chodorow, N. (1978) *The Reproduction of Mothering: Psychoanalysis and the Sociology of Gender,* Berkeley, University of California Press.

Dallos, R. (1991) *Family Belief Systems, Therapy and Change,* Buckingham, Open University Press.

Dallos, R. (1996a) 'Creating relationships' in Miell, D. and Dallos, R. (eds).

Dallos, R. (1996b) 'Change and transformation of relationships' in Miell, D. and Dallos, R. (eds).

Donaldson, M. (1992) *Human Minds: an Exploration,* Harmondsworth, Penguin.

Donaldson, M.L. (1986) *Children's Explanations: a Psycholinguistic Study,* Cambridge, Cambridge University Press.

Donzelot, J. (1979) *The Policing of Families,* London, Hutchinson.

Jacoby, R. (1975) *Social Amnesia: a Critique of Conformist Psychology from Adler to Laing,* Boston, Beacon Press.

Kaye, K. (1982) *The Mental and Social Life of Babies: How Parents Create Persons,* Brighton, Harvester.

Martin, J. and Roberts, C. (1984) *Women and Employment: a Lifetime Perspective,* London, HMSO.

Miell, D. and Dallos, R. (eds) (1996) *Social Interaction and Personal Relationships,* London, Sage

Mitchell, J. (1974) *Feminism and Psychoanalysis,* Harmondsworth, Penguin.

Morgan, H. and Thomas, K. (1996) 'A psychodynamic perspective on group processes' in Wetherell, M. (ed.) *Identities, Groups and Social Issues,* London, Sage.

Parsons, T. and Bales, R.F. (eds.) (1956) *Family, Socialisation and Interaction Process,* London, Routledge and Kegan Paul.

Sayers, J. (1986) *Sexual Contradictions: Psychology, Psychoanalysis and Feminism,* London, Tavistock.

Thomas, K. (1996) 'The psychodynamics of relating' in Miell, D. and Dallos, R. (eds).

Wetherell, M and Maybin, J. (1996) 'The distributed self: a social constructionist perspective' in Stevens, R. (ed.) *Understanding the Self,* London, Sage.

CHAPTER 5

TRIMODAL THEORY AS A MODEL FOR INTERRELATING PERSPECTIVES IN PSYCHOLOGY

by Richard Stevens

1 The diverse epistemologies of psychology

One feature which characterizes perspectives in psychology is their epistemology. By 'epistemology' I mean the form which any understanding or knowledge takes, the assumptions which underlie it and the methods used to establish it. In social psychology (as in other areas of psychology) we find not one but several quite different epistemologies or forms of understanding.

Much of the social psychological research which goes on in our universities and elsewhere, for example, is conceived of as 'scientific'. It is premised on precise measurement and on trying to elucidate cause-effect connections, usually by means of experiments. This approach might be termed *nomothetic* in that it is concerned to establish the fundamental cause-effect laws which are presumed to underlie human social behaviour.

This approach is not, of course, by any means the only one in social psychology. In other perspectives – psychodynamics and social constructionism for instance – we find a very different epistemology. Here, there are no measurements, no attempt to perform carefully designed experiments. Instead, we find an emphasis on qualitative accounts, on interpretation. Yet again, in the experiential or humanistic perspective (see Chapter 1 or Stevens, 1996) we see a third kind of epistemology. Here, it is not only a question of working with the qualitative (that is, the unquantifiable and therefore unscientific) but of questioning also the determinism of natural science. There is an assumption here that people are not merely the products of influences outside their control but that in a very real sense can take some responsibility for becoming what they choose.

These, then, are examples of three quite distinct ways of making sense of social life, each raising different kinds of issue and calling for different kinds of evaluative criteria. The question which arises is – Why is there this fragmentation? Why should social psychology (unlike the natural sciences) involve different kinds of epistemology? This chapter offers an answer to that question. It tries to show how taking into account different epistemologies can produce more effective understanding of human action. It also demonstrates how different perspectives or schools of psychology interrelate and can be mapped in terms of the trimodal model presented.

2 Three modes of human action

Why then the epistemological diversity in social psychology? One reason lies in the different intellectual roots of the perspectives and this aspect has been discussed in Chapter 2 of this book on the historical origins of social psychology. But the critical issue here is, I believe, that, in psychology, *epistemology is complicated because of the complex nature of our subject matter.*

Human beings are the product of a very long period of biological and cultural evolution. That evolutionary process has resulted in three distinctively different modes or bases for human action. Each mode has grown out of and has been made possible by the mode which preceded it, but in so doing it has taken on a distinctively different form. In other words, the second and third modes or bases of action I am to describe are *emergent processes*. (An emergent process is one in which the result of an interaction, a sequence of development, or a whole combined from parts may lead to new kinds of property which are not found in the developmental antecedents or interacting parts themselves. An example from the material world would be water, whose properties are different from the gases [oxygen and hydrogen] which constitute it.)

In the beginning was biology – what we might call the primary (or initial) source of behaviour. Here the basis for human action resides in the action of hormones, in the biochemical and psychophysiological processes which underpin behaviour. Such processes are profoundly influenced by genetic inheritance and major change is brought about only through evolution – in other words by mutation, and natural and sexual selection. In species low down the phylogenetic scale, behaviour is largely based on biological process. Even in humans, biological processes – hunger, thirst and sexual drives are obvious examples – influence the ways in which we act. There is also evidence, if often of a somewhat problematic kind, that the basis for complex consistencies of behaviour such as are described by 'intelligence' and 'temperament' can be influenced by primary processes of this sort. And, if the elegant arguments of sociobiologists have any basis, perhaps some social behaviours such as patterns of aggression and dominance or aspects of the way we relate sexually may also be influenced by our biological and evolutionary inheritance.

The extraordinary feature which marks the evolution of *homo sapiens* is the rapid growth in brain size from 400ccs or so in the first humans to three times that size in humankind today. This growth is associated with the emergence of language and this must have made possible an enormous increase in the capacity for complex symbolization. Far, far more than any other species, humans live in an inner world of symbols and conceptualizations; people act on the basis of the meanings which they attribute to their actions and the situations in which they find themselves. This marks a fundamental change in the nature of the basis for human action. Now this is not only biological but also *symbolic*. The chief source of action becomes communication and learning rather than genetic inheritance. Change is now effected through communication from one person, group or generation to another – a process of *cultural* evolution which makes possible far more rapid change than biological evolution.

We can see, then, that this shift from a biological to a symbolic basis for human action represents an *emergent process*. The capacity for symbolic thought is made possible by biological evolution but, once established, it brings about a fundamental change in the ways in which actions are generated.

It is useful, I think, to subdivide this symbolic mode. One secondary basis for action derives from *society* – from the values, beliefs, social practices and attitudes inherent in language, all of which we assimilate from the subcultures in which we live and grow up. (These are the phenomena of interest to social constructionists.) The other basis is more specific to each individual. These are the meanings assimilated during the particular experiences of a person's *childhood*, through interactions with siblings, parents and others who make up our personal worlds (the sphere of, for example, psychodynamic theories).

Out of this symbolic or secondary mode emerges a third. Our capacity for symbolization has developed so that it is possible for us to symbolize or conceptualize *ourselves*. We can observe, and monitor our own actions. We are capable of seeing ourselves as a person like any other. Above all, we become capable of *envisaging alternatives* – of knowing that we can act in a different way than what is expected of us: that we can be a different kind of person than we usually are. We become capable, in other words, of self-awareness and reflective choice. This constitutes a third kind of basis for human action – *reflexive awareness*. Here the basis is not biology, nor is it simply the meanings assimilated from our culture or during our childhood, but it is this human capacity to reflect on what we are doing and to contemplate and initiate alternatives and novel actions. Examples of human experience of this reflexive kind are awareness of our own existence and the existential issues with which such awareness confronts us. So we need to come to terms with our own mortality, for example, and the finiteness of our lives: and the fact that we make choices which may change our own or other people's lives. Another example of reflexive awareness is perhaps the heightened consciousness which can result from meditation or from intense reflection on the nature of an event and its consequences.

It is much more difficult to identify the processes involved in the emergent transition from the secondary to this tertiary mode, from the symbolic to the reflexive, but it is interesting to speculate about what kinds of cultural and personal factors may facilitate such a shift. Complex, modern cultures offer a plethora of information through books, media and travel – about beliefs and ways of being which are different from our own. By widening the alternatives open to us, this may facilitate reflexive choice. Perhaps living in what Luckman has called 'the multiple worlds of modern man' predisposes us to reflect on the different aspects of our existence and how they could be otherwise. The degree to which modern cultures stress and value individualism may also be a factor. Autonomy and the reflexive mode are institutionalized in both the notion of democracy and the legal codes of Euro-American and other societies. People are deemed to be responsible and accountable for their actions and contracts where these are entered into voluntarily and without coercion. At a personal level, certain types of education, good psychotherapy, experiential groups all *may* help us in the shift to a tertiary basis for our actions. Clearly, however, the capacity for reflexive awareness has been with us since written records began, certainly from the Greeks. And certainly also, for all of us, the capacity to act on the basis of reflexive awareness is fragile at best and is easily dominated by the other modes.

What I am suggesting is three modes or bases for action and human life – biological, symbolic and reflexive. These are fundamentally different bases which have emerged in the course of our evolution. They are emergent properties, in other words, each was made possible by its preceding mode but is distinctively different from it.

It is worth noting here that this trimodal model of the basis for human action enables us to reframe our usual way of classifying or conceptualizing human action. Typically, this has been classified in terms of its consequences. Altruism, for example, is defined as behaviour which benefits others. In trimodal terms, however, we can see that altruism can have different origins and therefore constitute different kinds of action. If a person behaves beneficially towards another merely as a result of convention and tradition (for example because he or she has been brought up to be good to others) then this is of a secondary or symbolic order and quite different from an altruistic act based on a contemplated moral awareness – in other words, of the reflexive, tertiary mode.

The trimodal model also helps us to become aware of the basis for some conflicts within ourselves and others. I remember, for example, on the occasion of the Falklands war, feeling very mixed emotions. On one side (my primary, biological predisposition to favour my in-group, coupled with the secondary influence of socialization that my in-group is my country) I wanted Britain to win. On the other (my tertiary reflexiveness), the whole conflict seemed destructive and misguided. Far better to redirect the enormous resources involved to resettling the islanders somewhere else in style.

In practice, most actions will be amalgams of two or more modes. But I have found it helpful in understanding a specific action or experience to attempt to analyse its degree of dependence on different modes. Also, people generally (maybe even cultures too) can be characterized, it seems to me, in terms of their relative dependence on biological, symbolic and reflexive modes, or combinations of these.

3 Three kinds of epistemology

How then does this trimodal model of the bases of human action relate to the central concern of this chapter – making sense of the epistemological diversity of social psychology?

In the case of biological explanations or primary mode analysis, action can be related, potentially at least, to specific biochemical and psychophysiological processes. These are tangible and therefore potentially observable and measurable. Hence the methods of natural science (that is, a *nomothetic* approach aimed at establishing causal laws) are entirely appropriate here. (The situation is complicated somewhat by the use of *functional* explanations, such as evolutionary and sociobiological accounts (see Toates, 1996), as well as causal ones. But this does not change the position, for functional explanations which look at origins rest on the assumption of a sequence of causally-related biological processes.)

At the secondary or symbolic level, however, the basis for action is not in the tangible processes of biology but in meanings. By their very nature, meanings are unmeasurable and unobservable. They can only be inferred, constructed, interpreted. We can only understand actions in this mode by attributing meanings (such as intentions) to the actor.

Freud began as a biological, nomothetic scientist seeking to establish the laws underlying personality. As a genuine scientist, however, he geared his approach to the nature of his subject matter. He did not attempt to impose the alien methods of natural science on the accounts and fantasies of his patients when the meanings in which he was interested could not be captured in this way. The result, psychoanalysis, uses an epistemology which is clearly not scientific in the sense of natural science. But it is appropriate to its subject matter – symbolic meanings – in a way that a natural science approach could not be.

This is the approach of interpretation. A term that has been used for this kind of epistemology is *hermeneutic*. This is borrowed from biblical studies where it refers to the unravelling of distortions imposed on a text by time and by translation. The hermeneutic approach in psychology seeks to interpret the meaning of an individual's actions and relate them to the underlying influences which gave them shape. For Freud, that meant the patient's childhood experience. For the social constructionist, who also operates with a hermeneutic approach, it lies in the beliefs and meaning systems of contextual culture. Hermeneutic epistemology – the epistemology of psychoanalysis and social science – lacks the precision of the nomothetic approach. Interpretations cannot be validated like a series of experiments can. And yet this is the epistemology required for understanding symbolic or secondary mode action. For, try as psychologists *have* tried, the symbolic cannot be reduced to the measurable.

When we come to the level of reflexive awareness, I want to suggest that we need a further, third kind of epistemology. Here, we are dealing not with the actual but the possible, not with how things are but with how they *might be*. Both nomothetic and hermeneutic approaches assume a determinism (action is determined in the primary mode by inherited biological process, in the symbolic mode by assimilated meanings.) At the tertiary level of reflexive awareness, however, actions are not determined but created by an autonomous person through his or her capacity to reflect on themselves and on events.

Psychology at the level of the biological or primary mode can be regarded as natural science, and at the symbolic or secondary level as social or 'personal' science. At the tertiary level, it is what we might call a 'moral' science, in that it is more concerned with how we choose to act: it represents a study not just of what is but of what *could* be and *should* be. An epistemology for this mode needs to focus on possibility and the future rather than present actuality in relation to the past, and it needs to assume autonomy not determinism. I call such an epistemology *'transformational'*. While the nomothetic approach of natural science is concerned to explain, and the hermeneutic approach of social and personal science is concerned to interpret, the transformational approach of moral science is concerned to facilitate possibility through encouraging reflection as a basis for action.

The propositions of trimodal theory discussed above are summarized in Table 5.1. There is a column for each of the three modes. Each row shows how they contrast with each other in terms of different features, Thus the bases they provide for action (i.e. biological or symbolic process or reflexive awareness) are contrasted in line 2 and the models of action they assume (i.e. determined or autonomous) in line 3. The subsequent rows summarize the kind of epistemology each requires and its aim, and the kind of science each mode might be considered to represent. Examples of the perspectives which each mode encompasses are indicated in the bottom row and are discussed further in the following section.

4 Trimodal theory and social psychology

Trimodal theory proposes that all three modes, primary, secondary and tertiary, are potentially involved in human action. Social psychology therefore needs to operate with three different epistemologies.

Table 5.1

Mode	Primary	Secondary	Tertiary
Basis for action	Biological process	Symbolic process	Reflexive awareness
Influence on action	Genetic inheritance	Meanings assimilated from society and childhood	Capacity to reflect on and be aware of actions and their consequences
Assumes	Determinism	Determinism	Autonomy
Kind of epistemology	Nomothetic	Hermeneutic	Transformational
Aim of epistemology	Explain (in terms of cause-effect laws)	Interpret	Facilitate possibility
Kind of psychology	Natural science	Social or personal science	'Moral' science
Examples of perspectives within mode	Psychophysiology	Social constructionism. Psychoanalysis	Existential psychology. Some humanistic, feminist and Buddhist psychology

What is important is that:

- We are alert to these different bases or modes of human action.
- We select the epistemology appropriate to the mode with which we are concerned. For example, if we are trying to explore how past experiences have influenced our ways of making sense of present events, then an interpretative or hermeneutic approach is called for.

Trimodal theory allows us to interrelate factors which otherwise may be regarded as oppositional: it shows, for example, how behaviour is *both* biologically and socially constructed, and how people are *both* determined and yet capable of autonomy.

The preceding sections made some reference to how different perpectives in social psychology fit into this schema. The biological model clearly maps onto the primary and nomothetic mode. Psychoanalysis and social constructionism are both concerned in their different ways with the meanings which underpin and generate social behaviour: they thus relate to the secondary mode and involve an interpretative or hermeneutic epistemology. The focus of existential and humanistic psychologies on personal change through reflexive awareness is clearly essentially tertiary and 'moral science', using a transformational epistemology. This applies also to the consciousness-raising strategies of much of feminist psychology and the meditation techniques of Buddhist psychology: in that these aim to bring about change through reflection and awareness, they operate in the tertiary mode.

Note, however, the mapping of the perspectives is not necessarily as clear cut as this analysis may make it appear. Some perspectives, for example, may be seen as bridging two or more modes. Thus, while existential and humanistic psychology might be classified as tertiary because of their focus on human autonomy and capacity for self-directed change, they nevertheless often rest on phenomenological accounts of personal experience which in themselves may be better considered as based in the symbolic or secondary mode. Also, psychoanalysis and social constructionism, to the extent which they seek to use their analyses to make possible self-directed change, may have a tertiary aspect. The experimentalist perspective also crosses the lines in that it operates with the nomothetic methodology of causal analysis but its concern is with the symbolic basis of the meanings we attribute to the social world. However in this case, in terms of the theory, this would be regarded as an inappropriate way to proceed.

Finally, it is worth bearing in mind the very different criteria for evaluation required by these different epistemologies and thus by the social psychological perspectives to which they relate. With the nomothetic mode used to explore the biological basis of action, the critical issue is 'the test of truth'. Do the predictions of the theory hold good? Is the understanding generated by the research valid? When we move to the hermeneutic strategies involved in the symbolic, secondary area, we still need to justify any analyses or accounts we give: to assess how far they effectively represent the meaning systems (the beliefs, feelings etc.) on which they are focused. We need to know that our account 'makes sense' of what the informants are doing, feeling or thinking, and to make some sort of sense ourselves of the way in which our account is similar to or differs from accounts which informants might themselves give of their experience. The criteria for determining validity here, though, are not obvious or straightforward; they are likely to involve assessments of plausibility and consistency and to rest on assumptions about the nature and bases of human experience and action. With the transformational epistemology appropriate to the tertiary reflexive level we are still subject to the 'test of truth', but the question becomes even more complex because we are often saying not that people are this or are currently able to do that, but that they are capable of being this or doing that; thus an appeal to current reality may not be decisive. What is at stake at the tertiary level is not so much whether an account is accurate, but whether it is possible or desirable. Ultimately, it is about inspiration: whether it can energise a person to open up the possibilities in their life. (The situation is further complicated because once a way of thinking about something is communicated, it makes it possible to think about it in that way, even if it had not been thought about in that way before. So some 'moral science' research and writing, as well as other forms of research, may therefore have a self-fulfilling quality.)

In conclusion, this chapter uses trimodal theory as a basis for making sense of social psychological perspectives in terms of the source of actions they emphasize (biological, symbolic, reflexive) and the epistemologies that they involve. Given the argument here that human personal and social life involves a mixture of all three sources, this would imply that we need a broad range of perspectives in social psychology in order to represent all three modes, and that such perspectives are therefore to be regarded as essentially complementary rather than mutually exclusive.

References

Stevens, R. (1996) 'The reflexive self: an experiential perspective' in Stevens R. (ed.) *Understanding the Self*, London, Sage.

Toates, F. (1996) 'The embodied self: a biological perspective' in R. Stevens (ed.) *Understanding the Self*, London, Sage.

CHAPTER 6
THEORIES OF MEANING

by Arthur Still

I Two theories of meaning

It is widely agreed that people, being social animals who speak and think and form part of a culture, 'live in a world of meanings'. But what is meaning and how does it arise? This question has been a major preoccupation of philosophers and logicians this century, as language has come to play an increasingly central part in their deliberations. Great theories from the turn of the century onwards about components of meaning (Frege, 1952), the constitution of meaning (Husserl, 1970), and the nature of significance (Peirce, 1992; Saussure, 1983) have been debated and refined. Psychologists themselves have contributed to this debate (Morris, 1938; Bruner, 1990), as well as writing useful guides to help colleagues find their way through its complexities (Russell, 1984). However, my purpose will not be to extract the significant results from this tradition, but to attempt something that is in principle much simpler – to uncover two broad, conflicting assumptions about meaning, each stemming from distinctive philosophical positions about the word 'meaning'. What is important from our point of view is not the philosophies themselves, but that each colours a contrasting approach to social psychology.

One approach or theory is characteristic of cognitive and experimental psychology (e.g. Lalljee, 1996), which takes the individual as the starting point; the other of social constructionism (e.g. Wetherell and Maybin, 1996; Wetherell, 1996) and related approaches which see the individual as emerging out of the social. These approaches are more than just different psychological theories, since they profoundly affect our view of the phenomena to be explained. They are metatheories. Thus there are different theories about the origins of aggression and gender differences, but at least there is usually agreement about the type of data. But this is not so in the case of meaning, where the metatheories of meaning seem to describe different phenomena and draw on different psychologies, though they confusingly share many words in common besides 'meaning'.

The first metatheory, characteristic of cognitive and experimental psychology, starts with the world of physics as the fundamental reality. Meaning is added by the brains or minds of the individual human beings who inhabit this world, by a process of cognitive construction. This theory is *cognitivism*. It is individualist, since the process of constructing meaning is by individuals, who are affected by, but still distinct from, the social world around them. Thus the subject matter of psychology is the minds and behaviour of individual human beings, and the social psychologist studies them in their social aspect.

The starting point of the second metatheory is with meaning itself. Human beings cannot be understood in isolation, able to construct meaning out of a meaningless physical environment, but only as beings already within a meaningful social environment. Likewise, the environment is not a pregiven world to which human beings have adapted through evolution, but is the setting for a form of life. What has evolved is the form of life as a system, which includes both individuals and environment in mutual interdependence. This is *mutualism*. The mutualist social psychologist starts with the social setting and studies how individual psychology, the self and its processes, emerges out of that setting through lifelong development (Still and Good, 1992).

Both metatheories of meaning involve construction: cognitive construction on the one hand, social construction on the other. It is easy to confuse the two kinds of construction and to use them interchangeably; it will be part of the purpose of this chapter to show that they, like their respective notions of meaning, are very different.

2 Cognitivism: the cognitive metatheory of meaning

In stimulus-response theories, and also in recent information-processing theories of perception and learning, the stimulus or input is, or could be, described in physical terms, as light or sound of a certain waveform, or a shape described mathematically. Pictures and words are used as stimuli, but even then the energies impinging upon the retinal surfaces are treated as physical, with meaning to be synthesized at a later stage. This implies that the world we inhabit is one that is best described in the language of physics, therefore, a world devoid of human meaning. 'How, in such an alien and inhuman world, can so powerless a creature as Man preserve his aspirations untarnished?' asked the philosopher Bertrand Russell, contemplating 'the world which Science presents for our belief' (Russell, 1953, p. 51) in a paper written in 1902.

What is the relationship between this and the world of meaning that we actually experience? How is meaning created in the jump between the inhuman and the human? The cognitivist answer which is still favoured by most cognitive psychologists was given over 300 years ago by John Locke.

2.1 John Locke and the parrot problem: meaning through ideas and mental representations

In 1689 Locke published *An Essay concerning Human Understanding,* which is often considered the first work of modern psychology. It is a systematic account of the mind and its capacity for knowledge, which is gained through experience rather than innate; hence Locke was an Empiricist. His book dealt with sensation, perception, memory, consciousness, but above all with ideas, which we might now call representations, since for Locke an idea in the mind stood for or represented its external object. The idea of a cat is a mental representation of a cat. He used the presence of ideas to distinguish between the mental life of animals ('brutes', as he called them) and humans. Consider the mental life of a parrot, which uses words, but does not have a language: '...Parrots, and several other Birds will be taught to make articulate Sounds distinct enough, which yet, by no means, are capable of Language' (Locke, 1975, p. 402). Why is this? What is it that gives meaning to the words of a human being, but is lacking in the words of a parrot?

You might find it helpful here to pause for a few minutes, and write down your own answer to this question, before reading Locke's explanation.   **ACTIVITY 6.1**

Locke's answer was that

> Besides articulate Sounds ... it was further necessary, that he should be able to use these Sounds, as Signs of internal Conceptions; and to make them stand as marks for the Ideas within his own Mind, whereby they might be made known to others, and the Thoughts of Men's Minds be conveyed from one to another.

Thus

> Before a man makes any Proposition, he is supposed to understand the terms he uses in it, or else he talks like a Parrot, only making a noise by imitation, and framing certain Sounds, which he has learnt of others: but not as a rational Creature, using them for signs of Ideas which he has in his Mind.
>
> *(ibid., p. 614)*

Was your answer to the parrot problem similar to Locke's? If so you are not alone. Every year I present the problem to my class of third-year psychology students and every year most of them come up with Locke's answer couched in modern terms. This is not surprising since it is a theory of knowledge and meaning widely held today. Consider the following two quotations, one from Locke, and one from a modern cognitive psychologist:

> Since the Mind, in all its Thoughts and Reasonings, hath no other immediate object but its own Ideas, which it alone does or can contemplate, it is evident that our Knowledge is only conversant about them.
>
> *(ibid., p. 525)*

More recently Attneave, who has been one of the pioneers of psychology's adoption of a computer metaphor for the mind, wrote that:

> [information] is mediated by receptor activity ... so that what we experience as the 'real world', and locate within ourselves cannot possibly be anything other better than a representation of the external world ... The statement that the world as we know it is a representation is, I think, a truism – there is really no way it can be wrong.
>
> *(Attneave, 1974, p. 493)*

2.2 Modern cognitivism

An important feature of this metatheory is that it is possible to trace the path between the world of physics and the world of human meaning as a causal chain. This has made it a potent basis for scientific psychology. The first requirement for connection between the two worlds is that various forms of physical energy stimulate the organism's sense organs. In the case of vision, energy in the form of light rays forms an image on the retina. The energy is absorbed by cells in the retina and transduced into nerve impulses which proceed along the optic nerve to the brain. The brain interprets these signals and constructs hypotheses about their causes:

> Nowadays we look upon visual perception as a piecemeal affair; our seemingly unified view of the world around us is really only a plausible hypothesis on the basis of fragmentary evidence. The transformations that go on in the retina and visual pathways are not merely reproductions, in high fidelity, of the visual image. At every stage a censor is at work, cutting with its scissors, and deleting with a red pencil, the unwanted visual message.
>
> *(Blakemore, 1973, p. 51)*

These 'plausible hypotheses' are the ideas or representations of the external world, and it is these that we experience, not the objects themselves. Sometimes the objects represented are quite simple, like pictures or words used as stimuli in psychology laboratories. Outside the laboratory they are generally more complicated. There are real dogs and trees, which are less simple than their pictures. Also there are other people, who are both complicated and unpredictable, which must be allowed for in the construction of their representations. Other people form the subject matter of social psychology, which thus becomes an important but not essentially different branch of cognitive psychology.

Notice that for cognitivism construction is necessary, since the fleeting pictures on the retina are far too sparse to do justice to the complexity of our experience of the world, especially the human social world. We have merely 'fragmentary evidence' and the cognitive work needed to make sense of it is complex. This may be based on innate mental structures, or, as with Locke himself, it may be constructed through experience. Lately, with the development of computers, the powerful language of cognitive science has become available for the description of this process of constructing representations. This has given fresh impetus to cognitivism and the massive increase of research generated on perception, memory and thinking is sometimes referred to as the 'cognitive revolution' (De May, 1992). Jerry Fodor has called the philosophy behind this 'methodological solipsism' (Fodor, 1980). Solipsism is a consequence of Attneave's 'truism'. It means we cannot know other minds or the world outside directly, only the representations in our own mind, and it is these representations, of things and other people, that, therefore, form the subject matter of psychology. We live in a world of meaning, but it is a private world of our own construction.

2.3 So is the outside world an illusion?

Although we may not know the outside world directly, most cognitivists, including Locke and many modern cognitive psychologists, believe in the existence of an outside world. This is a form of Realism (Chapter 7 in this volume), sometimes referred to as Representational Realism. For realists, although words get their immediate meaning by being linked with representations or mental constructions, these representations in turn correspond to real entities in the outside world, even though they cannot be known directly.

But since it is impossible to prove logically the existence of the external world, there have been philosophers and psychologists who have questioned its existence altogether. This theory that meanings are only in the head, and relate to nothing outside, is a form of Idealism sometimes called Psychologism (Johnson-Laird, 1983). Practically speaking, it makes little difference to cognitivism which is accepted, Realism or Idealism. It seems reasonable to compromise by supposing that sometimes our words refer ultimately to real entities, sometimes not. For a scientist, hydrogen, oxygen, and water refer to precisely defined entities which exist in the world. But words like freedom, democracy, love, friendship are less clearly defined. As a modern cognitive psychologist has put it:

> Are meanings in the mind or in the world? Is Realism or Psychologism right? ... The answer is that ... these questions appear to be false antitheses. The meanings of some words are mental constructions that are imposed upon the world in the absence of an objective correlate.

> Other words, however, ... pick out something in reality ... Language
> embodies no particular metaphysics; it embraces both Realism and Psy-
> chologism.
>
> *(Johnson-Laird, 1983, pp. 203–4)*

In philosophical terms, words have both sense and reference (Frege,
1952), or intension and extension (Russell, 1984). Extension is what the
word actually picks out in the world, so that 'dog' refers to any member
of the class of dogs; whereas intension consists of the properties (such as
having four legs, being a mammal) which place it in this class. For our
purposes, the important point to remember is that in cognitivism, our
acquaintance is always with ideas or representations, which are in the
mind. Even when a word picks out something in reality, we do not experience that something directly, but only its constructed representation.

3 Mutualism: the social theory of meaning

In mutualism, meanings are social rather than individual, and they exist
as potential actions within a social community rather than being located
in individual minds. It is a social theory but it does not just apply to
social material, such as the symbols used in communication. Even the
human meaning of physical objects and phenomena, such as stars, trees
and colour, are understood socially rather than cognitively.

The emergence of meaning cannot be illustrated directly as in
cognitivism, where it is an event or pattern within a mental mechanism.
Instead it is necessary to convey it by allusion and metaphor. A recent
master of the allusive style in the interests of a mutualist theory of
meaning (though he did not call it that) has been the philosopher
Ludwig Wittgenstein, an Austrian whose powerful influence has been
mainly in British and American philosophy and psychology (Bloor,
1983). Before Wittgenstein's philosophy of meaning became well known
in the 1950s, a number of social psychologists, most notably Mead and
Vygotsky (Wetherell and Maybin, 1996), were using a mutualist theory
of meaning, but they did not explore the theory with the uncompromis-
ing persistence shown by Wittgenstein. The pragmatist philosopher John
Dewey (Chapter 2 of this volume) spelt out the theory with a telling
quote from the anthropologist Malinowski, to illustrate that meaning derives from action rather than thought ('The meaning of the thing is
made up of experiences of its active uses and not of intellectual contemplation', quoted in Dewey, 1929, p. 205), and Richard Rorty (1982) has
brought out the affinities between Dewey and Wittgenstein in
developing his own version of a pragmatist theory of meaning.

3.1 Wittgenstein and the lion problem: meaning as use within a social context

If a lion could talk, we could not understand him

This puzzling claim was made in Wittgenstein's *Philosophical Investigations* (1953, p. 223). It goes further than Locke's very reasonable assumption that parrots do not have a language. Perhaps because lions, unlike parrots, do not utter words in real life, the thought of a lion speaking takes me straight to fictional lions in children's stories, which do speak and are understood. The children in C.S. Lewis's *The Lion, the Witch and the Wardrobe* have no difficulty understanding the lion Aslan when he speaks. Locke can easily explain this. As readers we treat fictional animals as though they were human and had ideas or intentional representations, which give meaning to their words, unlike real parrots. Wittgenstein invites a different act of imagination. What if you met a real lion and it spoke to you? Imagine yourself at the zoo gazing at a lion in its cage, murmuring 'Poor thing, stuck in prison like this,' and a voice comes from the direction of the lion, which sounds like 'Do you really care? Then get a hacksaw and help me to escape'. No trouble understanding the lion if this is fiction, or a children's cartoon, but we are assuming it is real. Try to imagine how you would react. Would it be different if you were visiting a human prisoner?

Now try another thought experiment. First imagine a cat. Many people will do this by forming an image of a cat, perhaps their own pet. Now say the sound 'onk' and as you do so make it mean cat. Did you manage to do this? Again many people do it by forming an image of the cat and somehow connecting the image with the word as they say it. Thus 'imagine' and 'mean' seem to involve similar mental processes, which would support Locke's theory, and its modern, cognitivist derivatives.

But meaning and imagining have important differences. Merely to form an image of a cat seems sufficient to imagine a cat, but not to *mean* cat. If 'onk' is to mean 'cat' it surely has to be understood and potentially used as such by other people. In other words 'onk' has to be used as 'cat' in a language in order for it to mean cat. So forming an image is not a sufficient condition. Is it necessary? Do you always have appropriate images when you speak? When I return home in the afternoon, and our cat mews and looks at his empty plate, I may ask my wife 'Have you fed the cat?' But when I do this I am not aware of any image. And what about the meaning not of a word but of a whole sentence, for instance the sentence 'If it doesn't rain I shall go for a walk'? Does this get meaning by corresponding to a sequence of ideas or images? Wittgenstein concludes that it cannot do so because it is not such a sequence that makes it part of a language, and it is only through being part of language that it can have meaning.

Can I say 'bububu' and mean 'If it doesn't rain I shall go for a walk'? –
It is only in a language that I can mean something by something. This
shows clearly that the grammar of 'to mean' is not like that of the expression 'to imagine' and the like.

(Wittgenstein, 1953, p. 18)

3.2 The social origin of meaning

What Wittgenstein is trying to convey with his stories and thought experiments is that although superficially the words 'mean' and 'imagine'
are similar, closer investigation shows that they are different. What is of
crucial importance is not the private image that may (or may not) occur
as you utter a word, but your ability to follow the accepted public use of
the word. One of Wittgenstein's most famous aphorisms was 'Don't ask
for the meaning, ask for the use'. He probably has in mind the traditional (cognitivist) way of asking for a meaning, which was to ask for a
concurrent event, a mental image or an event referred to in the world
outside. In contrast to this, to ask for use is to ask for the utterance's
place in the social context or 'form of life' in which the use is embedded.
'...[T]he speaking of language is part of an activity, or of a form of life'
(ibid., p. 12). The lion in the zoo does not share our 'form of life', and
that fact is implicit in the relationship between you and the lion. The activity when I say 'Poor thing, stuck in prison like this,' is different when
speaking to a lion and to a human prisoner; there is understanding
(which is part of the activity) in one case but not the other.

In mutualism our actions, including our utterances, have meaning given
by social context or form of life. As an assumption it does not explain
how meaning is given in this way, but indicates where to look, at social
interactions rather than in the brain. It is true that we can only act and
speak because of what goes on in our minds or brains, but according to
Wittgenstein it is not this that gives the acts and words meaning.

ACTIVITY 6.2   What do I have to do to make 'bububu' *mean* 'If it doesn't rain I shall go for a
walk'? In other words, what does it mean to say that the one expression
means the same as the other.

We cannot do it just by forming images and connecting them with
'bububu'. We could only do it by setting up what Wittgenstein called a
language game, in which players or participants speak and act, and connect the two in their speaking and acting, so that 'bububu' (meaning 'If
it doesn't rain I shall go for a walk') would be used by a group of people
on a dull Sunday afternoon – as a statement of intention to others who
understand it as such.

Thus, according to mutualism, the words I utter in conversation have
meaning not because of what goes on in my head, but because of the
part they play in the human community to which I belong. Locke's

parrot utters words, but is not a participant in any human community. This is not to say that the sounds made by animals never have meaning. The warning cry of a sparrow when a hawk flies overhead or the submissive cowering of a wolf cub confronted with a dominant male do have meaning, but it is given by appropriate use in a nonhuman social setting, rather than by the presence or absence of ideas in the head.

3.3 The role of the individual

What does this theory of meaning offer social psychology? Psychology is concerned with individual actions; what is the relationship between an individual action and the form of life that gives it meaning? This can be answered by a modern formula for the interaction between the human organism and its environment. It comes from Anthony Giddens, a contemporary British sociologist, in his theory of 'duality of structures'. He writes: 'Social structures are both constituted "by" human agency, and yet at the same time are the very "medium" of human agency' (Giddens, 1975, p. 121), where the medium constrains but does not determine action, and social structures and human agency are not fixed but undergo mutual change.

This formula may be generalized to form a scheme for mutualism: 'M is constituted by A, and yet is the medium of A' where we can substitute for M (medium) and A (action); social structures and human agency; language and talk; football and games of football; science and scientific activity, etc.

Because of this mutual interdependence, there cannot be social structures without human agency, or human agency without social structures. Thus there cannot be language without talk, or talk without language. Sometimes the constitutive impact of an action is quick and obvious, as in young childrens' games when the rules are still settling down. Sometimes it is small and uncertain, as in the evolution of a language when new metaphors become widely used and the words involved take on new shades of meaning.

On this view, social structures like language are not simply systems of rules. There are correct, accepted ways of using any word, but the boundaries are always fuzzy and forever being stretched and modified as people try to express themselves through metaphor and other novelties. If we followed strict rules, so that we spoke and acted according to rules and nothing else, then our language and other social structures could not be modified – we would be like machines. It is true that people do sometimes simply follow rules, but that is to act mechanically. This may be forced upon people in certain routine occupations, or upon children obliged to speak 'proper' English. By contrast, creative action is action that is constrained by the medium of action, yet changes it. Shakespeare was a product of the fertile literary culture of Britain in the sixteenth century, and changed that culture. To be constrained by the medium of action is not the same as to follow rules or to be causally determined.

Often the creative writer or scientist breaks what seem to be the rules of the time, yet achieves what is later acclaimed as the solution to a long-standing problem, and as having changed the science or literary culture of the time.

4 The relationship between cognitivism and mutualism

In mutualism there is mutual interdependence between agency and social structure, or organism and environment. In cognitivism the environment, described in the language of physics, exists independently of the organism which contributes meaning through cognitive construction. Both metatheories accept that we live in a world of meanings. But the account they give of meaning is quite different, and this difference is reflected by contrasting social psychologies. In cognitivism, the starting point is the 'alien and inhuman' world described by physics. This is our environment reduced to its bare essentials. The energies of this environment impinge upon us (and other animals) and are transmuted into meaningful experience through the activities of the sense organs and of each individual brain or mind. Social psychology is an extension of individual psychology, which deals with the aspect of the human environment that is made up of other human beings. It may be the most complex and important aspect, but no special principles are involved. The cognitivist theory of meaning underlies much of the work in social psychology on attitudes (Potter, 1996) and attribution (Lalljee, 1996; Dallos, 1996).

In mutualism, the starting point is the world of meaning itself. Out of this already meaningful world human beings have constructed the artefacts and institutions of culture. But this sense of construction is quite different from cognitive construction. It is construction through activity in the world, rather than by the cognitive machinery of the mind. It is not just the physical construction of boats and houses with hands and tools, but also the social construction of institutions, religions, sciences, through speech, writing, and the forming of social networks. By changing the world through our constructions we change ourselves, since we change the medium of our activities.

> What is the relationship between these two theories of meaning? Must we decide between them, or can they peacefully coexist, each playing an important role appropriate to its own particular perspective?

To conclude this chapter four possible answers to these questions will be described, and no attempt will be made to decide between them. That will be left to you, the reader.

1 Contradictory

The two theories are rival explanations of the same phenomena. They cannot both be right, so one is, or both of them wrong.

2 Supplementary

The two theories supplement each other, each describing a different domain or level of social reality (Chapter 4 of this volume). Thus the biologist describes the anatomical structure of an organism, as well as the physiological functions of the different parts, and its place within an ecological system. These are different aspects, and supplement each other to give a full description.

3 Complementary

One of the debates of modern physics that has become well known outside physics itself, is that between wave and particle theories. These seem incompatible, since one cannot be reduced to the other, yet both are needed to account for all the data. Neil Bohr's famous reconciliation is his principle of complementarity, which simply accepts the conflict as an inevitable part of the process of enquiry. In this case 'A rigorous space-time description and a rigorous causal sequence for individual processes cannot be realized simultaneously – the one or the other must be sacrificed' (D'Abro, 1951, p. 951). A familiar application of this is in the description of a sound, either as a weighted sum of frequencies, or as an instantaneous force. The first is a historical space-time description, the second the description of a moment in a causal chain. This principle, which Bohr derived from his reading of the psychologist William James (Chapter 2 of this volume), is actually very general, and can be applied to the debate between cognitivism and mutualism. In mutualism meanings arise historically, through human social activity, in cognitivism they are established as part of a causal chain by the moment to moment states of human brains or minds. They are different theories, even incompatible, but if this extension of complementarity is valid, they (or some other, more satisfactory version of them) are both necessary for a full account.

4 Phenomenological

The final possible resolution of the apparent conflict between the two theories comes from phenomenology (Chapter 2 of this volume), a movement which also derived ultimately from William James (1890), and which is dedicated to understanding how experience can form the basis of knowledge. Edmund Husserl, the founder of phenomenology, emphasized the simple but fundamental point that the starting point for all knowledge, including scientific knowledge, lies in everyday experience, or what he called the life-world. More recently this theme has been taken up in work by one of his students, Aron Gurwitsch (1974):

> Whatever activity we engage in, whether practical, theoretical, or other, is pursued within the life-world, whose simple acceptance proves an essential precondition of every activity.
>
> *(ibid, p. 114)*

> In the life-world, we do not encounter ... mere corporeal objects ... What we encounter are cultural objects ... buildings which serve specific purposes, like abodes, places of work, schools, libraries, churches, and so on. Objects pertaining to the life-world present themselves as tools, instruments, and utensils related to human needs and desires; they have to be handled and used in appropriate ways to satisfy those needs and to yield desired results.
>
> *(ibid, p. 143)*

As a consequence of this:

> All sciences, without exception, originate in the life-world on the basis of the findings encountered in it ... their purpose and sense are to provide a theoretical account of the life-world. More correctly expressed, each of the several sciences singles out and focuses on a certain segment or aspect of the life-world. However, those segments or aspects are not given beforehand in neat demarcation from one another. Rather, their delimitation and, along with it, the very constitution of the several sciences, are the outcome of theoretical work guided by theoretical interests. The first presupposition of the sciences proves to be the life-world itself, our paramount and even sole reality.
>
> *(ibid, p. 139)*

Returning to our two metatheories of meaning, it is clear that mutualist meaning arises out of the everyday social activities, the form of life, that constitute the life-world, and that cognitivist meaning is part of a scientific, theoretical account of an aspect of that life-world. But this account is thus part of a specialized form of life (science) within the life-world, dedicated to reducing social phenomena to mental or physiological processes. So while mutualism describes meaning as an essential part of the life-world, cognitivism attempts to describe the psychological or physiological structures necessary for participation in the life-world, and therefore for meaning to occur.

5 Concluding comments

In this chapter I have introduced two metatheories of meaning for social psychology. They are certainly different, but can they coexist, and what kind of coexistence is it if they can? Four possible answers to these questions have been described. In the first they are in direct conflict, rival accounts of the central aspect of human psychology. In the second they supplement each other, each explaining only a part of meaning, so that both are necessary for a full explanation. In the third they complement each other, in a sense similar to that of modern physics; they describe the same thing in incompatible terms, yet both are important for a full understanding of meaning. In the fourth, the phenomenological, mutualism attempts to describe meaning in the life-world itself, while cognitivism is a specialized activity within the life-world, which aims at a theoretical account of meaning. Cognitivism is thus a possible theoretical approach contained within a broad mutualist framework. But at the same time, it is the dominant approach to cognitive psychology, though not the only approach (Reed, 1991). As such it attempts to describe in its own terms the structural prerequisites (of the mind or brain) for any human form of life to take place.

References

Attneave, F. (1974) 'How do you know?' *American Psychologist*, no. 29, pp. 493–9.

Blakemore, C. (1973) 'Environmental constraints on development in the nervous system' in Hinde, R.A. and Stevenson-Hinde, J. (eds) *Constraints on Learning*, New York, Academic Press.

Bloor, D. (1983) *Wittgenstein: A Social Theory of Knowledge*, London, Macmillan.

Bruner, J.S. (1990) *Acts of Meaning*, Cambridge, Cambridge University Press.

D'Abro, A. (1951) *The Rise of the New Physics*, London, Constable.

Dallos, R. (1996) 'Creating relationships' in Miell, D. and Dallos, R. (eds).

De Mey, M. (1992) *The Cognitive Paradigm*, Chicago, Chicago University Press.

Dewey, J. (1929) *Experience and Nature*, London, George Allen and Unwin.

Fodor, J. (1980) 'Methodological solipsism considered as a research strategy in cognitive psychology', *Behavioural and Brain Sciences*, no.3, pp.63–100.

Frege, G. (1952) *Philosophical Writings of Gottlob Frege*, Oxford, Blackwell (first published 1892).

Giddens, A. (1975) *New Rules of Sociological Method*, New York, Basic Books.

Gurwitsch, A. (1974) *Phenomenology and Theory of Science*, Evanston, Northwestern University Press.

Husserl, E. (1970) *Logical Investigations*, London, Routledge and Kegan Paul (first published 1900).

James, W. (1890) *The Principles of Psychology*, New York, Holt.

Johnson-Laird, P.N. (1983) *Mental Models*, Cambridge, Cambridge University Press.

Lalljee, M. (1996) 'The interpreting self: a experimentalist perspective' in Stevens, R. (ed.).

Locke, J. (1975) *An Essay Concerning Human Understanding*, Oxford, Oxford University Press (first published 1689).

Miell, D. and Dallos, R. (eds) (1996) *Social Interaction and Personal Relationships*, London, Sage.

Morris, C. (1938) *Foundations of the Theory of Signs*, vol.1, no.2 of *Foundations of the Unity of Science: Toward an International Encyclopaedia of Unified Science*, Chicago, University of Chicago Press.

Peirce, C.S. (1992) *The Essential Peirce: Selected Philosophical Writings, vol. I (1867–1893)*, Bloomington, Indiana University Press.

Potter, J. (1996) 'Attitudes, social representations and discursive psychology' in Wetherell, M. (ed.).

Reed, E.S. (1991) 'James Gibson's ecological approach to cognition' in Still, A. and Costall, A. (eds) *Against Cognitivism: Alternative Foundations for Cognitive Psychology*, Hemel Hempstead, Harvester Wheatsheaf.

Rorty, R. (1982) *Consequences of Pragmatism*, Brighton, Harvester Press.

Russell, B. (1953) *Mysticism and Logic*, Harmondsworth, Penguin Books.

Russell, J. (1984) *Explaining Mental Life*, London, Macmillan.

De Saussure, F. (1983) *Course in General Linguistics*, London, Duckworth (first published 1916).

Stevens, R. (ed.) (1996) *Understanding the Self*, London, Sage.

Still, A.W. and Good, J.M.M. (1992) 'Mutualism in the human sciences: towards the implementation of a theory', *Journal for the Theory of Social Behaviour*, no.22, pp.105–28.

Wetherell, M. (ed.) (1996) *Identities, Groups and Social Issues*, London, Sage.

Wetherell, M. (1996) 'Group conflict and the social construction of Racism' in Wetherell, M. (ed.).

Wetherell, M. and Maybin, J. (1996) 'The distributed self: a social constructionist perspective' in Stevens, R. (ed.).

Wittgenstein, L. (1953) *Philosophical Investigations*, Oxford, Basil Blackwell.

CHAPTER 7
REALISM AND RELATIVISM

by Margaret Wetherell and Arthur Still

1 Introduction

In everyday life most of us take for granted that we are dealing with a real world – a world of events and objects which is independent of our thoughts about it. We constantly appeal, for example, to what *really* happened as we try to sort out the truth about a sequence of events. However, most of us would also claim that our view of things depends on our perspective. We recognize that news reports about the Gulf War in the early 1990s might well have been rather different in Baghdad than in Washington. We understand that two partners in a domestic dispute might have quite different versions of who started the argument. In these cases we may begin to doubt that there is any one universal reality underlying the different descriptions, or we may come to think that if there is a reality then the best we can do is develop an approximate version of its nature.

These beliefs and doubts are familiar ones in everyday life. They also form the substance of much philosophical discussion and are central to discussions about the status of scientific knowledge. Well over 2,000 years ago, for instance, Plato likened our everyday perceptions to shadows of objects cast upon the walls of a cave. Are the shadows cast by objects which constitute a hidden reality behind appearance, as Plato believed, or are the shadows that we experience all there is?

How do you know you are not dreaming at this moment? Write down as many reasons as you can think of for believing that you are not dreaming. Is it possible to *prove* that you are not dreaming?

ACTIVITY 7.1

The aim of this chapter is to consider the implications of debates about 'realism' and 'relativism' for social psychology. Naive realism is an unquestioning faith in the reality of what we perceive. More sophisticated realist positions would include the view that there are many biased descriptions and we may never do more than approximate to reality. Relativism denies that there is *any* single universal standard for judging the truth of different descriptions. These issues are important in social psychology because *how people know* and *what they know* are core topics in the discipline, along with an emphasis on the *constructed* nature of experience. Social psychology also claims to be a science – what does that imply about the researcher's relationship to the real? The next section will try to put some flesh on these debates about reality, construction and knowledge. We will then outline in the following sections three responses which have been important in discussions about the nature and aims of social psychology.

2 Constructs, shadows, truth and knowledge

Experimental social psychological research on cognition suggests that knowledge is often *partial*. What we see and how we label it depends on our pre-existing schema. People's constructions and interpretations arise from habitual thought patterns and from information processing strategies such as stereotyping which may distort their perceptions. The effects these researchers describe are often (but not always) described as 'misconceptions', 'preconceptions', 'biases', or 'illusions'. What does this particular choice of terms imply? It suggests a realist view, but not a naive one. It suggests that a distinction can be drawn between occasions when our understanding is blurred by our constructions and occasions when we do see clearly (veridical perception). It suggests that there is an independently existing reality to which we can get access, even though sometimes we may get it wrong.

It is worth noting that work on stereotypes, prototypes and attributions need not necessarily take this realist view of human perception. Cognitive researchers could see themselves as simply investigating the way things appear to us (the shadows) and how these sense impressions become organized in our minds, without making any assumptions about the veridical nature of these impressions. However, it is probably fair to say that the majority of experimental social psychologists working on cognitive processes would take a realist line and hence would be quite happy with terms like 'bias', 'illusion' and 'misconception'.

Let us turn now to an alternative tradition in social psychology – humanistic psychology and the experiential perspective (see Stevens, 1996 and Box 1.2 in Chapter 1). This approach, similarly, stresses the constructive work human consciousness performs. The emphasis here, however, is placed on *personal* constructions and *private* worlds.

ACTIVITY 7.2   Take a look at this statement from the humanistic psychologist Carl Rogers.

> Every individual exists in a continually changing world of experience of which he (sic) is the centre ... The world of experience is for each individual, in a very significant sense, a private world. The organism reacts to the field as it is experienced and perceived. This perceptual field is, for the individual, 'reality' ... The world comes to be composed of a series of tested hypotheses which provide much security. Yet mingled with these ... are perceptions which remain completely unchecked.

These untested perceptions are also a part of our personal reality, and may have as much authority as those which have been checked.

(Rogers, 1951, pp. 483–6)

What is assumed here about access to reality and what might be the implications for the process of conducting therapy?

Rogers describes a personal world which he sees as unique. What is important in his view is not any independently existing reality but reality as it appears to the individual. It is unclear, however, whether he thinks we can have access to an independently existing reality in the right conditions or whether all we have is reality as it appears to us. Therapy conducted from this perspective could go in two directions as a result. From a more realist position the concern might be with adjusting people's personal worlds so that there is a better match with a supposedly independently existing reality, perhaps cutting down the number of 'unchecked hypotheses'. From a more relativist position, one thing a therapist might do is argue that, since there is no single correct reality and no single truth, the task is to encourage people to define their own path in the most self-fulfilling way possible.

Constructs, however, are not just personal. There are also *family constructs*, and a great deal of research has been conducted on family belief systems – representations developed collectively by families about the nature of family members and their relationships (Dallos, 1996). Dallos argues that belief systems found in families can be dysfunctional and the source of symptoms of disturbance in individual family members. What does the possibility of shared constructs emerging from interaction suggest about people's access to reality? Does this mean that the family therapist, or an outside observer, can see the reality of a particular family's life more clearly than the family itself can from the inside? Who holds the key to reality?

A typical social constructionist perspective, similarly, looks at the complex web of judgements, myths, stories and theories (the meanings and practices) which make up a culture or a form of life. Wetherell and Maybin (1996) argue that these meanings and practices constitute our reality. The task of the social psychologist is to investigate a world made up of human interpretative practices and people's collective efforts over time - studying, for example, sets of objects, relationships, cultures and societies actively manufactured by people. Reality, from this perspective, is 'the result of the active, cooperative enterprise of persons in relationship' (Gergen, 1985, p. 267), rather than something God-given, or pre-existent.

Reality is not only socially constructed however; it is also multiple. Different cultures, and even different social strata within a culture, have different stories and practices, so they experience different realities. Although, as section 4 will demonstrate, there are social constructionists who take a realist position, of all the research we have considered this perspective offers the greatest challenge to realism. The possibility of multiple constructed realities suggests that there can be no absolute underlying standards against which local variations could be judged. If so, truth will always be relative. However, this does not mean that some realities will not be preferable to others. Given a choice, most human beings will prefer to live in a world as free from pain as possible, rather than in one whose 'reality' involves a vengeful god whose will is expressed in arbitrary torture and human sacrifice.

Overall, social psychological research on the nature of everyday knowledge encourages a sceptical position. We learn that our access to reality is likely to be incomplete, reflecting not only our personal history but also our social relationships. What does this mean, however, for social psychology as a science? Is the social psychologist's view similarly incomplete, dependent on their personal history and the communities to which they belong? Is it only 'ordinary people', the man or woman on the Clapham omnibus, who have a problematic relationship with reality? Does the social psychologist have some kind of privileged access?

When discussions about the nature of reality move from everyday knowledge to science, the debate tends to become heated and ancient arguments between long dead philosophers become repeated with passion. One reason for this is that to a large extent the authority and prestige of science depend on a claim to have special access to truth and reality. One of the main justifications for science is that scientists are developing a more and more accurate understanding of the actual nature of the world. The notion of scientific progress depends on this view. Relativism is a challenge to the power of science and to the claim that the activities of physicists, chemists, psychologists and biologists, for example, are different in kind from those of lawyers, journalists, spiritualists, and students of extra-sensory perception.

There are also moral and political issues at stake in debates about relativism. Relativism is often presented as a problematic position. Social constructionism is frequently described, for example, as 'sliding' into relativism (Harré, 1992), in danger of adopting a 'rubbery relativism' (Bruner, 1990), or advocating the 'extremes' of relativism. Why the concern? Relativism, as we have seen, is the claim that truth is relative to one's point of view and thus provisional. The worry is that if there are no objective grounds for choosing between points of view, then 'anything goes'. Any idea could be valid. This is a position which some see as leading to 'a passive, cynical and ultimately obstructive view of politics' and of the possibilities for human emancipation (Parker, 1992, p. 25).

In the rest of this chapter we want to look at three broad responses to debates about realism and relativism which are particularly relevant to the activities of social psychologists as scientists. The first response we describe as a 'no nonsense view'. This is a view which is happy to stake a claim for the real and for the specialness of science. The second view asks whether relativism is so bad after all and takes social constructionist arguments to their logical conclusion. In the final section we look at attempts to develop a new realism in social psychology in response to social constructionism. Arguments about realism and relativism are complicated and dense, with many sub-variants of positions. This chapter takes a schematic view and will ride over some of the complexities. We will also try to give some of the philosophical and historical background to these positions.

This would be a good point to pause and to try and clarify as far as possible your own views on these very difficult issues. Do you agree that we only get access to reality through our social, cultural and personal constructions? Would you want to make a distinction between the social world and the natural world in this respect? How would you justify such a distinction? Do you prefer the term 'bias' or the term 'construction' to describe phenomena such as stereotypes and cognitive schema? Do you think that scientific methods give us privileged access to reality? Do you think relativism will lead to political lethargy and cynicism?

ACTIVITY 7.3

---

3 Defending the real

One of the difficulties with arguing for realism is that the case against it seems so logically watertight. For eighteenth century philosophers the issue was one of how we can ever be confident that we are experiencing something real and not phantoms produced by our own minds. Did you find a satisfactory answer, for instance, to the questions about dreaming in Activity 7.1? Can we be sure that any belief in the existence of reality is not a result of social conditioning? We are so conditioned to treating the world which we experience as existing independently of ourselves that we feel that reality must be hidden behind the way things appear to us.

David Hume (1711–1776) argued that, in effect, all we know for sure are things as they appear to us, like Plato's shadows, and we construct a 'real' world based upon regularities in our experiences of these appearances. Hume challenged his readers to show him the reality behind experience, and naturally enough nobody has yet met this challenge, for direct encounter with reality becomes, by definition, part of the shadow world of experience. The fact that this world *seems* solid and persistent and not at all shadowy is due, Hume argued, to custom and habit, made possible because of these regularities. In this way, the purely *logical* argument for a reality beyond experience collapses, and 'reality' is a kind of construction.

Another great eighteenth century philosopher, Immanuel Kant (1724–1804), accepted the force of Hume's sceptical arguments (which he said roused him from his 'dogmatic slumbers'), but rejected Hume's conclusions. He developed a *transcendental* argument to explain why our experience of the world is both constructed and yet solid. He argued that human experience presupposes mental structures which make experience possible but are not themselves available to experience. When we categorize the perceived world, it is always in terms of objects extended in time and space, and subject to cause and effect. Kant suggested that we use these categories not because that is how the world is, but because that is the way our minds are organized.

And yet for many these various logical and philosophical resolutions did not seem satisfactory. Hume's sceptical position may be hard to refute, but this has not preserved sceptics from criticism and often enraged rejection. The rejections may be summarized quite simply – they all express the sense that scepticism does not do justice to human experience. For instance, Dr Johnson's response to the philosophy of Bishop Berkeley, which resembled Hume's scepticism about the evidence of the senses, was to kick a stone and say 'I refute him thus'. Most social psychologists act at least for part of the time as though they believe in the reality of the object of their investigations, and perhaps it is helpful for them to do so. Their realism is therefore pragmatic, and if confronted with logical arguments against realism they are apt to lose interest, to see these as metaphysical issues which are unfalsifiable.

In social psychology, the 'no nonsense' view articulated by Dr Johnson and others is reflected most strongly in the work of experimental researchers. Most experimental social psychologists are optimistic about the possibility of true knowledge of an independently existing real world. Their optimism arises from the value placed on science and its scope for ferreting out the truth. It is argued that reliable and valid (true) knowledge can be attained about the real nature of social life and people's psychology if the right procedures are followed. We can obtain an objective view of a world which exists independently of our observations. Indeed, false observations will be disconfirmed by evidence collected through observation and experimentation.

Many social psychologists would argue that they (and other scientists such as physicists, geologists and chemists) are investigating an ultimate reality, not a construction of their own making. They would take for granted that their concepts are more than constructs out of observations; certainly they talk and behave as though there really are such states or processes as memory and anxiety, attitudes and attachment.

Other social psychologists, while wanting strongly to defend the value of science and its privileged access to the real, develop a more qualified view. They accept a partial social construction based on a distinction between theory and observation. These social psychologists recognize that their scientific language is a product of social evolution, and that it could have been very different. They would agree with those philosophers of science who distinguish between observation language and theory language, implying that they refer to different levels of reality. Reality is thought to be a totality of facts, which are described by observation language, while scientific theories are a construction. In this view, a psychological theory like the theories of Freud or Vygotsky could well reflect the historical and social context in which the theorists worked. It might also reflect the personal preoccupations of the theorist. Freud's psychoanalysis and Vygotsky's dialectical view of child development can be seen as constructions, even as explanatory fictions. However, this view would argue that since the observations psychologists make refer to something real, theories could nonetheless be tested against the facts.

Paradoxically perhaps, this reliance on observations and on empirical evidence (evidence from the senses) as the guarantee of scientific method can be traced back to Hume's arguments for scepticism. Believing that all we had access to was the shadows (what he called 'impressions') Hume argued that we should focus on this immediate experience. The doctrine of 'empiricism' argues that the compelling entities of our world, like solid tables and chairs, physical laws, minds, and democracy are helpful (or sometimes unhelpful) constructions out of immediate experience. In social psychology, the term empiricism (sometimes described by critics as 'brute empiricism') is used as a shorthand to refer to emphases on observation and the importance of controlled investigation along with the belief that observations can be used to decide the facts.

However, from a realist point of view, one of the difficulties with emphasizing observations and empirical data is that there is no necessary guarantee that any actual underlying mechanisms (the nature of the real) have been discovered or properly identified. Take, for example, Babylonian astronomy, which over 2,000 years ago developed a precise and accurate set of predictions for eclipses. These predictions were based on Babylonian observations of the movements of the heavens and they worked. Yet Babylonian views of the movement of planets and the solar system were very different from the modern view of the earth rotating around the sun. Indeed, some scientists claim that modern quantum mechanics has just this feature of being a (brilliant) predictive theory for atomic events such as energy changes in atoms while having no model of the underlying mechanisms that produce these changes.

In response, realists might point to the cumulative record of science as it builds up over time. Imagine, for instance, telling the history of science backwards as a story which begins with Einstein's theory of relativity which is then disproved by Newton's physics which in turn is disproved by Babylonian cosmology. The fact that this retelling of history seems inconceivable suggests to many philosophers of science that as science develops and progresses a better and more accurate picture of the actual nature of reality and its workings does emerge. They would argue, in addition, that the scientific method has proved the best way of predicting and controlling the processes of nature, as new technology and new inventions demonstrate. Whether or not prediction and control is desirable, the products of science – cars, computers and hydrogen bombs – work in all cultures.

To summarize, in this section we have looked at a 'no-nonsense' view which believes in reality and the power of science to discover reality regardless of the difficulties of logically proving this thesis. This approach is associated with reliance on empirical procedures. But note that some empirically-minded social psychologists distinguish between theory and observations in this respect. Note, too, that empiricists need not necessarily be realists. Some experimental social psychologists have seen their own work in this light. Their research orders experimental results and observations and makes them coherent (much as the Babylonian astronomers ordered their impressions of the movements of the heavens) but it is not assumed that reality has finally been captured.

4 Exploring relativism

The aim of this section is to look at how relativist ideas have been taken up in social psychology. As we noted earlier, relativism is most often associated with the social constructionist perspective, which argues for the multiple nature of reality and the importance of human constructive work. As Jerome Bruner concludes, ' ...in most human interaction "realities" are the result of prolonged and intricate processes of construction and negotiation deeply embedded in culture' (Bruner, 1990, pp. 24–5). In effect, this view suggests that observations will always be contextual and dependent on some perspective.

What about Dr Johnson's point, however? One response you might want to make to social constructionist claims is to begin banging the table. 'Surely this table (or some other physical object) exists objectively, independently of my thoughts about it?' 'When I stub my toe against a rock, it still hurts doesn't it?' 'If the plane I am travelling in crashes into a mountain, I still die.' And, 'if there is this material reality then surely there can be truths independent of human interpretations which everybody could agree upon regardless of their culture?'

BOX 7.1   'Tables'

The realist thumps the table. What a loud noise! Much louder than talk. Much more gritty. Much more real. And yet we insist that this noise, being produced in this place, at this time, in the course of this argument, is an argument, is talk. As an argument, it takes the form of a demonstration:

> This (bang!) is real. *This* (bang!) is no mere social construction. Talk cannot change *that* it is or *what* it is. See how its reality constrains my hand (bang!), forcing it to stop in its tracks. Hear the inevitable result (bang!) of the collision of two solid physical objects. Need I say more?

All this is addressed of course to the relativist, the unbeliever, the heretic. And what is being asked of this unfortunate soul? Preferably, to recant (lack of response will, generously, be taken as a form of recantation). Failing this, the table thumping argument becomes a challenge:

> Show us (the challenger and the assumed audience-of-fellow-

---

realists) how we are wrong. Show us the contingent, could-be-otherwise, socially constructed, really-not-real character of this table – if you can!

Let us then accept the challenge. It is surprisingly easy and even reasonable to question the table's given reality. It does not take long, in looking closer, at wood grain and molecule, before you are no longer looking at a 'table'. Indeed, physicists might wish to point out that, at a certain level of analysis, there is nothing at all 'solid' down there, down at the (most basic?) levels of particles, strings and the contested organization of sub-atomic space. Its solidity, then, is ineluctably a perceptual category: a matter of what tables seem to be like to us, in the scale of human perception and bodily action. Reality takes on an intrinsically human dimension, and the most that can be claimed for it is an 'experiential realism' (Lakoff, 1987).

So let us remain at the human scale. When the table is assaulted it is not the whole of it that gets thumped, but only a bit of it under the fist or hand or tips of (some of) the fingers. What exactly is warranted by this – just the bit hit? What makes it a bit of a *table*? And for whom? How does the rest of the table get included as solid and real? And how does even that part that is hit get demonstrated as real for anybody but the hitter? And how exactly is this demonstration, here and now, supposed to stand for the table's continuing existence, then and later, and for all the other tables, walls, rocks, ad infinitum, universally and generally? A lot is being taken on trust here, however 'reasonably'.

(Edwards et al., 1995, pp. 28–9)

One response to table banging is given in Box 7.1. In general, social constructionists argue that we only come to know objects and events such as tables, chairs, plane crashes and stubbed toes through our human-made interpretations, we do not have any other access. More importantly, objects, events and the real world are not independent of human-made interpretations. Human constructions are *constitutive* of the nature of the world.

One good test case for this is the discovery of new land, such as people's various encounters with New Zealand and other islands in the South Pacific in the seventeenth and eighteenth centuries and much earlier (Wetherell and Potter, 1992, pp. 64–5). In one sense, there seems to be a material reality already there waiting to be discovered, bits of coast-line which boats bump into, and so on. But, in a crucial sense, we could also say that 'New Zealand' did not actually exist until it was discovered. Then, when it was discovered by Polynesian voyagers, by Abel Tasman, and most recently by Captain Cook (and given various different names), it entered into quite different interpretative systems, and became several different objects.

Furthermore, these interpretative and administrative systems had major consequences for the kind of country New Zealand became and, indeed, for the physical scenery. Maori groups had a much more animate and spiritual concept of physical land forms, while British settlers in the wake of Captain Cook would have been more likely to have viewed the land in terms of agricultural viability (sheep per acre and grain yields). This might differ again from the sensibility of the modern tourist guided by travel brochures and concepts of natural beauty. In other words, ideas and constructions matter. They become a material force as hillsides are swept away and landscapes remodelled in relation to changing ideas of agricultural management and modern tourism.

Social constructionists are not suggesting, therefore, that if someone thinks a piece of physical geography like New Zealand does not exist, it does not; nor that all there is to the real world is ideas. New Zealand is no less real for being constituted through human constructions – you still die if your plane crashes into a hill whether you think that the hill is the product of a volcanic eruption or the solidified form of a mythical whale, while if your reality construes the mountain as no more than a gaseous phantom, its practical limitations will have been tragically exposed. However, the real world is no less constructed for being able to get in the way of planes. How those deaths are understood and what is seen as causing them will be constituted through our systems of social constructions. And this constitutive process is particularly central to the kind of 'realities' social psychologists are studying.

Arguments like these and modern social constructionism owe a great deal to the philosophical movement of *pragmatism* which developed in the nineteenth century. Before the nineteenth century the traditional Christian realism about God and the moral order had given a context and a meaning to human life, in spite of all its pain and suffering. But this comfort became increasingly difficult to sustain. Darwin's version of Creation had little place for a living God, and some people began to toy with the idea that even God might be a human and cultural construction, a philosophical version of Voltaire's famous 'If God did not exist it would be necessary to invent him'. It was in this intellectual climate during the 1860s that one of the most eminent of the early psychologists, William James, experienced a depression in which he sought vainly for a meaning in life, and a reason for living. What is the point, he asked, if we are nothing but pawns of our biology and our culture? His recovery began with the conviction that meaning is established by acting in the world, not by intellectual reflection – this came as a revelation and he wrote in his diary that 'My first act of free will shall be to believe in free will' (James, quoted in Bjork, 1988, p. 89). This was the paradoxical beginning of the pragmatic claims sketched out in modern social constructionism that the appearance of truth and reality emerge out of living activity, they are not pre-requisites for it.

In the pragmatism developed by James and many others in the late nineteenth century and afterwards, human social activities were taken as given, out of which grew the knowledge and religions of different cultures. This was not seen as a one-way process, but as dialectical (reciprocal and transformative). As knowledge grows it affects social practices, including talk, which in turn effects knowledge and so on. This relationship between knowledge and its objects (referred to as mutualism in Chapter 6) was elaborated by John Dewey (1859–1952) throughout his long life, and it is essential to the thought of G.H. Mead, as well as to the Marxist Lev Vygotsky. To varying degrees these thinkers gave priority to the social over the individual as the basis of knowledge.

Modern social constructionism is also closely related to the development of the sociology of knowledge initiated by Karl Mannheim (1893–1947) and others. Mannheim's sociology of knowledge seems to have been worked out independently of Dewey, though there are clear affinities between them. Mannheim argued that since knowledge developed as a result of a social process, the origin or *sociology* of ideas and knowledge claims could be studied. The question became 'Why this kind of knowledge claim at this period in history?' rather than 'Is this idea true or false?'. Mannheim hesitated over whether all scientific knowledge was subject to social determination. Are physics and mathematics, for instance, socially determined? Modern sociology of science continues this distinction but on the whole is much less hesitant about examining the social basis of all science, including physics and mathematics.

We noted earlier that relativism raised particular moral, ethical and political issues. As a consequence, some social constructionists have wanted to distance themselves from the spectre of 'anything goes', and the view that all is relative. Others (compare Bruner, 1990; Gergen, 1985; Edwards et al., 1995; Sampson, 1993; Wetherell and Potter, 1992) want to challenge the implication that accepting a relativist position necessarily leads to moral and political quietism. But, on what basis can relativism be defended? Here again is Edwards et al.'s response.

> There is no contradiction between being a relativist and being *somebody*, a member of a particular culture, having commitments, beliefs, and a common-sense notion of reality. These are the very things to be argued for, questioned, defended, decided, without the comfort of just being, already and before thought, real and true. The idea that letting go of realism entails that all these commitments must fall, is no more convincing than the idea that life without God is devoid of meaning and value. Indeed the argument is remarkably similar ... as is the refutation: the death of God has not made the rest of the world disappear, but has left it for us to make. What we are left with is not a world devoid of meaning and value (or a world of absolute amorality where 'everything is permitted', as in the Nietzschian-Dostoyevskian conclusion) but precisely the reverse. It is a foregrounding of meanings and values, to be argued, altered, defended, and invented; including even the metavalue that some of these meanings and values may prof-

itably be declared universal and self-evident ('We *hold* these truths to be self-evident...'). Self-evidence here is the outcome rather than the denial of argumentation...

(Edwards et al., 1995, pp. 35–6)

In other words, Edwards et al. argue that taking a relativist position does not stop one from making assertions, taking stands, arguing for certain values and against others. If knowledge, reality and truth are seen as human constructions, there is even *more* pressure to think and argue, work out one's point of view, and learn how to defend it. What is lost is not values but what Bruner (1990) calls 'authorial meanings', or some final authority which can decide the truth outside argument, dialogue, debate and discussion.

Following the philosopher Richard Rorty (1982), Bruner explicitly acknowledges the pragmatic roots of his own view. He recognizes, first, that if cultures form minds, and if minds make value judgements, then some form of relativism is inescapable (1990, p. 24). In this context, the question social psychologists should ask themselves is not, 'is this view absolutely correct?', but, 'is this view of the world one we should hold?' We have to give up our search for an essential truth and learn instead to ask pragmatic questions about our grand (and not so grand) theoretical claims. Using Rorty's examples, Bruner suggests that truth is a matter of how things appear in practice, a matter of action rather than contemplation. When confronted, then, with statements such as 'History is the story of the class struggle', it would be more profitable to think about the consequences of believing that statement, its implications, and the other positions it commits one to, rather than beginning an impossible attempt to prove its absolute rightness or falsity (1990, p. 26).

Social constructionists would expect that their own knowledge claims should be open to the same kind of process of questioning and debate which Bruner suggests. Relativists, in general, are happy to live with the idea that their own claims to knowledge are constructed. They point out that it would be very odd to produce knowledge which does not explain its own emergence. Social constructionism is a perspective which can, in this way, turn its own knowledge on itself and ask, 'Why do we think that?', 'How have our knowledge and arguments been constructed to persuade an audience?'. This reflexivity has led to a new questioning of the way social scientists argue and write, constructing their own texts and canon of knowledge (see Ashmore, 1989, for an example).

On reflecting on these and related arguments, feminist theorists and other social psychologists with political commitments have noted that power and power inequalities are often missing from pragmatist and relativist visions of a world of argumentative cut and thrust (see Burman, 1992; Soper, 1990). These social psychologists argue that we need to study just who gets to set the agenda in different cultural and social communities. Whose versions of reality and whose notions of truth are most often accepted? Some working from this position (compare Billig, 1991; Gill, 1995; Wetherell and Potter, 1992) have argued, as a consequence, for what Rosalind Gill calls 'passionately interested inquiry' or 'politically informed relativism' – meaning that clear political commitments to anti-racism or for social justice are the centre-piece of the pragmatic approach advocated by Bruner and others, or placed at the heart of the process of arguing for meaning and value Edwards et al. identify. These commitments, of course, as befits a relativist approach, should not be seen as set in stone but as themselves open to debate, revision and discussion. This response, however, has not been sufficient for others, who though sympathetic to social constructionism still want to develop a 'new realist' position.

5 The 'New Realism'

Modern realists accept most of the findings of social constructionism (even call themselves social constructionists) yet still reserve a place for realism. Thus they readily accept that the discursive activities of travellers, inhabitants, historians and geographers have resulted in the social construction of what we now refer to as New Zealand. Nothing is denied but something is added. For many geographers there really was a New Zealand waiting to be discovered, and they might rephrase the sentence above as 'it might seem (to philosophers and social constructionists) that "New Zealand" did not actually exist until it was discovered, but in a crucial sense there was a material reality already there waiting to be discovered, bits of coast line which boats bump into, and so on'.

The modern realist does not try to prove the case, but relies on two kinds of argument, the transcendental (used by Kant) and the pragmatic (used by James). Some pragmatists, who give actions priority over thought, and practical results over abstract truth, could accept that belief in a reality beyond experience is justified if it 'works' or is useful. It would be useful, for instance, if it provides an indispensable way of organizing experience. More specifically, scientists may require a belief that they seek objective truth about reality in order to give purpose to their form of life, which has had such practical success. Their motivation (the pragmatist might argue) would be drastically curtailed if obliged to believe that they were merely weaving social constructions, rather than uncovering reality. Such arguments do not undermine relativism, since practical demands and possibilities vary from culture to culture, and so will pragmatic truth and reality. Thus pragmatism can give its blessing to the reality of everyday objects and of scientific entities, if belief in the reality of these is essential for the conduct of our personal lives or scientific activities. But in its full account of these realities, and why they are necessary, it would probably converge on a social constructionist account, showing how discursive and other activities constitute the forms of life that demand belief in an external reality. To take another example, pragmatists could applaud a social constructionist account of why people believe in God, but still accept the argument for belief in God's reality that it provides the background for a valid form of life (though this does not settle the matter, since others may reasonably dispute the value of believing in God).

Using a transcendental argument, the social philosopher Roy Bhaskar (1978) has reasoned that although scientific knowledge is a social product like 'motor cars, armchairs or books' (he calls these *transitive objects of knowledge*), knowledge is nevertheless '*of* things which are not produced by men (*sic*) at all ... If men (*sic*) ceased to exist sound would continue to travel and heavy bodies fall to the earth in exactly the same way, though ex hypothesi there would be no-one to know it. Let us call these ... the *intransitive objects of knowledge*'. It is this realism, the existence of intransitive objects of knowledge, that makes science possible (ibid, p. 22). Whether or not social psychology can be a science depends on whether or not it can find intransitive objects of knowledge (ibid, p. 44). In this way realism is a precondition for science to be possible. This is a transcendental realism for natural science, and the intransitive objects are there even before science investigates them. Bhaskar has little enthusiasm for a scientific social psychology, and would probably accept Gergen's (1985) argument that social psychology is history rather than science – in Bhaskar's terms, its objects are transitive.

More recently Greenwood has developed a realism to include everyday psychological entities – 'whatever entities exist in the natural, social, and psychological world exist independently of our concepts and descriptions of them ... The primary virtue of this account is that it enables us to understand how theoretical explanations can be genuinely explanatory (and fertile, etc.)...' (Greenwood, 1994, p. 26). Much of Greenwood's work is devoted to showing that social determination of, for example, emotions does not refute realism. In other words the way we express and talk about emotions is a product of social construction, and therefore socially and culturally relative, but it does not follow that emotive words do not refer to real processes or entities. Likewise pain may be real, even though its cultural expressions may be conditioned. How can we say all cultures have evolved social constructions around the experience of pain, unless there is some reality in common, pain, that links these constructions?

Transcendental arguments have been called upon to show that not just science and psychology, but even social constructionism presupposes a reality. Thus Harré (1992) argues that certain kinds of joint action are presupposed by social construction, and these include conversations. Whatever is socially constructed is theoretically dispensable within a social constructionist framework – it could in principle have been done otherwise. Science could have been constructed very differently or not existed at all. But this is not true of the joint actions involved in human conversations. These cannot be dispensed with if social constructionism is to get off the ground at all, and therefore cannot in themselves (as opposed to their content) be socially constructed.

6 Conclusion

Whatever you make of the various arguments for 'old' realism, 'new' realism and relativism (and we have not tried to provide any firm answers), the debates described in this chapter provide another way of understanding and organizing the diversity found in social psychology. Deeply held views about the nature of the 'real' and the possibilities for truth and knowledge often underpin social psychologists' choices of theory and method. As we have seen, there is a struggle going on in social psychology about the 'truth', just what it is, and who has the best access to it. This struggle gains its power because of the rhetorical potency of 'reality' and the way it is used to justify the 'big business' of science. There is a lot at stake, not least our understanding of the very nature and aims of social psychology itself.

References

Ashmore, M. (1989) *The Reflexive Thesis*, Chicago, University of Chicago Press.

Bhaskar, R. (1978) *A Realist Theory of Science*, Hassocks, Sussex, Harvester Press.

Billig, M. (1991) *Ideology, Rhetoric and Opinion*, London, Sage.

Bjork, D.W. (1988) *William James: The Centre of his Vision*, New York, Columbia University Press.

Bruner, J. (1990) *Acts of Meaning*, Cambridge, Mass., Harvard University Press.

Burman, E. (1992) 'Feminism and discourse in developmental psychology: power, subjectivity and interpretation', *Feminism and Psychology*, 2, pp.45–59.

Duncan, B.L. (1976) 'Differential social perception and attributions of intergroup violence: testing the lower limits of stereotyping of Blacks', *Journal of Personality and Social Psychology*, 34, pp.590–8.

Edwards, D., Ashmore, M. and Potter, J. (1995) 'Death and furniture: the rhetoric, politics and theology of bottom line arguments against relativism', *History of the Human Sciences*, 8, pp.25–49.

Gergen, K. (1985) 'The social constructionist movement in modern psychology', *American Psychologist*, vol. 40, pp.266–75.

Gill, R. (1995) 'Relativism, reflexivity and politics: interrogating discourse analysis from a feminist perspective' in Wilkinson, S. and Kitzinger, C. (eds) *Feminism and Discourse*, London, Sage.

Greenwood, J.D. (1994) *Realism, Identity and Emotion*, London, Sage.

Harré, R. (1992) 'What is real in psychology?', *Theory and Psychology*, 2, pp.153–8.

Lakoff, G. (1987) *Women, Fire and Dangerous Things: What Categories Reveal About the Mind*, Chicago, University of Chicago Press.

Parker, I. (1992) *Discourse Dynamics*, London, Routledge.

Rogers, C. (1951) *Client-Centered Therapy*, Boston, Houghton-Mifflin.

Rorty, R. (1982) *Consequences of Pragmatism: Essays 1972–1980*, Minneapolis, Minneapolis University Press.

Sampson, E.E. (1993) *Celebrating the Other*, London, Harvester Wheatsheaf.

Soper, K. (1990) 'Feminism, humanism and postmodernism', *Radical Philosophy*, 55, pp.11–17.

Stevens, R. (1996) 'The reflective self: an experiential perspective' in Stevens R. (ed.) *Understanding the Self*, London, Sage.

Wetherell, M. and Maybin, J. (1996) 'The distributed self: a social constructionist perspective' in Stevens, R. (ed.) *Understanding the Self*, London, Sage.

Wetherell, M. and Potter, J. (1992), *Mapping the Language of Racism: Discourse and the Legitimation of Exploitation*, London and New York, Harvester Wheatsheaf and Columbia University Press.

CHAPTER 8
FORMS OF LIFE: SCIENCE and SOCIAL PSYCHOLOGY

by David Devalle

1 Images for a science of social psychology

A major theme of this book is the relationship of social psychology and science. This chapter elaborates on this theme by looking at what it means to say that something is a science, relating this to the question raised in other chapters of whether and in what sense *social psychology* can be said to be scientific. One answer is 'it depends what you mean by "a science"'. This contains a recognition that different views about the kind of science social psychology is or should be have been advanced and opposed since the beginning of the modern subject. Looking at this contest and the reasons for it will naturally raise the third main topic of the chapter – *why it matters* whether all or some of social psychology is a science and what *follows* from saying that it is or that it is not.

Popular images of what we mean by the concept science tend to feature an image of science as what we think physicists and chemists do. Here, experiments involving systematic investigation produce evidence which is unambiguous and 'public' to anyone with the training to reproduce and understand it. Kelly's constructive alternativism (Kelly, 1953) and its image of man-as-scientist, with its ideas of progressive hypothesizing, testing and revision, is a way to grasp this process of how scientific reasoning works. Arguably it works, in an unbiased and value-neutral way, to add to our knowledge of the properties of the object under study and how behaviour may be controlled or predicted. 'Applied science' is more concerned with control and prediction to facilitate practical application of findings, 'pure science' more with properties and causal laws, but both draw on and contribute to the same knowledge base.

I am going to expand upon this conventional image of science and question the assumptions of this model. For example, a conventional image of science emphasizes truth as a central feature. In this book, however, there has been an emphasis on meaning, and the dialectic between truth and meaning is an underlying tension in this chapter. I adopt the narrative stance that science is a special form of life, and its features will be described by a refrain of 'logic' and 'history'. The structure of this chapter is that after discussing 'logic' features, there will be an interlude focusing on truth and meaning, raising specific issues relevant to the form of life that is social psychology. After this, the 'history' features of science will be discussed. The chapter finishes with issues about *authority* and why social psychologists should want to be called scientists.

If you recall, Chapter 1 ('Defining social psychology') introduced the multiple bases of social psychology by discussing three position papers. Three different ways in which the term 'science' has been used by social psychologists were identified :

1 *Science as method* – using the methods of the natural sciences (appropriately amended) to ferret out the laws of personality or intrapersonal process or social interaction or group/systemic behaviour, and adopting the neutral and disengaged stance of the natural scientist.

2 *Moral science* – concerned not so much with describing what people *do* as with exploring what they *could* do, how they *could* view the world and themselves, and perhaps how they *should* view the world and themselves.

3 *Political science* – concerned not with general laws but with uncovering power relations in what is assumed and taken for granted about human meanings, with an intent to change the existing social order or resist change to it.

Consider the following examples:

1 Psychoanalytic research and theory – based on the interpretations and self-analysis of 'psychoanalysts ... trained for many years to be observers of others and of themselves' (see Thomas, 1996, p.288) – where a similar *logic* is applied to that of more transparently scientific work but where the data are intrinsically and inescapably *constructed* through a process of interpretation and therefore not available to others without that training (who in acquiring it also acquire the stance of this body of theory).

2 The analysis of identity – e.g. Stevens (1996b) – which again depends on personal interpretations not necessarily available to other observers, but where the concern also appears to be not to establish laws but to search out possibilities and constraints, and the emphasis is less on interpreted data than on shared experience.

3 The analysis of racist ideology presented by e.g. Wetherell (1996a) – which is clearly based on data but equally clearly analyses the text in the light of preconceived theory and from a politically engaged rather than a neutral position.

The first of these examples (though perhaps not as obviously as the biological and experimental perspectives – see Toates, 1996 and Lalljee, 1996) would lay claim to 'science as method' – their aim *as scientists* is the dispassionate exploration of the human condition, although *as therapists* they may have other goals. The second and third also use systematic methods of enquiry, but they are not dispassionate about the field of enquiry. On the contrary, the analysis of identity fits well with the definition of *moral* science given above, and the analysis of ideology fits well with the definition of *political* science.

2 Scientia

Let us look in more detail at what science is. *Scientia* was simply the Latin word for knowledge. Modern usage of the word science has come to mean certain *kinds* of knowledge that are limited to 'the scientific method' and scientists (though the word 'scientist' was only invented by William Whewell in 1840 – prior to that they were natural philosophers). The modern idea of science emerges in the seventeenth century from medieval institutions and philosophical and religious activity. One of the oldest scientific institutions, established by royal warrant of 1663, is 'The Royal Society for Improving Natural Knowledge by Experiments'. The foremost feature of this institution was the public demonstration of experiments. 'Modern Science' had emerged and was influenced by people such as Francis Bacon, whose emphasis on 'the positive law of nature' shifted concern from scholastic deductive principles of logic and mathematics and simple observation into a systematic collaboration of speculation, articulation and experimentation.

Some would say that if psychology does not fit into this pattern, then it is not science. However, there is another idea about science, an older usage of the word that emphasizes a systematic approach rather than a research methodology with experimentation at its heart. This is the science of meanings, or hermeneutics. Here, what is important to notice is the difference between an explanation and an interpretation, a distinction between truth and meaning. It may be that we cannot find out the truth about our lives, but we can make out what they mean.

We find this tension present in the various perspectives of social psychology (Stevens, 1996a). When we start with meanings as our subject-matter and as the goal, we have to accept the sophistication of the subject-matter of our science. We do not find reality out there waiting for us, like the natural scientist; it has to be made present by creating something as 'data'. For example, Freud does this by treating dreams as 'raw data', along with other bits of evidence, and then goes beyond the appearances to look for the truth or meaning. In this case, because we create the subject matter we *interpret* the world in some way prior to studying it. As such, we assume our ontology and thus our methods involve evaluation. Furthermore, evaluation can have a reflexive relationship to our own lives; that is, we can change our lives and our ideas of what we 'actually' are, if we take seriously the implications of the concept of agency in the experiential perspective and/or the constructed self in the social constructionist perspective. This leads some to say that social psychology *cannot* be a science. How can it be a science if its subject-matter – in this case the self – changes as a consequence of being studied (see Winch, 1958)? Perspectives which favour hermeneutics, social constructionism and psychodynamics have attempted to meet such objections by evolving questions, methods and answers which have scientific aims – they generate knowledge – but do not follow the methodology of modern natural science in doing so.

Social constructionists would emphasize that evaluation is present throughout the practice of science. In natural science, as much as in social science, the personal beliefs of the scientist and the ideologies of the culture play a part in what is discovered. These values, it is said, come about through social processes. If you remember, from this perspective the very 'self' is distributed and constructed. Thus, there is no 'scientist', but rather a scientific self, constructed, like other selves, out of the materials made available by the prevailing processes. There is an emphasis here on bearing in mind what science is for and why it is done.

Various sociological and psychological explanations have been offered about the social structure of science and the motives of scientists. Merton (1977) was one of the first to describe the common values of the social world of scientists. The norms he proposed were *universalism, communism, organized scepticism* and *disinterestedness*. The norms he proposed are not always maintained, and when they are ignored is of importance in the evolution of science (see Mulkay, 1990). In this book, for example, the need for explanations to have universal applicability (universalism) is challenged by those scientists who favour a discourse approach of epistemological relativism where various competing and contradictory interpretations are held simultaneously; similarly, in psychodynamics events are multi-determined i.e. there can be several explanations which satisfactorily explain the 'causes' of the event. Merton also wondered why scientists rushed to be the first to publish findings, if they believed that the truth would come through the scientific process anyway. He decided it was their need for professional recognition, the highest form being *eponymy*, where a scientific theory or area is named after you. Merton's work on the social psychology of science inspired the flourishing research areas known as 'social studies of knowledge' (SSK – see Bloor, 1991 or Woolgar, 1988) and 'science and technology studies' (STS – see Latour, 1987 or Pickering, 1992).

2.1 Science as a form of life

Science itself is a social activity whose role has developed in the history of our culture, and it is a practice with political dimensions. Science's emphasis on method, reason and the appeal to evidence has established it as an authority superior to subjective experience or religious pronouncement. Science declares 'the truth', and it is difficult not to see this as a *purpose* of science, not just a description of how society behaves towards its scientists. Science is a particular form of life independent of other social and personal activities. It is a special kind of activity distinct from the life-world. You may remember this notion and Wittgenstein's idea of a *form of life* from Chapter 6 in this volume. The notion of a 'form of life' is complex, and you may ask how we distinguish between the various forms of life in which we participate, such as science, art and religion. There is not space here to go into this fully, but seeing science as a form of life means abandoning the idea of classifying a given activity as 'science' or 'not science' by some simple, essential feature common to all sciences, such as use of experimental methods, or disinterest. A form of life is not like a logical class or a social norm; it is more like a species (see Hull, 1988). Activities mutate, and it may be that various forms of life created 'social psychology' and that social psychology may come to evolve its own form of life. We shall return to this later. (What I am doing in this chapter is philosophy of science with special reference to social psychology, elucidating features of the form of life of science and social psychology. This is different from what sociologists do when they describe the different social phenomena that make up different forms of life (e.g. Mulkay, 1990), and it is different from clarifying the concept 'form of life', which is a problem for epistemology. Stevens, in Chapter 5, presents an epistemological proposal about the form of life which is psychology, with his synthesis of different epistemologies; disputes about this are epistemological. Sapsford's discussion of domains in Chapter 4 is also an instance of conceptual work in epistemology.) The life world has many forms of life that emerge and in which we participate. Understanding them requires participation. A little more discussion is probably needed to help us understand the idea 'form of life'.

If we see science and art as 'classes' with particular defining properties which belong to one class – some to science but not art, for example – then to know whether something is science or art we need to describe what the essential characteristics of science and art are. We might talk about kinds of explanation, or that truth is essential to science and meaning to art. We could then ask which social psychology was – a science or an art. But the *actual* arts and sciences have other features in common – for example systematic study, interpretation of evidence – and it may be that both use the terms 'truth' and 'meaning' in their discourses, and so this particular definition will not do the job we want it to do. More importantly, we might want to say that social psychology is *both* a science *and* an art; that is, features of social psychology resemble features of both sciences and arts. So the form of life to which social psychology belongs may not be clear-cut, and it may be that social psychology is a distinct form of life in its own right.

To illustrate this kind of idea, let us look at Wittgenstein (1953) discussing language in terms of 'language games'.

> 'You take the easy way out! You talk about all sorts of language games but have nowhere said what the essence of a language game, and hence of language, is: what is common to all these activities, and what makes them into language or parts of language?'... And this is true ... Instead of producing something common to all we call language, I am saying that these phenomena have no one thing in common which makes us use the word for all – but they are *related* to one another in many different ways. And it is because of this relationship, or these relationships, that we call them all 'language'.

He goes on to discuss 'games' and asks you to consider what is common to all games.

'What is common to them all?' Don't say there *must* be something common, or they would not be called 'games' ... but *look and see* whether there is anything common to *all*. For if you look at them you will not see something that is common to them *all*...

So there are similarities between the sciences but you will find no single distinguishing feature. There are similar features in the same way that members of the same family are similar; to use another of Wittgenstein's terms, there are 'family resemblances' between the sciences.

2.2 'Doing science'

In this book you have been introduced to perspectives, domains, and positions as terms to organize 'social psychology'. Additionally, you have encountered more traditional categories such as subjects and disciplines, and philosophical 'topics' such as epistemology and ontology. Understanding all this is the intellectual activity, the thinking and reasoning, of social psychology, however you are not 'doing science'. 'Doing science' must involve 'doing research'. Is this all it demands? If you are 'doing research' with a scientific attitude, are you now 'doing science'? We have to say no to this claim, for 'doing science' also involves belonging to a scientific 'community' where your activity contributes to the *inherited knowledge* which is argued about, believed, disbelieved and passed on.

A common positivist image of science is of static method and confirmed truths uncontaminated by historical and cultural processes. However, as scientific methods and theories are inherited by a scientific community you cannot stand outside of this history any more than you can stand outside of a culture. Even Comte, who crystalized the doctrine of positivism, stated:

The history of science is science itself.

(Comte, 1974)

This section has set up a tension between the 'notes' of logic and history that we shall explore in the rest of the chapter. We might ask what the value is of focusing on a point in history such as 'the rise of modern science' to help us understand science. My answer would be that we have to start *somewhere*! It is an important point in social and historical terms and shows the value of seeing science as a form of life as it describes science in terms of a 'given'. Social processes are the given, and the special activity of science arises out of these processes. The actual features of its form of life can change and evolve as conditions allow and necessitate, based on what we want our sciences and scientists to do and what they actually do. Society, science and the scientist are in a spiral of mutual interaction and evolution.

Using *form of life* to describe science allows the view that no one feature is necessary for an activity to be described as scientific, and though various features of the form of life of science are listed below, none of them is essential. In this reading, the old distinction between natural and social science – that is, sciences based on different subject matters, *nature* and *society* – is not seen as useful. So although it is used occasionally in this chapter, this is because of its historical legacy in discussion. There are many kinds of science, and there is no one feature that characterizes 'the natural sciences' in distinction from 'the social sciences'. The distinction between natural and social is too crude to be of great value in characterizing social psychology .

An issue which has been very popular in discussing science but which I haven't as yet touched on, is the contrast of science with *pseudo-science*. Popper described psychoanalysis and Marxism as *pseudo-sciences* in comparison to Einstein's work when characterizing the logic of science. Freud and Marx were pseudo-scientific because their theories couldn't be refuted and refutation, according to Popper, was an essential feature of the science practised by Einstein. As discussed earlier, physics is taken to be the typical science and by this model a criterion is derived in order for activities to be classified as science or as pseudo-science. For the contrast to work, there has to be some defining feature common to all sciences. Taking physics as the typical science means other sciences such as biology or geology or astronomy are open to the criticism that they are not like physics. Treating science as a form of life there are necessarily many kinds of science, each of which may in another's eyes appear to be pseudo-science. When there is disagreement *within* a 'science', such as psychology, then the term pseudo-science is often used as a term of denigration for another's efforts. Kitzinger (1990) argues that to call something pseudoscientific is a rhetorical device used to undermine competing views. More perniciously, such a characterization pays homage to an illusory monolithic method and maintains all the sciences in a state of 'physics envy'.

3 Features of the scientific form of life

The following features are discussed to help you think about science and social psychology and to consider what social psychology is or should be.

3.1 The scientific attitude

Science has to be taught; you do not naturally think scientifically. The conceptual reconstruction of experience that is science does not fit our actual experience. For example, intellectually we may know that the earth goes round the sun, but it still looks from earth as if the sun rises and sets. Until Copernicus established otherwise it was commonly thought the sun revolved around the earth. This is an example of how the scientific knowledge base is inherited. Much of science is 'uncommon' sense and 'counter-intuitive'. Although the man-the-scientist metaphor of Kelly suggests we do think scientifically about ourselves – that is we hypothesize and test our personal constructs against reality – it is only a model of how our personal constructs change. When we think 'naturally' we are not 'doing science', because it is assumed we are biased and not sufficiently sceptical and detached from our experience. It is assumed the results of your activity are not objective unless they can be clearly shared and supported by other research.

The conventional image of science stresses objectivity as a criteria by which to judge research and as essential for a scientific attitude. It assumes a person cannot be objective because of interpretative bias. Attribution research (Lalljee, 1996) describes how different explanations for action are given, and a different locus of causality is attributed, depending on the specific perspective of the actor. Depending on the 'outside' or 'inside' point of view, personality factors or situational factors are attributed as the cause of events. Therefore, a sceptical and detached attitude is held towards the objectivity of our own experience and opinions. We can speculate that it was partially this attitude, and a rejection of scholastic and religious dogma, which fostered the public demonstrations and experiments (and their replication) of the Royal Society which have been a major feature of science since. However, the issue of objective and subjective interpretation has been importantly contested and is a main feature of social psychology to which we will return later.

3.2 Research

There are many ways of getting at evidence, but a powerful approach (in many sciences) is the experiment. The nature of experiments is described elsewhere in this book (see Chapter 9). Briefly, an experiment is controlled *intervention* in a situation by the scientist, so designed that the effects of the intervention can be clearly distinguished from other possible causes of the outcome (in principle, though it is not always easy in practice). Often the situation will be an unnatural one, not occurring in people's everyday lives but specially designed to simplify the problem of excluding alternative explanations.

This method lies at the heart of the simple methodological stereotype of science with which this chapter began, the physicist or chemist in the laboratory. It is of course a far from complete description of scientific method, because many scientific studies occur in circumstances where experimental intervention is not possible. Field observation, for example, can be systematic and scientific even if not experimental, and some natural sciences are largely precluded by their subject matter from any possibility of experimentation – for example astronomy and geology. The same logic is expressed in systematic observation of nature: an element is isolated and its effects on another element described, even if the isolation cannot be more than a conceptual and analytic one. The key feature of scientific reasoning is the systematic analysis which takes us from general observation and opinion to 'saying how things are' in a way which can be backed with evidence. It is 'a push for closure': a push from opinions to truth, a closing down of the options of interpretation to a theory which will be accepted. The sciences are based on research activity; finding and analysing evidence is what 'polices' scientific thinking and divides it from mere speculation. Thus empirical work is a major feature of science.

3.3 Theory

In addition, though some have claimed otherwise, doing scientific research involves at least some prior thinking, a theory. Scientific theories have evolved out of received opinions and *interpretations* of these and the truth is sought. We also want to know what is worth talking about. This is a major contribution of the experiential perspective to social psychology (Stevens, 1996b): it calls our attention explicitly to dimensions of human life worthy of scientific effort. All science begins as a hermeneutic endeavour, an endeavour grounded in *meaning*. Even the most experimental of perspectives assume implicit meaning – they have to determine what *matters*, which problems and ideas it is profitable to investigate – and so declare some significant and others of no value. Ideally this is determined by scientific worth and human necessity, rather than financial criteria. We shall discuss this later.

The structuring of the language of science has been dominated by the separation of evidence from theory and has relied on the distinction between the description of events, or 'observations', and the statements that explain them. Sometimes this distinction is framed as 'what we see' and 'what we say', the distinction between appearances (phenomena, sense experiences) and what we can say about the reality that underlies them. Popper (1979) characterizes scientific explanation as *'the explanation of the known by the unknown'*. The epistemology of science demands that there be patterns or regularities and an underlying order, to be found or discovered. The usual ordering is by theories, where laws are theorems in a deductive system and the patterns of nature are revealed by experiment to test this theoretical ordering; without the possibility of such ordering there would be no point in doing science. It is the status of the ordering and how it comes about that leads to dispute. What is it that we are finding out? The key issues in the debate are about the *status* of theories and facts and the *means* by which these are contested and accepted by the scientific community. To what does a theory refer, and how does the theory come about?

At this point it is useful to characterize the debate by tracing some of its historical roots. Bacon's science was 'the spelling out of the book of nature'. Theories should be derived from an openness towards and a belief in the truth of nature. Bacon was challenging the kind of theories derived from scholastic practice based on Aristotelian deductive knowledge. Bacon's empirical method became a common view of science; it was based on induction, and empirical findings were seen as the bedrock of scientific reasoning.

Later arguments are about the 'reality' of theories and facts. The empiricist and rationalist differ over the role of evidence and the status of theory in creating the explanatory order[1]. Empiricists such as Hume insist that all theoretical ordering is grounded in experience; experience is the basis for our knowledge. Rationalists such as Descartes emphasize the role of reasoning in generating knowledge; for example, the concept of causality is necessary for the organization of 'experience' into theory and evidence. Kant synthesized rationalism and empiricism – he said we do 'see' causes in the phenomenal world, but they exist only in psychological reality, because of our innate 'cognitive' machinery. In this sense a cause is a construct of the human mind.

Positivists such as Comte and Mach were inheritors of the empiricist position and argued that the function of theory was merely to connect observed facts, and not to serve as causal explanation. The importance of Comte is that he extended the methods of physics to the study of society. Let us look in more detail at positivism, remembering that this is influential in psychology (see Chapter 1). Mach, who influenced the logical positivists, questioned the reality of the theories derived from the findings and the components of the theories. Theoretical statements are not 'real', theories do not represent the world and the components of the theory are not real. This positivism derives from Kant's phenomenalism: all science is derived from sensations, as all is part of the human mind. Mach reduces physics to psychology.

There is a constructionist flavour to the empiricist and positivist positions; theories are constructed out of the facts of nature, and this orientation stems from Bacon's natural history. However, Bacon's stress on the facts of nature is there in order that science can construct a picture of reality that accords with nature; it is a version of *realism* rather than constructionism, in that the causal order the theory describes is posited as something actually existing in nature.

Where some constructionists go further than the empiricists in their scepticism about the reality of theories and entities is by suggesting that theoretical order is not even *found* in nature, but *read into it*. This is because the meaning of the patterns observed depends on human reasoning and is not *derived from* the shadows of appearance. This is similar to Mach's positivism, however; he believed scientific laws, although only schematic, were still reformed by our experience of nature. The *social* constructionist makes a further claim that 'reading nature' is limited not because of our human senses but because the social process of constructing knowledge and the fundamentally *social* nature of the

---

[1] The accepted classification of thinkers into rationalists, positivists and other 'ists' is useful as a guide by taming the infinite variety of scientific thinking. But taming has its price and we can become imprisoned within our concepts like Rilke's caged panther: 'The world is made of bars, a hundred thousand bars, and behind the bars, nothing'.

human mind are subject to linguistic and social conventions. Here it is not a question just of what theories reference or represent, but also of how they are made. Sensing, observing and reasoning are situated in social practice. We are always inside language and inside society, and human reasoning and experience are dimensions of how we organize and make knowledge; we see through the blurred lens of our cultural representations.

Whether theories grounded in this latter kind of constructionist epistemological position can qualify as science is a point of debate within social psychology. Science as method grounded in the discovery of evidence needs 'uncontaminated' evidence to exist independently of the scientist. If we make knowledge and there is no independent source of clarification, then is what we have done to be counted as science? This is Bacon's *realist* emphasis on observing nature; nature is seen as independent of reason and experience. The interpretative view of science denies the possibility of knowing this independent reality, as theories and facts are sculpted from incognizable nature by logic and experiment (positivist) and by the norms of the scientific community (social constructionist).

There is disagreement about the implications of social epistemology – that is, the society and customs of scientists which play an important part in determining knowledge for the status of science. It is the 'trustworthiness' of the scientific community that is questioned. The cognitive authority and expertise of the scientist and the scientific community is doubted because scientists are subject to social influence. This is not to accuse science of being wrong, but simply that claiming to be a disinterested authority is less persuasive when a person is seen as saturated by social and psychological influence.

Nevertheless the constructionist would agree with the empiricist that 'science' is the activity of gathering evidence systematically and explaining it so that it can be understood by others. The findings and conclusions can be judged, challenged and used, and it is this social process that the social constructionist emphasizes and is sceptical toward. The structuring of the understanding may be rational or it may be simply a common language that is shared by the practitioners of the social and human activity we call science. In the latter sense a science may not be about truth found rationally or empirically, but simply an activity which answers questions systematically and in public. So, what you mean by science depends in part on your epistemology, in part on your notion of what reality is or could be, and in part on what its purpose is.

If we characterize 'science' as 'a systematic approach with a common language', then other activities such as artistic appreciation or literary criticism, which have these features, become sciences. However, although these activities have facts, theories, methods, evidence and are systematic, they are part of a different form of life – they are 'interpretative' arts. Conventional scientific reasoning believes the interpretations of scientists are warranted by objective evidence and thus carry authority (see Chapter 1). The realist reading of scientific activity asserts that scientific explanations describe reality (theory realism) and the component terms of the theory actually refer to things, for example atoms, which exist in nature (entity realism). These two readings characterize 'science' and help distinguish it from philosophy or the arts. However, the distinction has been blurred and the effects of this blurring are where different positions regarding the status of 'scientific' understandings are contested.

3.4 Ontology

A given science is characterized by a specific *ontology*, a specific view of what exists to be studied. It is the ontology which categorizes the different and particular into kinds or classes – for example atoms, species, behaviours, meanings – and so, in a sense, declares the furniture of the world. The different perspectives of social psychology have different ontologies; biology has 'bodies', experiential psychology has 'experiences'. This issue is one which characterizes social pschology as a 'multiple perspectives' discipline. A concept such as 'self' or 'person' can constitute an ontology, as in the definition of social psychology as the study of the person in a social world. The concept of the social or society raises other ontological questions such as whether the social is best described as a process or whether we should describe society as a real existent 'thing' (see Chapter 7, and also Bhaksar, 1989, and Searle, 1995).

The ontological distinctions in natural science evolved with its separation into physics, chemistry, biology and their interdisciplinary derivatives. Psychology, similarly, has had descriptions of its ontology as psyche, soul, mind, behaviour, self, and now person and identity. Just as the different branches of natural science have different methods, so do these different psychologies. Whether they are indeed different psychologies, or branches of a single subject, and whether they should aspire to a commonality of methods or each develop their own characteristic modes of operation, are matters open to question and debate.

One dispute centres on issues in the philosophy of language. If we hold that words or terms do not represent or refer to kinds or classes which actually exist but are merely terms of language, then this position, known as *nominalism*, would orientate theory and evidence in different ways. Positivists and empiricists are more sceptical about theoretical entities than rationalists and realists. Social constructionists vary on this; an emphasis on social process and discourse suggests we cannot describe the 'furniture of the world' because we are always 'inside language'. Some have nonetheless tried; for example, Harré (1986), a leading social constructionist, has a theory of language – linguistic realism – which posits a correspondence between discursive objects and a non-discursive world.

For a particular science to be a shared activity its participants must agree on certain central concerns, and one of these is its ontology – colloquially speaking, its 'reality'. Most natural scientists presuppose the existence and reality of nature. In terms that echo the previous chapter, they presuppose that nature is really there. Although concepts and theories are imaginal and social constructions, they still presuppose there is a 'something' to be constructed about.

It is where 'the real' is contested that issues arise for realism and constructionism. They disagree over the scientific status of how different perspectives conceptualize and interpret psychological life. For example, is seasonal affective disorder to be understood as a disease state and best approached from a biological perspective, or should the condition be viewed as partially socially constructed and personally experienced? How should we, and when is it appropriate to, turn 'ordinary experience' into concepts from a professional perspective? Different perspectives might recommend different treatments. Issues about the 'authority' of a perspective are important because of the conflict about which authority decides 'what is real' when the players in the interpretative repertoires are in dispute about 'the real'. The realist fears that constructionism will lead to all views being valid and that relativism will reign. The constructionist suspects that those who claim to be realists are assuming authority without warrant. The issue is complicated. 'Relativism of authority does not establish the authority of relativism; it opens reason to new claimants' (Rose, 1995).

3.5 Truth and meaning

At this point in the chapter the final note of the logic refrain is struck. Many sciences centre on truth; the social psychology in this book emphasizes meaning. We now start to particularize the form of life endemic to social psychology.

One way of approaching the question of why science is a source of authority is to point out that we have many possible *opinions* at our disposal which state why something has happened, what something is made up of or how to do something. We come across these opinions all the time; some are formed in the crucible of our own experience, some by listening to other people's experience, and some from our general education. It is because of this melee of opinion that we need and use the concept of truth; truth is assigned to those views we accept or believe. One way of establishing the truth is by finding out the facts.

A fact is a statement of, for example, what *actually* happened or happens. So the statement 'In 1066 King Harold of the Saxons was defeated by the Normans' is true. 'He was defeated at the Battle of Hastings'. This is also true. It is not true to say that the Battle of Hastings was in 1067.

Statements such as these are not just opinions, they are opinions which claim to be the truth. They may not be based on *our* observations, but they do purport to describe truthfully what actually happened or how things actually are. A fact is more than an observation; it is an *interpreted* observation. In scientific reasoning the argument goes, we interpret our observations in terms of what is real. When I describe the facts which I have seen myself, I do not describe what appears to my eyes, but I make a claim about what 'really happened'. I assert not just an opinion to which I am entitled, but what I regard as being the only true opinion, 'the facts about reality'. In so doing, if I base my claim on logical reasoning from evidence which is openly available, as the sciences in the conventional image say they do, then I make it possible for my claim to be examined.

A particular procedure for choosing between opinions and nominating some as the truth can be called a method. Two classical procedures are *reason* and *experience*; we met these earlier as rationalism and empiricism, where logic and method are accorded different roles in declaring the truth. The scientific method evolved through addressing questions of natural philosophy (physics) and is a particular procedure for judging the truth of different theories. A speculation is characterized as scientific if it can be examined in this way. The method of physics was so successful that it became the preferred way of selecting between opinions or speculations for other subjects and issues of interpretation are resolved by finding out the facts. The business of a scientific psychologist is to generate speculations about our lives; and develop research methods which justify or develop these speculations by finding out the facts.

It is certainly not difficult to agree that at least some social psychology follows this model in that it uses systematic methods – in some sense copied, often, from the methods of the 'natural' sciences. However in this book you have by now become familiar with the different perspectives and approaches in social psychology and will recognize the interpretative and reflexive nature of some of its subject matter. We need to look in more detail at scientific method, however, in order to see which kinds of social psychology follow this characterization of science.

Objectivity

Objectivity is a feature of fundamental importance in characterizing what science is. A claim to be scientific is a willingness to be open to public scrutiny and an acceptance that the conclusions put forward may be wrong.

> To claim objective truth is to lay one's cards on the table, to expose oneself to the possibility of refutation. It is to make it clear that one is talking about something, and saying that 'something is thus and not so'; this makes it possible for others to point out features of that something which are not as claimed, and hence disprove your opinion. All claims to objective truth are vulnerable in some way.
>
> *(Collier, 1994)*

However, how we decide that a conclusion is wrong is not as simple a matter as it might at first appear. In classical scientific reasoning, the facts or evidence are what is used to judge whether a claim can be maintained or a theory is true. It is accepted that the subject, the researcher, is biased in the sense of having his or her own values and expectations, so to make a universal, general claim to truth it is necessary to go beyond the judgement of the single researcher to a position of general agreement. The most easily acquired public scientific knowledge is obtained by watching the movement of objects. Remember Galileo and his demonstration involving objects falling from the tower of Pisa? Although different people view the event from different perspectives, it can be described in common values of measurement; 'objectivity' is possible.

The issue of general agreement however, becomes a problem when studying rare events and subjective experiences, not necessarily repeatable and often not even in principle accessible to other observers. The problem also exists where acquiring the techniques of measurement involves being socialized into the perspective which produced them. This problem holds true even in the 'natural' sciences. Nevertheless, one underlying metaphysical assumption common to all sciences is that knowledge is possible: there is a world of nature that we can study, it follows regularities that we can find or read into it, we can test our conclusions about these regularities. To call 'the social sciences' scientific in the 'methods' sense is to make the assumption that we can also do this with society and human lives with the hope of objective knowledge.

However this has been contested in psychology; objectivity is judged less important than understanding (*verstehen* in Chapter 2) as the goal of psychological knowledge. Here it is assumed that a person is an 'interpreted object' and is not best served by an image of determinism and predictability. Action and agency are key concepts, and understanding and interpretation are central to this kind of social psychology. This suggests that the form of life 'social psychology' has a feature not conventionally attributed to 'science'.

Interpretation

The point being made is that psychological explanations must involve value judgements. They are always *interpretations*, because they rest on metaphysical assumptions about the nature of persons and the best way to characterize them. Such questions are not resolved by scientific methodology; they require philosophical work. Additionally, reworking the narrative of 'who I am', a key activity in some perspectives (for example psychodynamic and experiential), requires us to maintain a reflexive openness to alternative interpretations and a scepticism about our preferred interpretation of our experience.

It is because of this that the distinction has been made between 'explanation' and 'understanding' (Von Wright, 1971). Understanding aims for more than scientific explanation, stressing the importance of subjectivity and inter-subjectivity for social psychology, as well as the more conventional scientific stress on objectivity. For example, the idea that I am a *person* is a definition that has been selected out of other possible descriptions – I could be named as a physical object, a body, or a member of the human species, or male, or British, or a human subject, etc. The selection of a particular form of identification or conceptual basis is what gives a science its ontology and a social constructionist would wish to draw our attention to how centrally this shapes the scientific process. And adopting a stance of inter-subjectivity for psychological research requires the scientist to participate in research in such a way that the discourse of 'understanding' is not given privileged status by claiming to be objective or explanatory.

In social psychology, as in everyday life, our utterances can represent both how things are and how we act upon and construe things. We explain ourselves and others in terms of motives, reasons and causes, and these make up interpretative discourse. It is central to the status of an interpretation that if it claims to be an *explanation* rather than a *speculation* there must be a way of deciding between different speculations. This is where we came in; the scientific method is our razor of truth to cut through the melee of opinion and get to the facts. But how do we choose between *interpretations*? This interesting question can be approached only by sacrificing the aid to judging between opinions that is supplied by the authoritative status of a science seeking *explanations*.

Basic metaphysical ideas such as the distinction between observer and observed, constitutive of the natural sciences and fundamental to the concept of objectivity, may themselves become matters of dispute within such a psychology. The idea of inter-subjectivity and the creation of meaning in a participatory dialogue, for example, attacks the very metaphysical assumptions that some would think fundamental to the creation of something which can be called a science; a science must in some way be *objective*, to merit the name at all.

The discussion about the Battle of Hastings in 1066 helped us to think about what we mean when we say something is a fact. We know the battle occurred and that it will not happen again. Beyond facts are conceptual issues, such as battle and skirmish, which involve interpretation. What is interpretatively important, though, is what the *consequences* of the Battle of Hastings were. In the scientific form of life this kind of interpretation tends to be classified as 'subjective'. Although science and history are similar in that they both ascertain the status of facts by various means and systematize the body of facts by general theory, it is in the logic of interpretation where procedures differ. Those interpretations that cannot be judged by objective means are seen as outside the jurisdiction of science; this is 'the limit to scientific understanding' (Medawar, 1985). Many theoretical physicists do make highly interpretative claims, but it is assumed they will be resolved by objective means; a scientist's speculation will be tested by 'evidence that speaks for itself'. A historian organizes and interprets facts to tell a particular story; what has to be justified is the facts used, the facts left out and the perspective from which the story is told. A historian's narrative is still justified by argument and subject to public examination. It can be *vulnerable* in some way and objective truth could still be claimed if the meaning can be refuted. But is this the same use of the term objective as understood in a scientific sense? The conventional scientific form of life wants such problems of interpretation resolved by referring to the 'objectively real', *the truth.*

Unfortunately, interpretating *the meaning* of our lives is seldom that simple. In conversation we argue, agree, and dispute interpretations of events and our lives. The narrative of the life course that emerges from this process how events happen, how they are explained, and their meaning has consequences for us. This sense making creates understanding and ideas of future possibility, it shapes our world and our lives. Disagreements and disputes over what really happened are why we have interpretative procedures which help us to decide what explanation to accept, and this is where psychologists and psychotherapists can become professionally involved. A desire for the one explanation about what really happened is hard to resist. Psychological science has understandably valued a procedure of scientific objectivity to resolve disputes between different explanations so that the truth about what really happened can be found and the *same* explanation be accepted. This explanation reigns as the sovereign explanation in the world of interpretation and the other explanations are discarded. But, as Bruner (1990) suggests, it is the interpretative procedures for adjudicating the *different* construals of reality inevitable in any diverse society that may be a more important matter and direction for human and social science. Social psychology, when it emphasizes the interpretative consequences of events rather than explaining why events happen, has a narrative role in our lives similar to history rather than science. In questions about the meaning of our lives it is not to science that we should look for answers (Medawar, 1985).

3.6 Doing social psychology: from progress to perspective

Modern science's form of life emerged around 1600, and some of its key features have been detailed. I hope the key section on truth and meaning showed the complexity of the issues. Hull (1988) suggests we should understand the emergence of a form of life rather like Darwin's theory of how a new species emerges, by adaptation to the environment. New forms of life emerge as adaptations to changing circumstances. In the example given above, modern science emerged because of conceptual change, changing social conditions and new technologies, and the 'medieval European world' transformed itself into the modern world. The accepted story of the emergence of psychology as a scientific subject has it emerging out of philosophy as experimental psychology in the mid-nineteenth century and become a branch of modern science (see, for example, Boring, 1929). However, Chapter 2 of this book reframes the conventional history by tracing older philosophical and religious influences (for example, St Augustine, Descartes and the Jesuit school).

This requires outlining features that represent a form of life, social psychology, not solely derived from the conventions of modern science. As Boring himself noted,

> the present changes the past; and, as the focus and range of psychology shift in the present, new parts enter into its history and other parts drop out.
>
> *(Boring, 1929)*

The following sections foreground the historical process of science to consider the influences upon the form of life emerging that is social psychology.

As was mentioned earlier in this chapter, scientists inherit a knowledge base. This increases as new knowledge is accumulated; we know more than we used to and believe what we know is closer to the truth. Progress has been made in knowledge. It was assumed that progress in scientific knowledge was made simply by this accumulative process. The actual content of science changed by the adaptation of theories as further evidence became available. Comte's (1974) positivism engages with the scientific inheritance in the way the scientist, detached from 'personal concerns', judges hypotheses and findings with standards of exactitude and common understanding, with the minimum of interpretation. However, more recent conceptions of how scientific knowledge changes have focused upon the influence of the socio-cultural dimension.

Kuhn's 1970 notions of 'normal science' and 'paradigms' challenged the belief that science progressed and changed by slow self-correction. 'Normal science' is firmly based upon past scientific achievements and is made up of research programmes, disciplines, journals, peer review, texts, universities, professional associations and government agencies. 'Paradigm' describes an accepted world-view that unites the activities of normal science. The educational process of scientists involves learning and adopting the paradigm; scientists are *socialized* into a paradigm.

Paradigmatic change (scientific revolution) occurs where the pattern of 'normal science' is disrupted by a new scientific vision of the world. Paradigm shifts occur; in other words, a new set of questions, assumptions and methods are brought to the structure of theory and knowledge, and a new way of looking at the world is generated. The direction scientific knowledge takes comes about as much from social processes and cultural influences (such as new technology) and different metaphysical speculations. It is not just a linear and logical 'unfolding of theory'. New insights and paradigms are generated by *science* and by *scientists*; we look for their genesis, therefore, to biography and to society as well as to scientific process.

So scientific knowledge changes over time and is constructed through a scientific peer process that agrees on what makes up the body of knowledge. The production of knowledge and the transformation of existing knowledge makes up a major component of the scientific form of life. In the conventional image of science, new paradigms emerge around a specific subject matter, a set of questions and ways of answering those questions, rather like a new 'discipline'. But, as Still reveals in Chapter 2, ways of thinking are also due to the influence of a particular area and of groups of people – that is, 'institutions'. Paradigm is sophisticated by the additional distinction between *discipline* and *institution* as two forms of influence that change science. A *perspective* incorporates paradigm and issues about disciplines and institutions to convey a current view of social psychology and a multiple perspective approach supports a pluralism often considered vital for a thriving science.

3.7 Disciplines

Kuhn's work, showed that scientists are socialized into their thinking. Each scientific discipline, though formalized in its ontology and methodology, is also maintained by social processes. Scientists have to understand each other; even paradigm shifts must be made intelligible to other members of the scientific community. The process of socialization, and its effects, we call 'following a discipline'.

Originally 'discipline' was the practice of a subject or a doctrine. As a term it has etymological roots in 'discipleship'. The term discipline, a particular kind of instruction in a subject, supports the idea of subjects as historically and institutionally emergent rather than logically formed from a particular metaphysical conception of reality. If you remember, in Chapter 2 Still says that in the early 1980s experimental social psychology was the particular form of life that dominated the 'discipline'. The discipline of 'social psychology' and what that entails now is what you, the reader, are being inculcated in and what we, the authors, are professing via this book.

The disciplines of physics and history seem to belong to different forms of life; science and art. But as all scientists inherit knowledge they are also historians. Arguments over what social psychology is use the history of psychology to privilege particular methods and approaches so as to form an acceptable canon of the discipline and for it to develop according to a particular line. The writers of each of the three manifestos in Chapter 1 might tell a different history of social psychology.

Social psychology as a form of life allows a more fluid approach to our 'discipline'. This is valuable, as the inherited knowledge of social psychology has been strongly influenced by the power of the form of life of modern science. The methods of social psychology should follow the methods of natural science and only then, it is argued, is social psychology science. This position is known as *scientism*, where social science apes the method of the natural sciences. It is the explanatory power of the laws of physics as detailing the 'real objective reason' for an event, in contrast to the biases and speculative reasons of human subjects or events, that is the source of the influence of the 'natural' sciences upon the 'social' sciences. 'Physics envy' has hindered the evolution of a sophisticated multi-faceted social psychology informed by a history prior to the rise of modern science.

Social psychology is a discipline without an a priori subject matter (or at least one which is commonly agreed upon). Different perspectives imply different subject matters or conceptions of the ontology of social psychology. A perspective incorporates subject, doctrine and discipline into an integrated view. Because of the different metaphysical and epistemological assumptions of various traditions in social psychology it has been found necessary to create these perspectives. Each perspective has the possibility of being a total vision of social psychology, but actually it is suggested they are best seen as *partial* visions. That is the value of the multiple perspectives approach. It accepts ontological and epistemological plurality, though there is debate about the relation of the perspectives. We have deliberately avoided stating that social psychology is a 'subject' so that it can be open to various orientations: for example the pluralistic model of 'domains of analysis'; or alternatively the relational order of tri-modal theory; or finally an epistemological relativism which assumes that no interpretative model of different perspectives is possible (see Chapter 4).

One way of resolving the problems of incommensurable paradigms and the lack of a unified science of social psychology is to adopt this multiple perspectives approach. This may be a mature response to the 'loose confederation of inquiries that constitute psychology' (Ryle, 1949), or merely represent the currently undeveloped state of psychology. Whether or not you accept this resolution will depend on your ideas about how science comes about, what it is and, most importantly, what knowledge and practice you want psychology to embody.

Chapters 1 and 2 in this volume demonstrate an orientation to this by presenting specific polemics for a science of social psychology and historically situating the various concerns from which social psychology has emerged. Conventional Social Psychology adopted the epistemology of natural science united by scientific method. In this book there is reference to a diversity of manifestos, perspectives and their possible relations. It is for you to use these to envision a different picture of social psychology and judge whether social psychology should be part of the form of life of conventional science or whether an alternative is needed.

Gergen's 1973 view is that psychology could easily have become a part of history rather than a part of science. A famous paper by Hempel (1965) discussed science and history in terms of their similarities and saw history as part of the 'methodological unity of all empirical science'. This harks back to Bacon's aim of the unified sciences, unified in method, creating a great system of understanding, the Great Instauration. The pluralist nature of this book and its emphasis on multiple perspectives suggest this is unlikely to be achieved and is not a desirable aim, though there is a trace of this tendency in Chapter 4.

In considering the discipline of psychology we should remember Newton, certainly a giant of modern science, who commented, 'If I have seen further it is by standing on the shoulders of giants', which alluded to a saying of Bernard of Chartres, '...we are like dwarfs on the shoulders of giants' from a time when science and art were both features of the religious form of life, and ask ourselves on whose shoulders does or should social psychology stand?

4 Authority of science

Why is this debate about the scientific nature of social psychology so important? What is at stake in claiming the title of 'science' is both the acceptance of a certain kind of duty or commitment and the search for a certain sort of power. What is the source of this power? Again, in common-sense terms it comes from the image of the scientist as being open to all possible results, objectively seeking new true knowledge. 'Scientists', arguably, put themselves on the line and lay themselves open to being provably wrong in public. It is values such as Popper's characterization of scientific knowledge as fallible, critical and open to refutation, or Merton's norms of organized scepticism and disinterest, that are the creed of the scientific community and have fostered the 'communal attitude' since Bacon's rejection of the authority of scholastic doctrine. Scientific authority is held in esteem precisely because science is equated with these values. In this chapter we have considered whether it operates in quite this way and asked whether it is even a desirable goal for social psychology. Nevertheless, it is still a socially privileged concept and historically,

> ...formal notions of objectivity were used not only to create knowledge but also to *legitimize*, i.e. to show the objective validity, of already existing bodies of information.
>
> (Feyerabend, 1987, my emphasis)

So, we not only have complexities in the issues of personal interpretation and objectivity to consider, but we also have to question why we seek the authority of science.

Today, it is not enough for a statement to be believed simply because someone states that it is true. We judge what is said by the authority of the sayer and the grounds on which that authority is maintained. To claim a prophetic text such as the Bible or the Koran as authority for policy or action is no longer a successful stratagem in modern Western societies. Reason, experiment and evidence, the very foundation stones of science, are what justify and give authority to a person's claim to know the nature of things and therefore suggest what should be done about them. Our society is so structured that we empower certain people to act on our behalf in decision making for the general good. Generally, these people are regulated by systems of qualification. At the current time, claims supported by scientific authority are highly regarded by these systems. Psychology claims to judge between opinions on the basis of evidence, through the way it arrives at a judgement by a combination of reason and experiment or observation. This is what gives it the authority of a science. It matters, therefore, whether social psychology is a science, because science is granted authority and *institutional* power in 'our' society.

4.1 Institutions

Nullius in verba, No man's word is final.

The Royal Society's motto has inspired generations of scientists. This sceptical challenge to the authority of empty words has also appealed to social psychologists, and they too have sought support for their word with scientific evidence.

Chapter 2 traced the roots of psychology with the hypothesis of the anima–animus distinction to understand what social psychology is. Many of Still's examples of intellectual propagation are prior to recent science, for example St. Augustine, Goclenius and Montaigne, when institutions had religious ends as well as scientific ones. There was also a sense in Chapter 2 of how institutions and communities of scholars propagated particular ideas, for example associationism. At several points of this book we have remarked on 'the two social psychologies', psychological social psychology and sociological social psychology, each with its own traditions, often housed in different departments. We distinguish two streams of influence, both intellectual and institutional, upon the evolution of social psychology.

We must consider the influence of institutions on science and, by extrapolation, the nature of the institutions which empower the science/form of life that is social psychology. The roots of modern science we have situated in social and historical processes, and so we focus not just on the common features of science but also on the changing interaction of scientists with society and on what is expected of them. This is especially true of social psychology in this century. Various types of institution – research councils, universities, multinational companies – foster it. Issues about the use of knowledge and its institutional propagation in social psychology are more fully covered in the two chapters in Part 3 of this volume, but mention is made here because it is an important feature of the form of life of social psychology (Fuller, 1991).

What influences are currently propagating social psychology? Which institutions are to authorize the criteria and content for an acceptable social psychology? The recent chartering of psychologists by the British Psychological Society is a case in point. What are the skills and competencies that a psychologist should have? How do we evaluate the truth and meaning of the criteria and content adopted by the institutions of psychology that sanction membership of this body? This is the key issue about the status of the authority of science and its influence on social psychology's form of life. Crudely put, what is the priority:

whether you speak the truth, or what implications your research has for profit and value?

'Big Business Science' refers to the current institutional framework of science (including social psychology), involving organizational processes, universities, research councils, editorial boards of journals, and associations. The principal function of the organizations of science is the generation of new knowledge. However, scientific organizations also serve other functions and interests. The debate between science as the pursuit of truth and applied science has been long standing. But the face of this debate has substantially altered. As Tolstoy illustrates,

> ...as an aftermath of the Second World War, science became an affluent enterprise and affluence has transformed it. Supported by and beholden to society on a scale undreamt of by previous generations, it has become thoroughly institutionalized. And so, ... the pursuit of scientific understanding is ... faced with the problem of distinguishing knowledge from institutional truth.
>
> *(Tolstoy, 1990)*

He continues, 'Some scientists may be driven by holy curiosity, but their paymasters serve a different god'. As corporate influences on science grow, what interests will actually inspire the direction of research? Furthermore, this influences the questions to be given research priority and therefore resources and funds. (In July 1995 the Conservative government put the Department of Science and Technology into the Department of Trade. The President of the Royal Society at the time expressed 'concern'.)

In addition to the critiques about the epistemology of science there are emphases which point out the practices and expertise of our social and scientific institutions are insidiously self-propagating – for example, in Michel Foucault's 'discursive practices' (see, for example, Wetherell, 1996b) and in feminism, (see, for example, Harding and Hinitikka, 1983, and Harding, 1991). A strong meaning-centred enterprise might abandon the idea of mere epistemological centring for understanding and doing psychology and lean towards an ethico-political centre. This type of vision is present when the claims for psychology as a moral and/or a political science are made (as in Boxes 1.2 and 1.3 of Chapter 1).

The assumptions in these visions, in contrast to the 'value-free' vision of conventional 'objective science', involve the necessity for psychologists to have a wisdom and an awareness of the importance of their interpretation of which questions are worth studying. Science, in these views, is no mere play activity, finding and making knowledge in a spirit of sceptical curiosity; it is a political and ethical enterprise situated within issues about the power of knowledge and the control of human lives. So, as well as recognizing that we have to evaluate and decide about theory and evidence, about what the answers are and how to get at the questions, psychology as moral and political science will have to take a position about the value and use of the knowledge that results from such a question-and-answer process. It may be that the ethico-political concerns of our manifestos posit other ends for social psychology than conventional scientific ones.

4.2 A final word

At the outset of this chapter science as a special form of life was established by distinction from Kelly's 'man-the-scientist' model. A scientist, or the 'scientific self' constructs theory and evidence and intervenes in the life-world in special ways. As persons we are in the life-world with many concerns and priorities that are not able to be addressed by the conventional scientist.

What if the scientific form of life is inappropriate to the problems faced in the life-world that we want 'psychology' to solve? Will the theories and methods we use be maintained simply because they emulate the model of the scientific form of life? Should we promise or even try to solve them? This is the debate around truth and meaning at the centre of this chapter.

A critical science of social psychology takes notice of the political dimensions of social institutions and how they describe and intervene in our lives, how they maintain specific narratives of understanding whilst privileging certain interests. Certain voices may go as far as saying the time has come to abandon the conventional image of science for social psychology. A focus on meaning calls into question whether truth is the priority, or indeed if it is what we need.

So the question of whether the form of life that is social psychology is a science involves ethical and political dimensions, and is not just a question of method. It involves confronting metaphysical issues which are far from simple and which normally remain buried in psychology's practice. In terms of methods, even though there are complexities, many branches of social psychology display characteristics of science in that they study evidence systematically to refute or confirm theories and aspire to do so in a manner which could be called 'objective'. However, it is clear that social psychologists are not 'value-free'; they are part of the culture which they study and are influenced by its dominant discourses such as the scientistic influence of the past. I suggest what they do *is* not and *should* not be neutral; it affects people's lives. In recognition of this, some social psychologists refuse to accept the name of scientist and dispute the authority of science. Others, however, work to make science aware of its own responsibilities as a *moral* and a *political* force within its culture.

Who shall have the final word?

References

Bacon, F. (1624) 'De Principiis Atque Originibus' (*On Principles and Origins*) in Spedding, J., Ellis, R.L. and Heath, D.D. (eds) (1857) *The Works of Francis Bacon*, London, Longman and Co.

Bhaksar, R. (1989) *The Possibility of Naturalism*, Hemel Hempstead, Harvester Wheatsheaf.

Bloor, D. (1991) *Knowledge and Scoial Imagery*, Chicago, University of Chicago Press.

Boring, E.G. (1929) *A History of Experimental Psychology*, New York, Century Co.

Bruner, J. (1990) *Acts of Meaning*, Cambridge, MA., Harvard University Press.

Collier, A. (1994) *Critical Realism*, London, Verso.

Comte, A. (1974) 'Course in positive philosophy' in Andreski, S. (ed.) *The Essential Comte*, London, Croom Helm.

Darwin, C. (1859) *The Origin of Species*, London, John Murray.

Feyerabend, P. (1987) *Farewell to Reason*, London, Verso.

Foucault, M. (1974) *The Archaeology of Knowledge* (trans. Sheridan, A.), London, Tavistock.

Fuller, S. (1993) *Philosophy of Science and its Discontents*, New York, Guilford.

Gergen, K. (1973) 'Social psychology as history', *Journal of Personality and Social Psychology*, 26, pp.309–20.

Harding, S. (1991) *Whose Science, Whose Knowledge?*, Ithaca, Cornell University Press.

Harding, S. and Hanitikka, M.B. (1983) *Discovering Reality: Feminist Perspectives on Epistemology, Metaphysics, Methodology and Philosophy of Science*, Dordrecht, Holland, D. Reidel.

Harré, R. (1986) *Varieties of Realism*, Oxford, Blackwell.

Hempel, C. (1965) *Aspects of Scientific Explanation and Other Essays in the Philosophy of Life*, New York, Free Press.

Hull, D.L. (1988) *Science as a Process: An Evolutionary Account of the Social and Conceptual Development of Science*, Chicago, Chicago University Press.

Kelly, G. (1953) *A Theory of Personality*, New York, W.W. Norton & Co. Inc.

Kitzinger, I. (1990) 'The rhetoric of pseudoscience' in Parker, I. and Shotter, J. (eds) *Deconstructing Social Psychology*, London, Routledge.

Kuhn, T.S. (1970) *The Structure of Scientific Revolutions,* Chicago, University of Chicago Press.

Lalljee, M. (1996) 'The interpreting self: an experimentalist perspective', in Stevens R. (ed.).

Latour, B. (1987) *Science in Action,* Cambridge, MA., Harvard University Press.

Mach, E. (1885) *Analysis of Sensations,* Chicago, Open Court.

Medawar, P. (1985) *The Limits of Science,* Oxford, Oxford University Press.

Merton, R.K. (1977) *The Sociology of Science,* Chicago, Chicago University Press.

Mulkay, M. (1990) *The Sociology of Science,* Bloomington, Indiana University Press.

Pickering, A. (ed.) (1992) *Science as Practice and Culture,* Chicago, University of Chicago Press.

Popper, K.R. (1963) 'Conjectures and refutations' in *Conjectures and Refutations: The Growth of Scientific Knowledge,* London, Routledge and Kegan Paul.

Popper, K.R. (1979) *Objective Knowledge. An Evolutionary Approach,* Oxford, Clarendon Press.

Rose, G. (1995) *Love's Work,* London, Chatto.

Ryle, G. (1949) *The Concept of Mind,* London, Hutchinson.

Sarton, G. (1962) *History of Science and the New Humanism,* Cambridge, Mass, Harvard University Press.

Searle, J.R. (1995) *The Construction of Social Reality,* Harmondsworth, Penguin.

Stevens, R. (ed.) (1996a) *Understanding the Self,* London, Sage.

Stevens, R. (1996b) The relexive self: an experiential perspective' in Stevens R. (ed.).

Thomas, K. (1996) 'The defensive self: a psychodynamic perspective' in Stevens R. (ed.).

Tolstoy, I. (1990) *The Knowledge and the Power: Reflections on the History of Science,* Edinburgh, Canongate.

Von Wright, G.H. (1971) *Explanation and Understanding,* London, Routledge and Kegan Paul.

Wetherell, M. (ed.) (1996) *Identities, Groups and Social Issues,* London, Sage.

Wetherell, M. (1996a) 'Group conflict and the social psychology of racism' in Wetherell M. (ed.).

Wetherell, M. (1996b) 'Life histories/social histories' in Wetherell, M. (ed.).

Whewell, W. (1840) *The Philosophy of the Inductive Sciences,* London, J.W. Parker.

Winch, P. (1958) *The Idea of a Social Science and its Relation to Philosophy,* London, Routledge and Kegan Paul.

Wittgenstein, L. (1953) *Philosophical Investigations,* Oxford, Basil Blackwell.

Woolgar, S. (1988) *Science: The Very Idea,* London, Tavistock.

CHAPTER 9
EVIDENCE

by Roger Sapsford

1 Introduction

This chapter describes a range of different methods which have been used by social psychologists (and others) in their research. It is not a complete catalogue, but a fair diversity of approaches is covered at least briefly. Its aim is not so much to show how to use these methods, but to discuss what we typically *say* about them: how we describe them, how we justify their use and what claims are made for them. Its aim is to raise useful questions about the nature of research, which is a central activity within social psychology, as it is in other disciplines which might aspire to the status of sciences.

In a sense the chapter is about how we judge or evaluate reports of research. It does not, however, give criteria for telling good social psychology from bad social psychology. Nor does it suggest how we may tell a valuable report from a less valuable one, nor attempt to enter into the minds of those who make such judgements; reports are judged by many different kinds of people, for many different kinds of purpose, and using many different criteria of what is valuable. As its title suggests, the scope of this chapter is strictly limited to the judgements we make about the *evidence* in research reports, and to how we establish evidence as plausible and sufficient for its purposes.

Having read other chapters in this book as well as the preceding words, however, you will not be surprised if my answer to the question of how we judge evidence touches on wider questions about the nature of social psychology and even the nature of truth. This is because 'research' is not some technical exercise carried on by social psychologists as an aid to their arguments, but a central part of the arguments themselves. The collection of evidence is integral to the process of building theory, and vice versa. The position taken in this chapter is that what distinguishes social psychology from, for example, the philosophy of mind or moral philosophy is that it shares with the natural sciences a fundamental need to *ground* theory in evidence at every point, not just to rely on argument or to present cases used as a starting-point or an illustration. The description of the social world is therefore an integral part of building a theoretical understanding of it – there is no theorizing without description, and 'describing' is a 'theoretical' activity.

On the other hand, a research report starts with a *question* or a *problem* and ends with an *answer* or *solution*. It gets from the one to the other *via* evidence relevant to the question which is plausible as support for the answer. A mystique has grown up around the notion of research, but in essence 'research methods' consists of ways of rendering the evidence plausible to the reader – ways of showing that the conclusions *can*, logically, follow from the evidence in a research paper and therefore supporting the contention that they *do* do so. In other words, a research report consists of a series of nested arguments. The overall argument of the report will be that the conclusion is correct, given the evidence. Within this lie a series of (sometimes implicit) arguments about why the evidence should be believed.

Judging research is not just a technical matter, however, but also partly a philosophical one. If you took the view that the social world is something sometimes unknown but not problematic *in its essence*, something potentially *discoverable* by accurate and imaginative measurement, then the problems would all be technical ones, of how to measure and discover. As you have seen, however, an equally tenable position is that facts may be the test of theories, but they are also the product of theories, because what we do as researchers is crucially determined by the theories we hold and the 'models of the person' and 'models of the social order' which they express. This statement is as true in everyday life as in research – as George Kelly (1955) has pointed out (among many others), the 'person as scientist' sees the world through a pre-existent construct system. It is not possible to take any action without already having some view of the world in which the action is taking place, but we then alter our judgements on the basis of the responses to our actions; in other words, we change our theories when the evidence proves them wrong. In the same way, research is framed within a 'map' or 'world-view', and the map determines what is seen as appropriate for the researcher to do, but is often modified by the results of the research. (Much applied research appears unproblematic and untheoretical – it does not discuss the nature of the person or the social world, but takes a 'common-sense' position for granted. Common sense is not a-theoretical, however; it embodies coherent models of what the person and the world are like, even if it does not bring them forward for discussion.)

Thus the standpoint of this chapter is that while all theorizing in social psychology is grounded in evidence, at the same time all evidence is gathered from some theoretical position. In other words, 'theorizing' and 'researching' are not separate activities. This is a point to which we shall return as the chapter develops. Let us look first, however, at some of the very different ways in which evidence has been gathered within social psychology, and at the arguments which 'warrant it' – in other words, how researchers make the claim that their conclusions are true and are supported by their evidence.

2 The variety of methods

As well as accommodating a wide variety of perspectives, social psychology makes use of a very wide range of research methods. Social psychologists have used specially constructed situations – experiments – in 'the laboratory' or in the outside world to test theories. They have observed behaviour in natural settings, as participants or without themselves intervening. They have set up conversations – interviews – and counted the incidence of certain expressions, or fitted what was said into predetermined categories, or aimed for a more naturalistic interchange and looked afterwards for patterns of meaning in what was said. They have used conversational settings as a way of exploring current feelings and past experiences to get beneath what is said to 'underlying processes' – the therapeutic or diagnostic interview. They have used 'structured conversations on paper' – 'tests', questionnaires and interview schedules – ranging from lists of broad free-response questions to very specific inventories of beliefs or attitudes or preferences or feelings which have to be answered within predetermined categories. They have analysed 'text' – written or printed materials, or naturally occurring conversations overheard or recorded – and again studies range from the highly quantitative ('content analysis') to the highly interpretative ('critical analysis' or 'discourse analysis'). Almost any method of data-collection which has been used anywhere in social research has been used at one time or another by a social psychologist.

A traditional way of classifying research methods is as 'quantitative' or 'qualitative' – as concerned with numbers and measurement or with description and understanding/appreciation/interpretation. Quantitative data-collection is normally associated with a 'scientific' style of research, and indeed its methods do attempt to resemble those of the physical sciences, but the association is not absolute. Researchers who would not naturally think of what they do as 'like the physical sciences' are nonetheless able to count and report (for example the proportion of informants reporting a given belief or feeling), and 'scientific' researchers have used qualitative or 'appreciative' means on occasion – see for example Luria's use of diaries and interviews to characterize the *experience* of suffering a certain kind of brain damage (Luria, 1972). Many data-collection procedures combine features of both – Kelly grids, for example, explore highly individual conceptual worlds in a quantified way amenable to statistical analysis – and many predominantly quantitative studies using questionnaires or even experimental procedures will include a qualitative element such as opportunities for respondents to comment freely on answers or 'de-briefing' interviews in which they can talk about the *experiences* which underlay their quantified responses. I shall use the 'quantitative'/'qualitative' division as an organizing principle below, but it is as well to remember that a given piece of research will probably be not 'one or the other' but located between the two extremes on three related but separable dimensions:

1   *Naturalistic/controlled*: some research, particularly when looking for causal influences, controls the situation presented to informants/subjects – by limiting possible behaviours, in experiments, or by limiting possible answers, in the questionnaire – so that the outcome is readily interpretable and easily compared between different informants. Other studies are very eager to disturb the natural setting as little as possible, to observe behaviours and elicit remarks in a context as near as possible to that of real (unresearched) life.

2   *Structured/unstructured*: on the face of it this is the same dimension as the previous one – experiments and highly quantified surveys structure the situation, while naturalistic research imposes the minimum of structure. However, it is possible that a situation may be highly structured by the researcher and yet naturalistic for the subject – in some field experiments, for example, where an unobtrusive intervention is made. On the other hand, some naturalistic situations are also highly structured and therefore untypical of behaviour as a whole – for example weddings, or funerals – and all natural social situations exhibit *some* degree of structure.

3   *Specific/generalizable*: this might be seen as two related but non-identical dimensions. Virtually all research in social psychology aims at *some* kind of generalizability; the research aims to tell us something about the human and/or social condition. Studies differ, however, in the *breadth* of their aims: some studies aim explicitly to describe the characteristics of the human species, some to describe what happens in a given culture, while some may be concerned only with a particular (and rare) kind of person or situation. Studies differ also in the *evidential base* for generalization: some draw large samples from the relevant population, designed to stand a calculable chance of representing it exactly in microcosm, while some may present data from a few or even a single case. (This does not map perfectly onto the 'quantitative/ qualitative' distinction which I use below. Some studies of single cases are strongly quantitative and designed like experiments.) While on the whole those studies which aim for great breadth tend to use formal sampling methods to ensure that the evidence for their generalizability is satisfactory, this is by no means always so; some studies of single cases aim to say something about a whole species or culture, while some large-scale surveys aim only to describe a limited population (a particular institution, for example). The important thing, in reading research reports, is to *think* about the extent to which the results may safely be generalized, and not to assume that a sample of middle-class students necessarily tells us much about working-class life, or that results from a sample of men necessarily tell us much about the experiences of women, or that a sample from one place and time will necessarily represent what will happen in a different culture, in a different period.

2.1 'Scientific' research

The essence of 'scientific' research is clear measurement and logical design. (The force of the inverted commas is not only that this kind of research lays explicit claim to be scientific – meaning 'like the natural
sciences' – in a way that other forms of enquiry are not, but also that the
claim, and the definition of 'science' that goes with it, would be disputed
by some other researchers – see Chapter 8.) It takes the nature of the
social world as no more problematic than the nature of the natural
world – partly hidden, contingently, but in principle open to discovery
by properly fashioned studies. What is essential, in this view, is

1   that we be very sure what it is that we are measuring, and

2   that the design of the study be such that the researcher's conclusion,
    and *only* the researcher's conclusion, can follow logically from the
    evidence.

Thus when designing a way of measuring something – a personality inventory, for example – we shall want to be able to report on its reliability, precision and validity. *Reliability* is the extent to which the
measuring instrument gives the same readings when used repeatedly to
measure the same thing. *Precision* is the extent to which the reading can
be specified in great detail, as opposed to just 'hitting around a target' in
a probablistic manner. A ruler marked only in inches, with no marks for
the fractions of an inch, is imprecise: you cannot read off an exact score,
but only approximate to the nearest whole number or guess the score in
between. A tape-measure made of rubber, on the other hand, is unreliable: what measurement you get depends on how hard you stretch the
tape as well as on the height of the object to be measured, and you are
liable to get a different reading each time you use it. If it is people's
heights you are measuring, you need a reliable measuring instrument
and preferably one that is reasonably precise, if you are to produce *valid*
results. More than this, however, you need to measure the right thing –
height from feet to top of head, not breadth across the shoulders. (In the
more likely case in psychology where what you have is *an indicator* of
the dimension to be measured, length of leg would be a better indicator
of height than breadth across the shoulder. It would not be entirely
valid, however – length of leg does vary a bit between people in proportion to total body-length.)

So when constructing an inventory to measure, say, anxiety, I should
want to show (and the reader would expect to be told) that the measure
would produce similar scores when used repeatedly on the same person
(which can be tested by literally administering it twice, or by comparing
two random halves of the test to see if they produce similar scores, or in
other, more complicated ways). I should want to know the extent to
which it was the actual *score* that was reliable, not just (say) the rank
order of scores within a group – the precision of the test. Most of all, I
should want to deliver some proof that the test did indeed measure
anxiety and not some other trait. The simplest way of establishing this

claim would be to point out that all the items looked plausible as measures of anxiety – face validity – but as evidence this is clearly a weak claim. It would be stronger to show that the test produced similar results to some already validated test (*concurrent validity*) – another question-naire, perhaps, or clinical diagnosis. (This is sometimes called 'criterion-related' validity when the alternative measure is agreed to be unam-biguously valid.) Stronger still would be to show *predictive validity* – that the test could predict who would later suffer from anxiety attacks, or whose behaviour would be disrupted most by circumstances which we know disrupt the behaviour of anxiety-prone people.

We should note how the foregoing paragraph betrays the extent to which psychological theory quite explicitly underlies the act of measure-ment. We have set off to measure a theoretical construct, 'anxiety'. (In the example the construct is not very clearly defined; it starts off looking as though 'anxiety' is a current measurable state of a person, but as we develop the idea it becomes clear that we mean not a current state but a potentiality – a proneness to certain kinds of behavioural disruption.) Ultimately we can show that the measure is successful only by having a well developed theory of anxiety already – so that we can validate the measure by predicting behavioural disruption, for example – so that the theory is conceptually prior to the test.

Beyond the question of measurement comes the question of *who* is being measured. Many social psychological studies use 'samples of opportunity' (for example, available students) and claim implicitly or explicitly that what is true of them is true of the population as a whole, or even the species as a whole. Where what is at stake is what a person *can* do or feel or cope with, this kind of argument will do well enough. Where it con-cerns what people *do* normally do or feel or cope with, or what they are like, it is clearly weak in terms of logic; all too easily, the subjects of the research could be untypical of the population to which the general-ization is being made. A substantial technology has grown up around the selection of samples to be representative of their parent populations within calculable bounds, and studies which claim to describe popu-lations from samples are expected to draw on this.

Beyond this again is the question of the design of the research study – which is to say, the logic of the argument which will be presented in the research paper. If what we want to say is 'The population is like this', then we can go out and measure (probably using sampling to bring the task down to manageable proportions). Where we want to say 'This leads to that' (a causal hypothesis) or, more strongly, 'If my theory is correct then this group should differ from that, or this manipulation lead to that effect', then more is needed. Looking at whether males and females differ, for example, I can go out and take measurements, and assert that the differences are sex differences. However, there could be other differ-ences between the two groups.

1   Suppose, for example, that the women in my sample tended to be from 'higher' social classes, on average, than the men: then any dif-ference between the two groups could be due to social class.

2 Women tend on average to be a bit shorter than men; suppose the difference was due to height.

3 Suppose the difference was due, not to biological sex or anything necessarily associated with sex, but with how our society happens to socialize its women differently from its men, or to behave towards them as adults.

The first of these alternative explanations could be eliminated by better – more representative, less haphazard – sampling from the population. Alternatively, we could *control* for it by statistical means: we could look for an effect of social class, irrespective of gender, and then for an effect of gender within social class. Similarly, we could control for height by statistical means, comparing tall men with tall women and so on; while there is a sex difference in *average* height, a substantial number of women are taller than the average man. The third cannot be controlled by either sampling or statistics, however; socialization, stereotyped reaction and biological sex are confounded in this notional study and cannot be disentangled. It would take a different kind of study to determine which was more important.

The strongest argument that the researcher has correctly interpreted the effects of some factor obviously occurs when it is the researcher who has made (precisely controlled) changes to this factor and observed the results while being in a position to assert that nothing else has changed except the factor. A design of this kind is what we mean by *an experiment*, and all studies of causation aspire to the logic of the experiment, even if they cannot achieve it in its entirety. In the pure experiment, a number of logical claims are made:

1 *I made this intervention in the situation, and observed this change.*

By itself this would not be sufficient; logically, the change might have happened anyway. So a second claim is needed:

2 *Another group were observed in whose situation I did not intervene, and the change did not occur.*

The existence of this second group (or some other comparison-base of similar status) is what defines the true experiment; the experiment *consists* of a comparison of a treatment condition with a 'control' condition where the treatment was not experienced. The two claims together are still not as strong as they might be, however, because any difference between the two groups could be pre-existing or could be due to some other factor. Two further claims are necessary, therefore:

3 *The two groups were, for all practical purposes, identical before the intervention was made, and*

4 *they received exactly similar treatment during the course of the experiment, except for my intervention in one group's situation.*

If all four of these claims can be substantiated, we have a very strong argument that the researcher has correctly interpreted his or her data –

that the supposed cause or antecedent did indeed produce the effect which is claimed.

2.2 'Qualitative' research

The orientation which underlies social-psychology-as-science, as I have said, takes the fundamental nature of the world as given and unproblematic; the problems are those of accurate measurement, to *discover* what is 'out there' and *describe* it correctly. In our ordinary lives, a researcher of this kind would say, we discover the world by looking at it – in more detail and in more complex ways when we consider something is hidden from us. In one interpretation, Kelly's 'people as scientists' are not fundamentally different from this in how they behave. True, they *start* from a theory of the world rather than data, but they use this theory as a basis for action, part of whose purpose is to gather data in order to make the theory describe the reality better. Similarly, in our social psychology the business of the scientist is to gather data to test theories, with the intent eventually of building a 'working model of the social world'.

From a constructionist standpoint, however, things are not this simple, for three reasons.

1   Taking Kelly's 'scientist' metaphor a stage further, we do not know with certainty when we are *right* about what we 'discover'. Everyday models of the world are *tentative*, by their very nature: they are 'the truth about the world' only till something turns up to force modification on them. A constructionist would say that 'scientific' theories are no different.

2   We are not separate from what we research, nor from the circumstances under which the research is carried out. The 'scientific' model assumes a scientist who is objective, in the sense of being (a) unbiased, (b) free of preconceptions, and (c) able to carry out the research without altering the nature of the substance or phenomenon under investigation. To the first of these we would all aspire; research is of little value if our preferred outcomes are necessarily confirmed and there is no space in the design for us to be proved wrong. A constructionist would argue, however, that the second and third conditions for the existence of the 'scientist', in the sense in which the word is used here, cannot be met in social research. It is not possible to be free of preconceptions, because we live in a symbolized world which is defined within historically provided discourses and ideologies, and our power *not* to take these for granted is limited. Further, our research exists in a symbolized world, and for the people whom we investigate the research will become a part of what their world means, so by the act of research we necessarily change the nature of that which is under investigation. (Even 'unobtrusive' research changes the world once accounts of it are disseminated.)

3   Research is not neutral. It is particularly true of *social* research that it does not just discover facts but creates possibilities. In 'describing' the human condition, we add our voices to one side or the other in a whole range of political and moral debates; *we help to determine what the human condition shall be*, rather than just passively describing it. The researcher's role as a moral and political agent is not avoidable; those who are not aware of it still play such a role, but unwittingly.

People who take this kind of standpoint tend to be suspicious of 'scientific' research because it prejudges the nature of what is under investigation in ways which may not be morally or politically neutral. Such people would also point out that social situations shape behaviour, and the experiment and the survey are social situations, with known rules (for example of deference and compliance) which are *not* the rules of everyday life. Those who take this point of view tend on the whole to use more 'qualitative', 'appreciative' techniques of research.

The classic form of 'qualitative' research, though not in fact greatly used as yet by social psychologists (but for an imaginative example see Vetere's (Vetere and Gale, 1987) study of family life, which involved observers actually living in people's homes), is *participant observation*. Here the researcher becomes a participant in the situation, either overtly (with the role of researcher declared) or preferably, from the point of view of avoiding 'research as a social situation', covertly as a full and equal participant. He or she then takes notes of what is going on and what people say, interpreted from the personal knowledge gained by participating. (For a description and discussion of this kind of research in action, see Chapter 3 of Banister et al., 1994.)

The main aim in this kind of project is to make the research naturalistic – to disturb the situation as little as possible – and to examine the *whole* situation, trying to cover the full complexity of the many ways in which actors interpret and describe their own world and the nature of what they unknowingly take for granted. The researcher tries for the impossible and contradictory stance of being at the same time a full participant – so that the understandings of the actors are shared – and marginal to the action so that what the actors take for granted and 'pay no heed to' can be seen as worthy of notice and comment.

The 'negative virtues' of this kind of approach are that it avoids the 'demand', 'volunteer' and 'experimenter' effects which Banister et al. discuss in their first chapter, if the research is covert and the actors do not know that research is going on. If the research is overt then these effects still occur to some extent, but their force should be lessened as compared with quantitative survey or experimental research, because the situation in which the researcher is working is not the artificial setting of the laboratory or the artificial social situation of the questionnaire interview, but as close as can be obtained to 'real life' for the actors. We should note that covert research raises ethical problems: it is often easier to carry out and yields very rich and useful data, but at the cost of a feeling that you have been using your friends or co-workers for research purposes without their permission – a feeling as if you had stolen something from them. On the positive side, while the fact that the researcher is studying the situation rather than just living in it gives him or her perspectives on it which may not be available to the participants themselves, the fact that he or she *is* living in it provides some chance for the participants' own perspectives to be understood, on their own terms.

Reflexivity is the main warranty of the extent to which naturalism has been achieved and to which the researcher has understood the situation in the participants' terms and yet not been absorbed by the participants' understandings. By the term 'reflexivity' I mean the constant awareness, during the research and when reporting on it, that the account to be presented will be the researcher's story as well as the participants' and that what the researcher does and believes will affect the nature of the data and their interpretation. So it will encompass, insofar as it can, an awareness of the researcher's own theoretical position and previously taken-for-granted preconceptions. It will cover the way the nature of the research was presented to the participants and what sense they appear to have made of it (or an account of how they were prevented from knowing about the research and how successful this was). It will include an assessment of the role the researcher played in the situation, in general terms and also in terms of detailed actions and unguarded comments that may have affected the course of the relationship. In general, it will try to uncover how the social situation was constructed and the extent to which the researcher was a party to that construction. (In other words, it will try to identify any possible 'demand' and 'experimenter' effects, as discussed above.) 'Naturalism' is of course an impossible goal – and perhaps not even a fully desirable one (see Chapter 3 of Banister et al., 1994) – but having it as a methodological aim alerts us to the interaction of the research itself and that which is being researched and protects us from the illusions of invisibility and value-neutrality.

Note that the idea of meaning within relationships (including research relationships) as personally and interpersonally constructed is a core concept in several branches of social psychology. It lies at the heart of Kelly's 'construct psychology' – for example, in the proposition that two people can communicate only to the extent that they can share each other's way of construing the social world – and the idea that groups develop constructs as groups which are different from those of an individual member is discussed by Rudi Dallos (1996). Kerry Thomas (1996) makes a more fundamental case, from a psychodynamic perspective, for reflexivity as the core of therapeutic relationships as well as research ones. Clients, in this view, 'impose' aspects of past problematic relationships on the therapist. Therapists need to be aware both of this process of transference and of their own reactions to it, and to bring under control their own human tendency to express their own past problems in the relationship with the client. The same can be said of research relationships and the analysis of observation data, noting that what has to be brought consciously into the analysis is not just the personal side of the relationship but anything which is shared and mutually understood (or *mis*understood) which could have a bearing on the conclusions.

Note also that the requirement of reflexivity in qualitative research is not different in essence from what is needed in quantitative, scientific research. When an experimenter works on the design of an experiment to make sure that there is no alternative explanation for the obtained results other than the experimental manipulation, or the survey researcher constructs questions or other data-collection procedures so that they are unambiguous and do not 'force' the respondent into one answer rather than another just because of the way the questionnaire is constructed, or interviewers are trained to administer questionnaires in a standardized way so that inter-interviewer variability does not confound the results, a form of reflexivity is being displayed. Reflexivity is examining the research process itself, to detect which of the apparent results are artefacts of the procedures used and the way the research was carried out in practice.

The other main form of qualitative research is 'open' or 'depth' interviewing – long interviews as conversations, with perhaps an agenda of topics to be covered but no detailed schedule of pre-formulated questions to be asked in a given manner and a given order. This has been a very common tool of social psychologists in the last thirty years. It is a less naturalistic method in that the situation is quite clearly 'research', but every effort is made to make the conversations feel natural and to let the informants develop their own agenda in their own words rather than imposing the researcher's way of viewing the topic – and generally, indeed, to give the informants some control over what topic areas are discussed. The method is inferior to participation in that it deals with words and rhetoric, not actions, but superior in that it allows the participants to put forward their *considered* views and because it can deal with the past and with future aspirations as well as with present circumstances.

Beyond this, many methods could be considered in this section which are hybrids between the scientific and the appreciative stance but which have a great deal in common with open interviewing. While the classic open interviewing was concerned with participants' accounts of the world and prided itself in putting forward accounts with which the participants would agree, essentially similar techniques are also used by those who do *not* believe that participants' accounts of their worlds are necessarily authoritative. Marxists, feminists and other 'critical scholars', for example, sometimes analyse interview data not for the sense that the participants make of their worlds but for the underlying and perhaps unconscious order which their surface views betray – for the power of ideology to deceive people about their own interests, or the power of discourse to structure the situation for them and limit the range of ways of seeing the world which they have available. Psychodynamically informed researchers and therapists routinely carry out relatively open interviews, in clinical practice, with the intention of trying to uncover feelings and motivations of which the informants are unconscious, and this lies at the very root of their form of theory. Here the agreement of the participants would not necessarily warrant the researcher's conclusions, and their disagreement would not necessarily invalidate them, so reflexive awareness by the researchers of how their own reactions contribute to the data and their own preconceptions were imposed on the situation is even more important.

A great deal of recent research in social psychology is concerned with the analysis of texts, and here the same range of methodological considerations apply as in interviewing. (Indeed, the interview transcript *is* a text to be analysed.) It is possible to analyse texts quantitatively, counting the incidence of particular words, or inches of text given to particular subjects, in order to test pre-formed theories in a scientific way. It is possible to analyse texts with the intent of summarizing and presenting the views of their authors, bringing material together in a synthesis which the authors would recognize as a fair portrayal of their views and models. It is possible also to use what is said in texts as symptomatic of underlying unconscious motivations, ideologies, discourses, world-models or whatever (as in discourse analysis or some psychodynamic analyses of biographies and autobiographies – or, indeed, the analysis of what is said in clinical interviews). Just the same considerations apply as to the conduct and analysis of interviews, with the added problem that forming a reflexive awareness of how the texts were produced and for what purpose may itself be a considerable research project.

The reflexive analysis of the circumstances under which the data were produced is a major tool in establishing the credibility of their interpretation – a major form of argument that the data are fit to support the conclusions drawn from them. A second tool frequently employed is *triangulation* – taking more than one bearing on a problem. Thus if it can be argued that the behaviour or the social characteristics of the interviewer are likely to be a major factor shaping the data, then use of more than one interviewer differing in behaviour or social location gives us more confidence in the results, if they are similar irrespective of which interviewer collected the data. If it can be argued that the analyst is importing his or her own biases into the analysis, then 'blind' analysis by more than one researcher may increase our confidence. If the particular form of research is likely to produce particular kinds of results – interviewing, for example, being prone to tap into a rhetoric not necessarily connected closely with people's actions, a 'context of justification' more concerned with *accounts* of actions than with the actions themselves – then investigation by a range of methods (interviews in another context, analysis of diaries, observation, getting the views of others on a person's actions, etc.) may increase our confidence. Similarly, if it can be argued that the texts produced for one purpose (for example government reports and discussion papers) are prone to certain influences because of the purpose for which they were produced, then we might want to supplement or continue our analysis with material from another source with different 'demand characteristics' (ministers' or civil servants' diaries or autobiographies, campaign and conference speeches, television discussion programmes, perhaps even personal interviews). Throughout, the aim is to demonstrate, as well as can be done with the materials at hand, that the evidence we have cited is rightly interpreted and that it can play the part we wish it to play in the argument that links the original problem to the conclusions we put forward.

There is a tendency nowadays in social psychology for some authors to prefer qualitative methods to quantitative ones – to prefer participant observation to experiments and less formal and structured interviews to questionnaire work – because of the greater richness and naturalism of the data. The point is worth making, therefore, that there is good and bad qualitative research just as there is good and bad quantitative research – that no method is right for all purposes, and no method will satisfy the requirements of evidence if the research is badly planned or conducted. In some ways qualitative research is more difficult to carry out than quantitative studies, because the researcher's nature and behaviour are more explicitly involved in the gathering and interpretation of the data. It is the more necessary, therefore, that a report of participant observation or 'open' interviewing should give a detailed account of how the data were collected, of the relationships entered into, the views and changes of view of the researcher(s) and how all parties construed the nature of the situation. One purpose of the research report is to give the evidence, and the conclusions based upon it, but another is to 'warrant' the evidence by the best means possible – to argue, to the best of the writer's ability, why the results should be trusted and why the interpretation of them is appropriate and useful.

There are particular problems with this in the kind of qualitative research which puts forward the researcher's account of a situation as a fair representation of participants' accounts – classic participant observation and open interviewing. Here the way the *researcher* perceives the situation is clearly a central factor, and one not obviously open to check or verification. In qualitative research of this kind we have to take a great deal on trust – the researcher's perceptiveness, self-awareness and basic honesty (his or her desire to *test* a conclusion rather than just illustrate it). The problem is even more acute in psychoanalytic research or discourse research, where we cannot even rely on the agreement of participants/informants/authors as a warranty of the truth of the account. However, all researchers do the best they can to warrant their results – to persuade us that their conclusions are valid – with the material and arguments available. You will notice, in any of your own work which requires both a quantitative and a qualitative phase of analysis, the quite different problems you face in doing this.

We should note that 'scientific' research also has its problems in this area. If you have carried out any kind of research which involves 'coding' text or open-ended questionnaire responses, for example, you will be well aware of the subjective, even idiosyncratic nature of the judgements which have to be made even in preparing the quantitative data. Because the data are presented in numerical form, they appear less open to interpretation or mis-interpretation and more like objective measurements of what is there to be measured. However, as we have seen (a) 'what is there to be measured' is at least in part constituted by the theory which underpins it, and (b) the validity of the measuring instruments is also always open to doubt and in need of justification. Beyond this, we still have to trust the basic honesty of the researchers – the more so because we seldom know in detail how the figures were *actually* collected and collated. Scandals such as the Cyril Burt affair, where a very eminent psychologist was accused of inventing data to support his conclusions, do not cause such excitement because cheating is unthinkable, but because it is all too thinkable and all too easy!

At its simplest, 'warranting' evidence means arguing plausibly that what it says is true – and, as we have seen in earlier chapters, the concept of 'truth' is one which leads to debate between realists and relativists in a variety of shades! We often present the debate between 'realism' and 'social constructionism' as if the two were complete polar opposites, but when considering research this opposition may perhaps be less extreme. When talking about research a certain minimal realism is inevitable. We have to be able to say that the results aim to be *true* – to correspond to how the world *is* – if the activity of 'doing research' is to make any sense at all. Even if you wish to take the position that what is being researched is the way that the informants' social constructions *create* the social world, you still need to be able to say that your presentation of how they *do* create it is as near to true as you can get it. The question of how we *know* that our conclusions from research correspond to the real world remains open, of course. My own position tends to be that 'the map is not the territory' – that what we say about the real world is an abstraction from it and a conceptual construction, something which makes useful sense of the infinite variety of experience by simplifying it and pointing to patterns and regularities. Other positions are possible, however, as you have seen.

Similarly, we have to say that the *first* aim of research is to produce truth, if we are to make sense of the activity at all. At various times it has been the fashion to say that research should be judged not as a neutral, 'scientific' activity but as a political one, with good research being that research which has a desirable political impact. This has been argued, for example, by some Marxists and other socialists since the 1930s and by feminists since the 1970s. It seems to me a valid point that intellectual work takes place in a real and political world and that scholars and researchers should be conscious of the nature of their world and take an active part in its conflicts. If the conclusions of research are to be politically useful, however, they must first be warranted as *true*; else why undertake the research in the first place?

Special problems of warranting occur where the research which is being described is in any way emancipatory. Here what is being claimed is not that the human species (or some particular part of it) *is* like this, but that it *can become* like this. Here a degree of relativism is inevitable: if you are claiming that such and such 'works for you', it is a logical possibility that it may not work for me, without invalidating your claim. Indeed, a degree of relativism is always inherent in such positions, without prejudice to whether those who put them forward are realists or not in their epistemology, because the acceptance of such a theoretical position must always be a question of choice in the first instance. In putting such a position forward you will always be saying that I *should* agree with your viewpoint – on evidence, but evidence is not logically compelling when applied to 'ought' questions – and then such and such will follow if I do so and so – on evidence, but the evidence will still not determine whether I *want* such and such to follow. The ultimate position of the emancipatory theorist is the one that G. K. Chesterton (1909 – see, for example, p.45) put forward a long time ago in defence of Catholic theology and belief against the materialists – that the materialists' position was logically unassailable but trapped them in an unnecessarily narrow range of experiences and actions, and that if they could 'come out into the light' they would not only know their error but be happier and more human at the same time.

References

Banister, P., Burman, E., Parker, I., Taylor, M. and Tindall, C. (1994) *Qualitative Methods in Psychology: a Research Guide*, Buckingham, Open University Press.

Dallos, R. (1996) 'Change and transformation of relationships' in Miell, D. and Dallos, R. (eds).

Chesterton, G.K. (1909) *Orthodoxy*, London, John Lane.

Kelly, G.A. (1955) *The Psychology of Personal Constructs*, New York, Norton.

Luria, A.R. (1972) *The Man with a Shattered World*, New York, Basic Books.

Miell, D. and Dallos, R. (eds) (1996) *Social Interaction and Personal Relationships*, London, Sage.

Thomas, K. (1996) 'The psychodynamics of relating' in Miell D. and Dallos R. (eds).

Vetere, A. and Gale, A. (1987) *Ecological Studies of Family Life*, Chichester, Wiley

PART 3
APPLYING SOCIAL PSYCHOLOGY

Preface to Part 3

This final part of the book is about the *use* of social psychology. One of the tasks of this part is to reassert the importance of 'applied social psychology' in a book which has, necessarily, been dominated by more academic theories. It goes beyond this, however, to look in general at the uses that are made of social psychology and the impact of social psychology on the nature of contemporary life. The message of both the chapters in this part concerns power – not interpersonal domination but the power of an academic discipline to inform and support social practitioners and to shape our ideas about our social worlds and our own capabilities. At the same time both are also concerned with *resistance* to power – the use of social psychology to empower individuals and give them some control over their own lives.

Chapter 10 asks the question 'Who uses psychology?' and explores the relationship of social psychologists to the management and solution of social problems. It presents the discipline as one which, from its very outset, has been 'a science with practical aims' and for which practice and application have always been the core purpose of the endeavour. The chapter emphasizes the political nature of social psychology's involvement in the professions which care for and control people's lives. At the same time it looks at the scope for social psychology's application in our personal lives and what we can get out of it that will be of use to us.

Chapter 11 takes up some of these themes but gives them a different slant. Its initial focus is on social psychologists – along with psychologists studying individuals and clinical psychologists – as part of the structure of social control. It picks up the discussion in Chapters 8 and 10 of social psychology's institutional base and looks again at its formal involvement in therapy, education, assessment and supervision, and in the training of professionals to handle these tasks. It is also concerned with the way that ideas from social and clinical psychology shape the social world by becoming the 'taken for granted' basis of popular thinking. For example, Freudian models of self and models of mental and personal capacity constructed by the psychologists of the early years of the twentieth century (by, e.g., Galton, Pearson, Binet and Spearman) have come to be taken for granted as received truths about the human condition and so condition how we act and how social institutions act upon us.

At the same time this chapter emphasizes the possibility of resistance to control and to the 'taken for granted' – an emphasis made possible because the roots of resistance have always been well nurtured within the discipline itself. The history presented in this chapter is a history of resistance. It briefly describes the resistance to received psychiatric ideas in the 1950s and 1960s, the resistance in the 1970s to 'received wisdom' which embodied a dehumanized and depoliticized model of the person, and the resistance of the 1980s to the cultural dominance of a particular historically and socially constructed form of individualism and to its political and psychological consequences. The end of the chapter attempts to come to grips with the resistance of the 1990s to the tyranny of 'grand theory' and to explanations of the human condition which are over-influenced by a view of social or psychological structures and ignore the importance of the detailed working-out of individual lives and group interactions. In all of this a strong element of sociological determinism is present, but at the same time the possibilities are pointed out for concerted resistance against the tyranny of the Social.

A message of the book as a whole is that social psychology must be understood as both an *applied* and a *critical* discipline. The diversity of perspectives comes not just from the creativity of psychologists, nor from academic imperialism aimed at hegemony merely within a field of ideas. Where we differ in our perspectives, it is because our understanding of the world as social psychologists have *effects* on the world. Social psychology is the root of many applied technologies which aim to change people – in the areas of education, of work and management and of clinical treatment and counselling, to name just a few. Psychologists adopt one perspective rather than another, therefore, because they find it gives them more insight into what can be changed and more tools for doing so; a relevant question to ask of any area of social psychology is *'What works?'*. At the same time, however, social psychologists study what it means to be human in current social relations with the intent of enlarging our understanding of our condition and therefore our power to change it – to uncover the myths and ideological presuppositions by which we are bound. The 'model of the person' in a psychological perspective is not just a useful tool, but to some extent a self-fulfilling description; to the extent that people believe the model and act accordingly, the model becomes true. A second relevant question, therefore, is *'What are the consequences of my theoretical stance?'* The tension between these two questions is not something to be resolved, but something inherent to the discipline – its great problem, but at the same time its greatest strength.

CHAPTER 10
USING SOCIAL PSYCHOLOGY

by Jeannette Murphy

I Introduction

This chapter reviews some of the ways in which social psychological theories, methods and findings have been used. (Although mention will be made of some of controversies and debates surrounding such applications, this aspect will be developed more fully in Chapter 11.) I have deliberately called this paper 'Using social psychology' rather than 'Applied social psychology' because I did not want to become too enmeshed in the debate as to what counts as applied social psychology. The chapter adopts the position that while only *some* research is designated as applied, in principle, *all* of social psychology may be used. What then, you might wonder, is meant by *applied* social psychology? The term is often used as the antithesis to *pure* (or *basic*, or *theoretical*) research.

What criteria are invoked to distinguish between basic and applied research? The traditional view has been that basic research is carried out to test hypotheses, while applied research is carried out to solve a social problem. Although this distinction sounds clear–cut, many theorists are not happy with such a hard and fast distinction.

> The history of the natural sciences demonstrates that many of the most important and far-reaching applications of research have stemmed from basic research findings which have revolutionised or changed the way in which the world is perceived and understood. ... Logically there is no reason why basic research may not be used and have practical consequences for policy-making, any more than why applied research may not throw light on more basic theoretical issues and problems.
>
> It is more satisfactory to think of a range of different kinds of 'research', rather than a simple dichotomy between 'basic' and 'applied'.
>
> *(Bulmer, 1982, p. xii)*

One can visualize a continuum ranging from theory-driven research at one extreme to research focused on social problems at the other. Some researchers tend to operate with a theory in search of exemplification, whereas others begin with a phenomenon and try to conceptualize its features, often with reference to one or more existing theories. *However, the two approaches are often in various stages of transition so that the distinction between them may become easily blurred.*

(Jones, 1985, p. 93, emphasis added)

But while there is no hard and fast distinction between the two approaches, it is interesting to observe how in the history of social psychology the pendulum has swung between basic (theoretical) and applied work. At times of social crisis or upheaval, for instance, applied work has tended to flourish: 'As the depression of the 1930s deepened and as the war clouds darkened in the second half of the decade, the questions of interest in social psychology took on a more applied character' (Pepitone, 1981, p. 976).

As we will see later in this chapter, the years of the Second World War produced a diversity of applied work on such topics as intergroup relations, leadership, propaganda, organizations, political (e.g. voting) behaviour, economic (e.g. consumer) behaviour and environmental psychology. The value placed on such applied work has fluctuated. Applied fields of work, says Pepitone, have at times been accorded a low status by those wanting to make social psychology a laboratory-based science because applied psychologists have tended to use surveys and other field methods rather than laboratory experiments.

Pepitone defends applied research against its critics by pointing out some misconceptions: 'Unfortunately, the attribution of the label *applied* carries the implication that such areas are atheoretical, thus causing some scientifically oriented social psychologists to stay clear of the phenomena ... Such phenomena, however, are hardly without relevance to the development of basic theories of human social behaviour' (1981, p. 976).

A different set of objections to some applied social psychology stems from worries about the moral and ethical underpinnings of research which is commissioned by those who are involved in social control. Cina (1981), for example, has serious doubts as to whether social psychologists who accept money from the military or from industry can avoid assimilating the values and goals of their paymasters.

Bulmer (1982) suggests that part of the confusion about how social research is applied stems from a mistaken analogy between the applied social scientist and the doctor or engineer. These latter provide technical solutions which are applied in real world situations, but this is seldom, if ever, true of the social psychologist. Rarely does a social psychologist have the brief or the know-how to design better social mechanisms or structures to cure society's ills. Instead, they provide 'enlightenment and understanding, an angle of vision upon the problems of the world which may influence decision-makers and the policy process.' (p. xiii)

BOX 10.1   Using social psychology:

Here is a summary of some of the work discussed elsewhere in the book which has social relevance. This list is not meant to be comprehensive but is meant to remind you of some of the uses of social psychology; it should also stimulate you to think of additional linkages.

The perspective of experiential psychology (Stevens, 1996a) has an applied dimension in that it explicitly sets out to provide guidance and insight into the ways in which we live our lives. Not only has it had a considerable impact on the practice of psychotherapy and counselling, it has also changed the ways in which many people think about themselves and their relationships. Writers such as Carl Rogers have sought to develop techniques to help us to change and live more fulfilling lives. (The question of using social psychology in personal life is looked at later in this chapter.)

Many other kinds of social psychology may also be applied to personal life or to institutional contexts. For example, some of the cognitive experimental research outlined by Mansur Lalljee (1996) has direct relevance for staff in residential establishments. And the insights and practice of psychodynamic therapies explored by Kerry Thomas (1996a) are clear examples of applied psychology (though predicated on quite different assumptions from humanist–influenced therapies). Work carried out in the biological tradition on addiction (see Toates, 1996) offers yet another example of how work centred in the domain of the person could have a social use (developing rehabilitation programmes).

A proportion of psychological theory derives from social psychologists involved in clinical practice and, in turn, is used in this context: family therapists and counsellors draw on this domain of social psychology. Research on relationships is used to help individuals, couples and families to change. (An interesting question is whether such work also provides people with methods of resisting change – see Chapter 11 of this volume.) At the same time, there is no reason why work in this domain cannot be used directly by individuals who want to understand and influence their personal relationships. Many of the ideas about relationships developed within clinical or academic contexts have been popularized and absorbed into the general culture. The mass media are aware that there is a market for books, articles and television programme about personal relationships. Popular accounts of clinical work ensure that these ideas are disseminated to a very wide audience.

Looking beyond personal uses, work on relationships is also used by social policy analysts. For example, social psychological work on social support and social networks reviewed by Miell and Croghan (1996) has been of interest to those working on health policies. What has captured the attention of health analysts is the accumulating evidence to show that social relationships impinge on health. And studies on the family life-cycle, summarized by Rudi Dallos (1996), provide valuable insights for those working in the field of family policy. In view of the enormous social and economic changes which families have faced over the past twenty years, government departments and voluntary agencies are concerned to make sense of the way in which families are coping and the impact of family life on the next generation. And those whose work requires some understanding of family process (e.g. social workers, doctors, nurses and teachers) also draw upon work on this done by social psychologists.

Psychological research on group and social structures also often comes from an applied tradition. Hedy Brown (1996) provides many examples of work that was initiated in response to social problems. In the field of experimental studies of small groups, many research areas have been funded because of their timeliness. Conformity, obedience to authority and work on bystander apathy are examples of research that was triggered by social concerns. Likewise, many of the classic field studies on group dynamics were aimed at providing insight into the psychological bonds which integrate individuals into their social and political worlds. Both Jonathan Potter (1996) and Margaret Wetherell (1996a) provide a critical rethinking of some of the central concerns of social psychology. Margaret Wetherell queries the way in which racism has been equated with individual prejudice. In place of this way of making sense of intergroup hostility, she argues the need to look at ideologies and group membership. Helen Morgan and Kerry Thomas (1996) provide examples of the way in which the psychodynamic perspective can be applied to organizations. (In reflecting back over the ground you might ask yourself whether the material is more likely to be of direct interest to policy makers, to employers and trade unions or to individuals.)

2 Social psychology's social role: key issues

In thinking about the way in which social psychology comes to be used, there are a number of distinct lines of enquiry we might choose to pursue. How, you might wonder, do areas of applied social psychology become carved out? How do the findings of social psychology become translated into practice? What is entailed in using or applying theoretical knowledge? When I started to try to map out this area, it struck me that there are at least three different ways of thinking about the uses of social psychology, each of which lead to rather different sets of questions and a different route through the literature and the course material.

Using social psychology to solve social problems

The first set of questions concerns the ways in which social psychology is used.

- How is social psychological knowledge used?

- Who uses social psychology?

- How is social psychology used in Britain and in Europe, compared to North America?

- How is social psychology used today, compared to 40 or 50 years ago?

- How are the results of the academic work disseminated?

Such questions imply the need for *factual information and historical data*. If we want to know how the discipline has been applied, we need examples, trends, statistics, and evidence. Section 3 of this chapter provides a sketch of the ways in which the findings of psychology have been applied to social problems.

Personal uses of social psychology

The second type of question which might intrigue you relates to a more personal form of application.

- How might I use or apply the social psychology I have learned from this book?

- How can I use social psychological insights in my career or in my personal life?

- How does one go about translating theoretical, abstract knowledge and principles of social psychology into usable methods and techniques?

What is required here are *methods* for identifying useful material and relating it to your own specific circumstances. How can you extrapolate from a research report or a theoretical perspective to the reality of your own life? There is no simple formula to tell you how to test the relevance of research to your personal circumstances. The best we can do is to point to some of the perspectives which would seem to have potential in terms of personal application. Firstly there is humanistic psychology, which deals directly with personal growth and self-actualization. You may have some prior acquaintance with humanistic or experiential ways of applying social psychology to personal life, since much of popular psychology borrows from this tradition. A second perspective, the psychodynamic approach, cautions us that much of the self is hidden and that our subjective experience of selfhood is partial. What is the significance of such a claim to the ways in which we live our lives? Kerry Thomas (1996) challenges us to think about whether we do have a unitary, *real* self. The psychodynamic perspective also offers us a way of looking at relationships and a way of thinking about what goes on in groups and in social organization. Work on family systems is the third obvious starting point for applying social psychology to personal life. Some of the other perspectives you have encountered (e.g. social constructionism) have something to say about how we relate to other people and 'how society gets inside our heads'. The issue of personal relevance is developed later in section 4 of this chapter.

Appraising social psychology's social role

Moving on from personal applications, we might want to speculate on broader issues surrounding the nature of social psychological knowledge and the consequences of applying social psychology.

- How is social psychological knowledge generated?

- How do social psychologists select their research topics?

- Who funds the research?

- What determines the balance between basic and applied research?

- Who sets the agenda for the discipline and how do shifts occur?

- What has been the impact of social psychological research on society?

To answer these questions we need to appraise social psychology's *social* role, which means making evaluations or value judgements. We have to go beyond the historical facts and our own personal agenda to reflect on the way in which social science is part of the social world but at the same time may exert an independent influence upon the world. Questions such as these get us into the sociology of knowledge, the politics of research and the various critiques which have been made of 'social psychology in action'. These issues are developed more fully in Chapter 11 of this book, but a few observations will be made in section 5 of this chapter.

3 Social psychology and social problems: an historical survey

Although the main focus of this chapter is the way in which *social* psychology is used, this section will start by considering the relationship between modern academic psychology and the various traditions of applied psychology. The reason for approaching the topic in this way is because the general history and background of psychology has set the agenda for social psychology. The main focus is the changing social expectations as to what psychologists should do and what psychology should offer society.

In tracing the way in which applied psychology[1] emerged, there is one misconception which needs to be challenged immediately. It might seem plausible to assume that basic theoretical, academic psychology preceded applied psychology by at least several decades. During this time it might be presumed that academics consolidated their knowledge base, perfected their research methods and elaborated their theories and that, eventually, this basic research gave rise to applied psychology. Although this account may seem plausible, it does not square with the evidence. The origins of applied psychology, as demonstrated in Table 10.1, are much older than one might imagine, suggesting that academic psychology and applied psychology have co-existed from the time psychology was accepted as a discipline in its own right.

Table 10.1 Some key dates and events in the history of applied psychology

(Derived from Leahey, 1992; Lück, 1987; and Schönpflug, 1992)

Date	Event
1870s	German research on urban life (including content analyses of advertisements)
1884 International Health Exhibition in London	Galton offered the British public the opportunity to test their mental faculties
1893	Sully started the British Child Study Association
1893 Columbian Exposition	American public given the opportunity to take psychological tests
1896	First psychological laboratory opened in Britain at University College, London, to work with schools First psychological clinic opened (to diagnose children with problems) at the University of Pennsylvania
1901	First talk on the psychology of advertising marked the application of psychology to business and industry
1905	Vineland Training School opened – Binet test introduced to the USA

[1] For the purpose of this discussion, applied psychology can be equated with the various specialist branches such as educational psychology, clinical psychology, occupational psychology, etc.

Table 10.1 Some key dates and events in the history of applied psychology (continued)

Date	Event
1907	Stern acted as a court-appointed expert in cases where children were involved as witnesses (Germany)
1908	Start of the 'mental hygiene' movement (publication of Clifford Beers' book *A Mind That Found Itself*)
1909	First child guidance clinic opened in Chicago – attached to a juvenile court
1911	Taylor published *Principles of Scientific Management* (based on studies initiated in 1878)
1913	Munsterberg published *Psychology and Industrial Efficiency*
1915	Psychologists began to use tests to pick workers for particular jobs
1917	Psychologists engaged to select officers, classify men, develop proficiency test for military jobs and administer IQ tests to all recruits
1919	Research initiated into consumer psychology in Germany (studies of window dressing)
1920s	Elton Mayo and his group carried out research at the Hawthorn Plant of the Western Electric Company
1921	Myers established the National Institute of Industrial Psychology
1922	Munsterberg published his jury studies

Note: This table is meant to draw attention to the early origins of applied research; it does not purport to catalogue *all* the major milestones.

Reading through this chronology, it is clear that nearly all of the applied branches of psychology – educational psychology (including psychometrics), consumer psychology, industrial psychology and child/adolescent psychology – were established before the First World War.

An agenda for applied social psychology

Social psychology's subject matter at any given time, claims Gergen (1973), is largely a function of the dominant societal issues of the day. At the time of the First World War, for example, the social issue was to sort, classify and train the two million military conscripts and recruits. Faced with this task, psychologists developed the technology of IQ testing. In the period after the First World War, mass testing was extended to the educational system. In the United States, psychologists also became engaged in controversies about immigration policy and eugenics. Psychologists were pulled into these arenas because the data collected during the First World War seemed to provide scientific proof of the innate inferiority of various racial and ethnic groups. (This conclusion was to be hotly debated and rejected by a later generation of psychologists who demonstrated that, far from being tests of general, 'natural' intelligence, these tests were culturally biased.)

These early examples of psychological involvement in real world issues may give the impression that, when it came to applying their expertise, psychologists inevitably lined up with conservative or reactionary groups. This was certainly not the case. Many European social psychologists sought ways to unite their scientific and political visions. Marie Jahoda (1983) described the way in which social scientists of her generation in Vienna were wedded to the view that humanitarian, democratic socialism was possible. Reich (1933), in his book *Mass Psychology of Fascism*, attempted to explain the appeal of National Socialism in terms of the character structure of lower middle-class and working-class Germans.

Similar patterns can be detected in North America. During the 1930s there was a noticeable shift to the left. American social psychologists became associated with various liberal causes, in particular the fight against racial prejudice. Their goal was to use social psychology to achieve racial and ethnic harmony. A commitment by social psychologists to improve intergroup relations was to continue up until the civil rights movement and race riots of the 1960s, which called into question many of the psychological assumptions about the causes of prejudice. (The challenge of finding ways of combating racism which do not give undue emphasis to psychological processes is explored by Margaret Wetherell (1996a).)

The significance of the social context in dictating the agenda for applied research was striking during the Second World War. Helen Morgan and Kerry Thomas (1996) describe the way in which the outbreak of war in Europe initiated new lines of research in psychiatry. War was no longer confined to the battleground but was brought to the home counties directly through bombing as well as through the improved media communications.

> ...the British Government feared a loss of morale among the military, and widespread psychiatric breakdown. They believed there was an urgent need to understand matters of morale, conflict, leadership and

group behaviour. The traditional views of psychiatry and social organization theorists were felt to be unequal to the task.

(Morgan and Thomas, 1996, p. 52)

This concern to deal with the problems that it was anticipated would be thrown up by the war led to an independent group being established (made up of staff from the Tavistock Clinic) to conduct research into the behaviour of individuals in groups. An offshoot of this work was the appointment of Bion and Rickman to Northfield, a military psychiatric hospital, where they reorganized the training wing. This activity was to provide the theoretical basis for the therapeutic community movement and for group analysis. (Bion was to continue his work as a therapist with small groups of patients at the Tavistock Clinic after the war.)

In the USA also, the Second World War shaped the type of research undertaken by social psychologists:

> There can be little doubt that the most important single influence on the development of social psychology [was] ... the Second World War and the political upheaval in Europe that preceded it. The smoke had hardly cleared from Pearl Harbor before the government began recruiting social psychologists to assist in the solution of problems faced by a nation at war.

(Cartwright, 1979, p. 84)

Cartwright identified a wide range of research areas which were funded by the government: 'Building civilian morale and combating demoralization; domestic attitudes, needs, and information; enemy morale and psychological warfare; military administration; international relations; and psychological problems of a wartime economy' (p. 84).

The Second World War opened up new fields of investigation such as organizational psychology, economic behaviour and political behaviour. 'It provided concrete examples of the practical usefulness of social psychology' (p. 84). Consequently, in the post-war period, the prospects for social psychology were bright, particularly in North America.

It is difficult to make similar generalizations about pre-war British social psychology because much of what we might today consider as social psychology was done under the aegis of other academic departments. In Germany, social psychologists were active in a wide range of research activities during the war. In the wake of post-war devastation, it was to take several decades for research to flourish again.

From the point of view of applied social psychology, what is puzzling is how quickly academic researchers in the post-war years redirected their attention from large-scale social issues to much narrower, technical questions which could be studied under laboratory conditions. Brewster Smith's (1983) account of the post-war period in the USA raises the fascinating question as to *why* some seemingly promising research areas failed to develop, most notably work on the relationship between character, social structure and ideology (the 'authoritarian personality' tradition at Berkeley, California). This work had sought to unite psychodynamic insights with the work of the Frankfurt School on politics and ideology. He speculates whether the abandoning of work which looked at the intersect between individual psychological processes and socio-historical trends '...may have helped to confirm subsequent experimental social psychology in its ahistorical, narrowly natural-science-oriented ways' (1983, p. 173).

Brewster Smith contrasts the demise of this work in Berkeley with the success of another group of social psychologists at New York University (NYU) who had 'a strong commitment to bring social psychology to bear on social problems, in addition to a readiness to regard psychodynamics as relevant' (p. 173). Members of this group included Marie Jahoda, who later set up the Psychology Department at Brunel and then went on to became Professor of Social Psychology at the newly established University of Sussex, and Kenneth Clark, who was at the forefront of the struggle to bring social psychological knowledge to bear in the legal fight against racial segregation in North American schools. Examples of the problem areas the NYU group tackled were interracial housing and juvenile heroin use in its social context. But the pioneering work of the NYU group did not take root either and the group disbanded in the early 1960s. Writing in the early 1980s and reflecting on the post-war period, Brewster Smith sounds the death knell for this type of applied social psychology in North America.

Other observers have also documented a decline of interest after the Second World War in the study of social issues. Reich (1981) claims there was a major shift away from the practical concerns necessitated by the war to a preoccupation with theory, measurement and methodology. Reich seems to think that the post-war flight from the field to the laboratory was a response to fears that demand for relevance and application was outstripping the development of theories and techniques. The president of the American Psychological Association touched on this concern in his 1946 address:

> But we must remember ... that, in the overwhelming majority of instances, steps forward in scientific theory have been independent of practical application. The hope that is here being expressed is that the new psychologists will in general not allow themselves to become *mere technicians* using psychological methods and techniques for accomplishment of practical ends, that in training of the new generation of psychologists we take care to cultivate an interest in theory as well as in practice.
>
> *(Quoted by Reich, 1981, p. 53)*

Reading papers from this period, one gets the impression that social psychologists were also driven by the fear that their work lacked the status of the more 'scientific' fields of psychology.

The impact of the war on psychology was quite different in Europe. As a result of the Second World War and the political events that preceded it, social psychology became almost nonexistent for several decades. Many of the key figures in post-war American (and British) social psychology in fact were individuals who had left Europe to escape Nazi persecution. (At one point nearly all the social psychology chairs in British universities were held by academics who had fled from the Germans.) It took several decades before a European approach to social psychology was to re-establish itself. In 1963 it proved difficult even to identify a core group of European social psychologists (Tajfel, 1972, p. 308).

Until the late 1960s the USA played the determining role in the structuring, orienting and driving of social psychology, so it is hardly surprising that the focus of the discipline was heavily influenced by the social problems confronting North American society (Apfelbaum, 1992). The effects of these social problems upon the content of research would be readily apparent, suggests Cartwright, if one were to do an archaeological dig through the accumulated literature of social psychology. Writing in 1979, these are the layers he identified:

- sex roles and the status of women – dating from the 1970s

- urban unrest, violence and riots – deposited during the 1960s

- research on conformity – from the heyday of McCarthyism in the 1950s

- problems arising out of the Second World War.

Running vertically through this literature he identified research on continuing problems such as:

- intergroup relations

- prejudice

- racial and ethnic stereotypes

- discrimination

- social conflicts

- the inefficiencies and pathologies of social institutions

- the detrimental effects of modern society on mental health

- the problems of delinquency and antisocial behaviour.

Having studied social psychology in Britain in the late 1960s and early 1970s, I know from personal experience that most of what was taught in Britain in these days was imported from North America. Our textbooks were American and our curriculum made very little reference to British society. (Perhaps the most notable exceptions were Himmelweit's work on mass media and Bowlby's research on maternal deprivation.) This situation was to change dramatically by the mid-1970s. As European social psychology took root, a growing body of literature developed which looked at social issues in British society.

The end of the age of optimism

If the early days of social psychology (the 1920s to the 1950s) were characterized by unbounded optimism about the prospects of using the findings of the discipline to improve society, tempered by a more back-to-the-laboratory period in the 1960s, the period from the 1970s onwards may be depicted as a period of doubts and loss of confidence. Starting in the mid 1970s, we find continued reference to a 'crisis in social psychology', much of which hinged on uncertainty about the relevance of the discipline or its social purpose (see for example Armistead, 1974; Elms, 1975; House, 1977; Minton, 1984; Sherif, 1977; Strickland, Aboud and Gergen, 1976). This internal angst was triggered by a period of massive social change in North America and Europe. The Vietnam War, the antiwar movement, the rise of youth culture, student protests, the beginning of the women's movement, the civil rights movement and the development of Black power and Black consciousness – these events set the scene for a reappraisal of social psychology: 'Against the background of turmoil and alienation of the late 1960s ... psychologists fretted that they were not doing enough to solve the problems of society' (Leahey, 1992, p. 479).

At first the doubts were confined to fringe groups and to younger members of the profession. However, by 1969 the concern about psychology's social role and its social relevance prompted George Miller, as president of the American Psychological Association, to raise it at the annual conference. In a much quoted speech, Miller argued that rather than set themselves up as experts who apply their science, psychologists needed to 'give psychology away' to the people. Not everyone, however, agreed with Miller's proposal. Indeed, as Leahey points out: 'Some Americans, especially conservative ones, did not want what psychologists were giving away. Vice President Spiro Agnew (1972) blasted psychologists, especially B.F. Skinner and Kenneth Clark, for proposing "radical surgery on the nation's psyche"' (1992, p. 481).

A decade after Miller's address, a symposium was held to see what progress had been made in giving psychology away.

> Most of the reports were rather gloomy; even the optimists thought little had been accomplished. Two authors were especially scathing. Sigmund Koch tore Miller's speech apart. He argued that, if anything, psychology was being given away too well in pop psychotherapy and a flood of self-help books. Koch said, 'In sum, I believe the most charitable thing we can do is not to give psychology away, but to take it back'. Michael Scriven, a philosopher turned program evaluator, issued psychology a failing report card. Psychology failed for being ahistorical, for not applying to itself the standards it applied to others, for fancying itself value-free, and for continuing indulgence in the Newtonian fantasy. George Miller, who was there to introduce Koch and Scriven,

was depressed: 'Two men who I admire enormously have just de-
stroyed my life'.

(Leahey, 1992, p. 481)

Yet despite soul searching and negative appraisals, applied psychology in
all its different guises continues to flourish.

In Britain, the majority of applied psychologists work in the following
main areas:

- clinical and counselling psychology

- educational psychology

- industrial (or occupational) and organizational psychology

- government services (e.g. as prison psychologists).

If you are interested in learning more about these different application
areas see Hartley and Branthwaite (1989) or Colman (1995).

Using social psychology: the British and European tradition

A glance at the history of social psychology suggests that, from the very
earliest days, ideas, theories and researchers have readily crossed national
frontiers. Thus, the ideas of Wundt and his colleagues were familiar to
British and North American scholars, as was the work of Binet and Freud.
McDougall, an early British psychologist, had a significant impact on
American social theory and several of the prominent Gestalt psychologists emigrated to North America. In the 1920s it was quite common
for aspiring American academics to spend time studying in Germany
(Minton, 1984). A host of European psychologists such as Kurt Lewin,
Fritz Heider, Theodore Adorno, Marie Jahoda, Erich Fromm and Erik
Erikson emigrated to North America as a direct consequence of the rise
of fascism in Europe. British academic departments also assimilated a
number of European social psychologists who were to make a significant
contribution to the discipline (e.g. Hilde Himmelweit, Henri Tajfel and
later Marie Jahoda). Finally, in the post-war years, many Europeans
routinely did post graduate training in North America. As Marie Jahoda
put it, 'social psychology feeds on culture-contact' (1974, p. 70).

In view of the international nature of much of modern social science, it
may seem dubious to include a separate section on a British/European
tradition. Can we identify a distinct or separate British or European approach to using social psychology? Over the last twenty years there has
been a growing recognition that early American domination of the discipline led to what Moscovici called a 'colonial pact' which hampered the
development of a European way of looking at social psychological
phenomena.

Starting in the mid 1960s, there was an expansion and a reappraisal of social psychology in Britain. Writing at the time of the setting up of a new psychology department in Britain (at what was then Brunel College), Marie Jahoda had some interesting observations to make about the importance of applied psychology. Having recently arrived from the United States, what struck her about Britain was that psychology (apart from clinical and educational psychology) seemed to be divorced from practical concerns. She made a plea for making a greater effort to use the findings of psychology to improve the quality of life: '...there are few, if any, work situations in society – be it work, learning, teaching, industrial production, or acquisition of skills in schools, universities, factories, local government, hospitals, etc. – which could not benefit from the efforts of an appropriately trained psychologist' (1962, p. 26).

Her assessment of the potential contribution psychology could make to society was reflected in the way in which she tried to shape the course at Brunel:

> the implication is that the education of young psychologists should include not only the learning of concepts and theories and the performance of essential laboratory experiments, but opportunities during the academic course for asking in a variety of situations one basic question: How do psychological concepts and theories relate to the actual behavior of people?
>
> *(p. 27)*

It was at this time that British social psychologists began to seek opportunities to collaborate with their European counterparts. As Jos Jaspers at Oxford put it, the belief was 'that social psychology needed another forum, intellectually independent from the one provided by our colleagues in the US' (1986, p. 3). The European Association of Experimental Social Psychology aimed to provide this arena and to promote a different approach to social psychological research. One of the early publications from this group was a two volume set of readings edited by Tajfel which provided a blueprint for the direction European social psychology was taking. A hallmark of this collection was its belief that what was needed was an integration of the study of the individual and society: '...social psychology can and must include a direct concern between individual psychological functioning and large scale social processes which shape this functioning and are shaped by it' (Jaspers, 1986, p. 10).

Tajfel, Fraser, Jaspers and their colleagues were anxious to recast social psychology, and to move away from the notion that the social world could be equated to the presence or absence of a few strangers in unfamiliar laboratory surroundings. European unease about American social psychology stemmed from the view that methodology tended to dominate the discipline at the cost of ideas and social relevance. As Jaspers put it: 'Should not ideas, problems, issues come first? Perhaps this is in part where the difference in focus between European and American social psychology is to be found. The most noticeable contributions to

European social psychology ... *took on problems of a much wider scope'* (p. 14, emphasis added).

Their redefinition of the discipline had implications for the nature of their empirical and theoretical work and its relevance to social life. Tajfel's two volume collected edition, for example, included work on children's thinking about socio-economic systems, unemployment, religion, ideology and group processes and intergroup relations. A superficial impression of all this research might be, says Jaspers, that Tajfel included a good deal of applied social psychology. However, Jaspers repudiates the idea that this sample of emerging European social psychology could be classed as *applied*. Tajfel (1972) was quite opposed to linking the new European social psychology too closely to applied research, whose terms of reference tend to be defined by their patrons, be they commercial, industrial or national. Yet, despite the fact that no chapters were devoted explicitly to 'applied' topics, the contributors were clear about the social relevance and applications of the ideas and research they were presenting. Jaspers contrasts this European collection to the American tradition as exemplified in Lindzey and Aronson's *Handbook of Social Psychology* (1985). In Tajfel's work there was 'No separate volume devoted to applications, but topic by topic an attempt to integrate theory and application; individual and society' (p. 10).

Jahoda (1974), in her comparison of American and European handbooks, makes a similar observation about the different ways of handling applied issues. She maintains that the Europeans have been better at integrating theoretical and applied issues. She herself has never been happy with the 'pure' and 'applied' dichotomy, and her own research shows that it is possible to merge the two traditions.

So is it now possible to point to a distinctive European tradition in social psychology? And, if so, has this led to a different way of using social psychology? Most European social psychologists would say that what has emerged in Europe over the last thirty years is a social psychology which places greater emphasis on the *social dimension* of individual and group behaviour. A move away from the 'self-contained individualism' of North American work should have implications for the way in which findings get taken up and used. Graumann predicts that social psychology will develop a new social purpose: '...since social psychology ... started off with a much wider scope and agenda but "narrowed down its tasks to gain scientific acceptance by employing experimental methods"' (Jaspers, 1986, p. 13), it might now gain acceptance as a *social* science by readdressing real social issues' (1988, pp. 17–18).

The end of the century: a more committed social psychology?

As we approach the end of the twentieth century, it is interesting to speculate about whether social psychology has recovered from the crisis of the 1970s and found a new social role. In Britain there are signs that social psychologists are committed to doing research which has a bearing on important social problems and issues of the day. Most of the contributors to this book see themselves as engaged in work that provides the basis for social critiques, social change and personal growth. Although not everyone would be happy to march under the banner of 'critical social psychology', there is still a sense of engagement, both in terms of the topics chosen for investigation and in the way in which the authors seek to relate their perspectives and their research findings to issues which concern politicians, policy makers, educationalists, and ordinary citizens. The box below provides support for the claim that social psychology is addressing matters of social concern.

BOX 10.2 British social psychology in the 1990s: researchers and research areas

Glynis Breakwell – investigations into pressures on employees in sexually atypical employment

Michael Billig – work on fascism and ideology

Richard Eiser – investigations of risk and attitudes

Colin Fraser – studies on unemployment

Howard Giles – research into language dynamics

Stephen Reicher – research on crowds

Throughout this book we have stressed the way in which accounts are socially constructed and how it is usually possible to generate more than one version of events. An account of how applied social psychology has developed and where it is heading is, itself, a construction and, of course, not everyone would agree with this interpretation of contemporary trends. In the early 1990s a group of European social psychologists organized a conference in Paris to consider what they felt to be the neglect of socio-cultural issues (such as the upheavals in Eastern Europe). This group claimed that at the close of the twentieth century social psychological research is 'disconnected from the problems of political, or other, influence in our society' (Blanchet et al., 1992, p. 526). They suggested that one factor which determines whether social psychologists research macro socio-political events (e.g. the rebirth of nationalism and racism) is institutional research rewards (i.e. prestige, funds, contracts, facilities and research teams). Clearly, the funding of social research (as well as the aspirations and commitments of professionals) has a bearing on what social psychologists study.

4 The search for personal relevance

As suggested in the introduction to this chapter, social psychology can be used in different contexts and for different purposes. Most of what we have looked at so far concerns how psychology is used to deal with social problems. Another way of applying social psychology is through therapy or counselling. Compared to two or three decades ago, it is far more common today for individuals to seek professional help to gain insight into their own behaviour and motives. (And there is no longer a stigma attached to having therapy or counselling.) However, in addition to seeking professional help we can also seek to relate the models and evidence of social psychology directly to our personal lives, our interpersonal relationships and our social roles.

One way of trying to understand and to change oneself is by reading books about personality, personal development, or personal relationships, or by enrolling on a course. Judging from the amount that is published (not just self-help books, but also the scores of magazines and newspapers which contain advice columns or include articles with a self-improvement or self insight angle), people in our society are very interested in reading about social dynamics and personal change. But can you draw upon what you have learned of social psychology to help in the process of living? The different perspectives you have met have somewhat different insights to offer about how to incorporate social psychology into personal life.

What follows below is not meant as an exhaustive account of what might be learned from social psychology which is of relevance to personal change and development. Rather, it is intended to remind you where in this book ways of thinking have been presented which are not just about *society* or *social groups* or *'other* people', but about you yourself, your personal world, your social networks and your location as a person.

Humanistic social psychology: growth and openness to change

The suggestion that psychology can be used for personal growth is a theme developed by Richard Stevens (1996a,b) among many others. At the heart of this approach, which advocates using psychology for personal ends, is the belief that change is possible: individuals can change, relationships can change and society can change. There is a potential *use* to humanistic psychology since it provides us with both insights into ourselves and other people and with some goals towards which to strive.

What are these goals? Humanistic psychology stresses the importance of certain ways of relating to others: openness, acceptance of the uniqueness of others and a willingness to take responsibility for your contribution to the relationship. Another idea developed by Stevens is the way in which techniques developed in therapy and counselling may be applied to personal relationships. Getting in touch with your own

feelings is important both in therapeutic situations and in intimate relationships.

Humanistic psychology is not the only perspective to make claims about
applying knowledge at a personal level. Nearly every perspective has implications for how to live your life. What is interesting to consider is the
different types of insight and the different orientations that the different
perspectives offer.

The significance of embodiment: the view from biology

The message of Frederick Toates (1996) is that we cannot ignore that we
are biological beings and that events and processes within our physical
body limit our agency. How do we integrate this way of thinking about
ourselves into our personal lives? Toates suggests a number of areas
where a biological perspective can help to illuminate the content of our
personal world. His first example is jealousy. He uses an evolutionary
framework to explain how the contexts and precise trigger stimuli that
arouse jealousy differ between the two sexes. Other studies he cites show
the complex interdependence between the external environment,
internal events and subjective feelings. Moods, for example, arise though
an interplay of biological and social factors. When you feel upset or
bored or emotionally flat, do you try to disentangle the factors that are
associated with your mood? Do you think, 'Oh, it's that time of the
month', or 'I'm still feeling low because I didn't get that job', or 'It's the
after-effects of that flu I had last week'?

Perhaps the most compelling insights from the biological perspective relate to the use of drugs and alcohol. Did you find that the account of
the adaptive value of addiction helped you to make sense of why individuals find it difficult to give up drugs? What is interesting about the
biological perspective outlined by Toates is that it does not lead us to
conclude that change is impossible or that our behaviour or internal
states are determined by biological processes. Instead, we are reminded
that we are what we are as a result of dynamic interactions between ourselves and our social and physical environment. Translating this into a
personal agenda would mean taking into account events in several different domains.

Social constructionism: locating yourself in the world

Social constructionism offers a way of joining up our personal, individual
biographies with the wider social context in which we are located. The
net result is a way of relating personal and social change. For instance,
Wetherell's (1996b) analysis of masculinity has implications for how you
make sense of your life and how you go about trying to change. The thesis put forward is that 'change does not come about from a rational process of rethinking one's life alone, or from individual therapy'. The
message is that you need to also work on your social relationships *and*
your social context. These ideas are endorsed by Arlene Vetere (1996).

She makes the case that family therapists need to help individuals move beyond thinking in terms of personal inadequacies and to question socially prescribed roles which may constrain relationships and hinder personal development.

One part of the quest for self understanding involves digging out the personal significance of external social events. The constructionist approach should help you to understand how you 'make your identity'. After reading such work you should be more alert not only to other people's constructions, narratives and stories, but also to your own. You may find yourself listening in a new way to the stories that you tell others about yourself. If you are a parent, social constructionism may also offer you new insight into how your child actively constructs his or her understandings through interaction with others.

The life-cycle model: handling transitions

While it is fascinating to read how other people manage their lives and their relationships, can we derive insights from such material which is relevant to our own lives? A model such as the family life-cycle might be used in three different ways. It might help you to:

- reflect upon or make sense of past events in your life (e.g. to understand your own childhood)

- gain insight into current events and relationships (e.g. how to deal with parenthood)

- anticipate and prepare for future life events (e.g. children leaving home or your retirement).

The psychodynamic perspective: confronting anxieties and irrationality

Although it developed within a clinical context, the psychodynamic perspective presented by Kerry Thomas (1996a,b) and by Helen Morgan and Kerry Thomas (1996) has a great deal to say that is relevant to everyday life. Thomas sets herself the task of demonstrating how the concepts of psychodynamic theory offer a way of making sense of much that seems mysterious or contradictory about our inner worlds, our social relationships and our experiences in groups. One of Thomas' primary concerns is to get you to appreciate how the psychodynamic perspective differs not just from 'common-sense' views but also from other psychological perspectives. The challenge thrown down at the outset is that 'things are not as they appear'. Our sense of agency, of being in control of our lives, is deemed to be largely an illusion. Self knowledge is beyond our reach because much of what we are is hidden deep in our unconscious and it is this that is the major driving force in our lives. Irrationality, according to Morgan and Thomas, is not just confined to the domain of the person. They introduce the idea that the behaviour of the group is also determined by unconscious as well as conscious factors.

How are you to go about assimilating such subversive views? Perhaps the main thrust of this perspective is that we must proceed with caution when it comes to making sense of our own and other people's consciously constructed accounts of their subjective experience. Thomas stresses that subjective experience is problematic because consciousness is 'only the tip of the iceberg, and biased'. Much that we assume or take for granted about ourselves may, in fact, be false. The same applies to relationships: 'Our everyday relationships depend to a large degree on what is carried over from the past'. If this is true, where does this leave us in our day-to-day life? Compared to other perspectives which hold out some prospect of change, does a psychodynamic view mean that we are trapped in the past?

Psychodynamic writers do not rule out the possibility of change, but they maintain that to understand a relationship or to understand an individual's experience of relating needs the help of an outsider. An intellectual grasp of the concepts and principles of the psychodynamic method do not, by and of themselves, produce change.

BOX 10.3 Possible personal outcomes from studying social psychology

This checklist is not meant to be exhaustive. It is presented to stimulate you into thinking about what you have taken away from social psychology. So please feel free to disagree!

1 Developed increased awareness of the different kinds of influences on your actions and experience (e.g. origins in biology, childhood and society). Such awareness may facilitate your ability to do something about such influences, or at least enable you to appreciate why things are as they are.

2 Developed awareness of the ways in which society can help to structure your sense of identity or the pattern of your relationships (e.g. gender issues). Awareness in turn may make it possible to immunize yourself or take steps to counteract the influence.

3 Gained awareness of the possible influence of biological factors on your behaviour and relationships (e.g. patterns of sexual relating, jealousy).

4 Became aware of biases in the ways you categorize and process information, e.g. fundamental attribution error.

5 Appreciated the importance of giving other people scope to make their own decisions.

6 Stimulated you to think about the human condition.

7 Alerted you to the potentially self-fulfilling nature of ideas.

8 Pointed you towards new ways of thinking about aspects of being that you may have been aware of but had not really reflected upon (e.g. the discussion of existential issues presented by Stevens (1996a).

> 9   Stimulated you to think about your own potential – about ways in which you *might* be.
>
> 10 Increased your awareness of possible techniques for change which are available and how they work (e.g. psychodynamic therapy, humanistic counselling, family therapy).

This section was not meant to be a comprehensive review of social psychology. I hope, however, that it has shown that it is possible to tease out the personal relevance of the perspectives presented by the discipline. How you go about translating research evidence or the perspectives of social psychology into your personal life depends on what you are seeking and the problems you are facing. Do you want to understand yourself or your relationships or both? Do you want to make changes in your life, to keep from repeating certain patterns or making certain mistakes? Do you want to improve the quality of relationships, for example, to overcome power imbalances or develop more equitable, less exploitative relationships or find a way of getting more out of relationships (personal, social, business, work, family)? Is your goal to avoid conflicts and stress or is it to experience a greater sense of freedom or well being?

In the process of thinking about the ways in which we, as individuals, may use social psychology, I was reminded of a folk saying which asks for 'the power to change things that are open to change, the fortitude to accept things which cannot be changed and the wisdom to distinguish between the two'. It occurred to me that perhaps there is another way in which social psychological research might be used to construct a personal life philosophy. Instead of focusing on change, another function of the discipline might be to help us to identify or recognize areas of behaviour, beliefs, or values which are *not* amenable to change.

As suggested earlier, some perspectives, such as humanistic psychology, give positive messages about the possibility of change; others are less sanguine. If you were to reflect on the perspectives you have met, could you readily identify examples that fall into either category? Do you think that the different perspectives have identified areas where we need to be able to reconcile ourselves to insurmountable social, biological or psychological realities? (If you are stumped by this question, you might cast your mind back to two perspectives you are met: the psychodynamic approach and the biological approach.)

So far in thinking about personal uses, the assumption has been that our motives are pure or uncontaminated. That is, we are seeking to change in order to improve ourselves, to be happier, better, more fulfilled individuals. But we can identify another strand of personal use which emanates from an individualistic, competitive ethos of modern capitalist society. In discussing the work of Galton, Danziger (1990) draws attention to this other use of psychology. At the 1884 International Health Exhibition in London, at a charge of threepence per person, Galton invited people to test their mental faculties in his laboratory. In return, each individual received a card containing the results of the measurements that had been made on him or her. In all 9,000 individuals were tested. What were the public getting?

> What [Galton] contracted to provide his subjects with was information about their relative performance on specific tasks believed to reflect important abilities.
>
> *(Danziger, 1990, p. 55)*

> Why did individuals want this information? What use was it to them? In a society in which the social career of individuals depended on their marketable skills any 'scientific' (i.e. believed to be objective and reliable) information pertaining to these skills was not only of possible instrumental value to the possessors of those skills but was also likely to be relevant to their self-image and their desire for self-improvement.
>
> *(p. 56)*

So individuals may want to use psychology in order to further their self interests and to advance themselves, rather than to understand themselves or to develop more satisfying interpersonal relations. This not only applies to psychological testing; the same personal utility may be sought in any area of applied psychology. For instance, parents may turn to child psychology in order to bring up their child in a way which enhances the child's potential or they may seek ways of speeding up their child's development in order that the child may succeed in life. In turning to social psychology, individuals may have mixed motives, some of which are altruistic and some which have to do with self aggrandizement.

Reflections on the utility of social psychology

Philosophers interested in epistemology have pointed out that one way in which forms of knowledge may differ is between

> knowing how (procedural knowledge) and
>
> knowing about (theoretical knowledge).

Just think for a moment about the different ways you might use the word *know* and the different status and use of different forms of knowledge. For example:

> I *know about* the history of mathematics
>
> I *know how* to calculate the area of a circle
>
> I *know how* to use a calculator
>
> I *know* the rules of tennis
>
> I *know how* to play tennis

There are no simple answers to the question 'What use is social psychology' or 'How can I use social psychology'. How will you use or apply the knowledge you have gained from social psychology? What value will it have for you? There are quite a range of answers which might come to mind, for example, it may:

- enable you to pass exams

- help you advance your career

- be useful for persuading people, winning arguments, exercising power or controlling people

- enable you to play games, enter quizzes

- be a means of impressing people.

5 The social impact of social psychology

As you might imagine, excursions from the relatively safe, protected world of the university to the arena of social policy are not without their problems. From the very early days, psychologists found themselves caught in a conundrum. On the one hand, psychology has been criticized for not having social relevance and for not being sufficiently applied, but on the other, when psychologists undertake to apply their knowledge by acting as policy advisors or expert witnesses, they are also apt to come under attack. During the 1970s the issue of the social responsibility of social scientists became a matter of public concern and academic debate. There was disquiet about the funding of social research by the military and by large foundations, and the uses to which such findings were put. Critics focused on military applications, along with educational uses, industrial applications and clinical methods. Some of the examples of psychological research unearthed by the critics make for quite disturbing reading. Cina (1981, p. 279) describes 'before' and 'after' psychological tests being administered to US soldiers who were made to observe A-bomb test explosions. In the UK, the involvement of psychologists in prisoner interrogation in Northern Ireland was also a matter of controversy. The disquiet about the use and funding of social psychological research is developed in Chapter 11 of this volume.

6 Conclusion

Social psychology has always straddled the line between theory and application. Many natural science psychologists would no doubt (privately if not publicly) cast most of social psychology in the 'applied' camp. On the other hand, those in the applied fields of clinical and organizational psychology often look to social psychology for basic concepts and general principles. To an important extent, then, what is basic and what is applied are features of the observer's orientation. Furthermore, the same research can often be titled and described in basic or applied terms.

(Jones, 1985, pp. 93–4)

From the evidence looked at in this chapter and what you have met elsewhere, it is clear that social psychologists are engaged in research which has implications for the way in which we organize our social institutions and the way in which we live our lives. Psychologists, whether engaged in basic or applied research, have attempted to tease out the social relevance of their perspectives. But at the same time, the nature of applied research has changed over the course of the twentieth century. If you were to look at a social psychology textbook from the 1940s alongside a 1990s equivalent, what would you be likely to find? Would the areas of application be the same? What new areas have emerged? What areas have been jettisoned? Some areas have been abandoned (e.g. the authoritarian personality work) and some areas have been recast (e.g. work on attitudes and attitude change; studies on intergroup relations). In addition, some topics are of very recent vintage, for example work on disability, research on child abuse and ways of interviewing children, and the growing field of health psychology. Finally, even in research areas where there appears to be continuity, what you are likely to find if you look more closely at the work being done, the questions asked and the methods used is that as the social problems are redefined, so too the social psychological research is transformed.

If we look upon social psychological knowledge as a collection of *scientific facts* or *laws about human behaviour* which are independent of the researcher, the research method, the culture in which research is set or the historical time frame, then you will be seeking universal applications. However, once you begin to see social problems as being socially constructed, social perspectives as social constructs and research as a social process, the issue of applying social psychology takes on an entirely different complexion.

Sarason (1978) has caricatured the way in which social scientists have gone about trying to solve social problems.

> For 20 years after World War II, the social sciences became, and with a vengeance, vigorous, quantitative, theoretical, and entrepreneurial. If you wanted to solve in a basic and once-and-for-all way the puzzles of individual and social behaviour, you needed resources of the wall-to-wall variety. True, it would take time to learn to ask the right questions, to develop the appropriate methodologies, before you could come up with the right answers. What we were after were those bedrock laws of social behaviour and process that would allow a society 'really' rationally to diagnose and solve its problems. Give us time (and

money) and you will not regret it. In the meantime, if you think we can be helpful to you with your current problems, please call on us. And call they did, and go they went.

(Sarason, 1978, p. 324)

And what were the results? According to Sarason they have been discouraging and shattering: '...discouraging because of the lack of intended outcomes and shattering because they call into question the appropriateness of the scientific-rational model of problem definition and solution in social action' (p. 324).

Sarason takes social scientists to task for failing to understand that in the social world there are *intractable* problems which have to be 'solved' over and over again. To accept intractability is tantamount to accepting the imperfectibility of human beings and of society. He identifies the following sources of intractable problems:

- our sense of aloneness in the world

- our need for other human beings

- the inevitability of death.

Sarason considers that these are psychological and biological 'givens' which cause problems but they are not the kinds of problems that fit into science's problem-solving models. According to Sarason, each society defines and copes differently with these problems and as a society changes, the nature of the definitions and copings change. Although the problems which Sarason identifies, which overlap with the problems Freud identified in *Civilisation and its Discontents* and with the existential issues outlined by Richard Stevens (1996a), are assumed by Sarason to be universal, he insists that they are not problems that people have created.

Sarason's list of intractable problems may appear somewhat biased because it focuses exclusively on problems in one domain – that of the person. You may wish to expand the list to include problems which arise from the other two domains. For instance, you may feel that issues relating to social structure, social history, social inequalities, social divisions and the economic organization of society lead to problems which are never permanently solved.

If we accept Sarason's basic premise that social problems are different in nature from the puzzles that natural scientists and engineers confront, what are the prospects for using social psychology to change society and to improve the quality of our lives? His message is that we must accept that there are some problems which can never be eliminated or ignored: '...any planned effort to effect a social change ... that does not recognize and understand the history and the dynamics of these three problems will likely exacerbate rather than dilute the force of these problems' (p. 10).

His advice to scientists who enter the arena of social action is that they need to be guided by the values they attach to the facts of living.

The social constructionist perspective developed in several chapters of this book provides further insight into the dilemmas of the applied researcher or anyone who seeks to find ways of using the findings of social psychology. Social constructionism reminds us that it is not just the social problems themselves that change from one era or generation to another, but our perception of the issues, how we frame them, also changes. Imagine the difficulties liberals from the 1940s or 1950s would face in trying to understand where the debate has moved in relation to race, ethnicity, gender or disability. The task of making use of social science findings is more than a technical exercise of matching problems to evidence. We need to be able to understand the *story* behind the problem (how the problem has come to be constructed in a particular way) and the *story* behind the research (how particular individuals happened to become involved in researching a given social problem).

References

Apfelbaum, E. (1992) 'Some teachings from the history of social psychology', *Canadian Psychology*, vol. 33, pp.529–39.

Armistead, N. (ed.) (1974) *Reconstructing Social Psychology*, Harmondsworth, Penguin.

Blanchet, A. (1992) 'Organizing the international conference on the history of social psychology', *Canadian Psychology*, vol. 33, pp.525–8.

Bowlby, J. (1951) *Maternal Care and Mental Health*, World Health Organization, London, HMSO.

Brewster Smith M. (1983) 'The shaping of American social psychology: a personal perspective from the periphery', *Personality and Social Psychology Bulletin*, vol. 9, pp.165–80.

Brown, H. (1996) 'Themes in experimental research on groups from the 1930s to the 1990s' in Wetherell, M. (ed.).

Bulmer, M. (1982) *The Uses of Social Research: Social Investigation in Public Policy-Making*, London, George Allen and Unwin.

Cartwright, D. (1979) 'Contemporary social psychology in historical perspective', *Social Psychology Quarterly*, vol. 42, pp.82–93.

Cina, C. (1981) *Social Science for Whom? A Structural History of Social Psychology.* (Doctoral dissertation, State University of New York at Stony Brook.)

Colman, A. (ed.) (1995) *Applications of Psychology*, London, Longman.

Dallos, R. (1996) 'Change and transformations of relationships' in Miell, D. and Dallos, R. (eds).

Danziger, K. (1990) *Constructing the Subject: Historical Origins of Psychological Research*, Cambridge, Cambridge University Press.

Elms, A.C. (1975) 'The crisis of confidence in social psychology', *American Psychologist*, vol. 30, pp.967–76.

Freud, S. (1930) *Civilisation and its Discontents*, revised edition by Strachey, J. (1963), London, Hogarth Press and the Institute of Psychoanalysis.

Gergen, K. (1973) 'Social psychology as history', *Journal of Personality and Social Psychology*, vol. 26, pp.309–20.

Graumann, C.F. (1988) 'Introduction to a history of social psychology' in Hewstone, M. et al. (eds) (1988) *Introduction to Social Psychology*, Oxford, Blackwell.

Hartley, J. and Branthwaite, A. (1989) *The Applied Psychologist*, Milton Keynes, Open University Press

Himmelweit, H.T., Oppenheim, A.N. and Vince, M. (1958) *Television and the Child: An Empirical Study of the Effects of Television on the Young*, London, Nuffield Foundation.

House, J.S. (1977) 'The three faces of social psychology', *Sociometry*, vol. 40, pp.161–77.

Jahoda, M. (1963) 'The establishment of a new psychology department', *Bulletin of the British Psychological Society*, 48, pp.25–9.

Jahoda, M. (1974) 'Social psychology: national or international? A review of "Sozialpsychologie", vol. 7 of *Handbuch der Psychologie*', *European Journal of Social Psychology*, vol. 4, pp.503–8.

Jahoda, M. (1983) 'The emergence of social psychology in Vienna: An exercise in long-term memory', *British Journal of Social Psychology*, vol. 22, pp.343–9.

Jaspers, J. (1986) 'Forum and focus: a personal view of European social psychology', *European Journal of Social Psychology*, vol. 16, pp.3–15.

Jones, E.E. (1985) 'Major developments in social psychology during the past five decades' in Lindzey, G. and Aronson, E. (eds.)

Lalljee, M. (1996) 'The interpreting self: an experimentalist perspective' in Stevens, R. (ed.).

Leahey, T.H. (1992) *A History of Psychology: Main Currents in Psychological Thought* (3rd edn), Englewood Cliffs, New Jersey, Prentice Hall.

Lindzey, G. and Aronson, E. (eds) (1985) *Handbook of Social Psychology* (3rd edn), vol. 1, New York, Random House.

Lück, H.E. (1987) 'A historical perspective on social psychological theories' in Semin, G.R. and Krahé, K. (eds) *Issues in Contemporary German Social Psychology*, London, Sage.

Miell, D. and Dallos, R. (eds) (1996) *Social Interaction and Personal Relationships*, London, Sage.

Miell, D. and Croghan, D. (1996) 'Examining the wider context of social relationships' in Miell, D. and Dallos, R. (eds).

Minton, H.L. (1984) 'J.F. Brown's social psychology of the 1930s: a historical antecedent to the contemporary crisis in social psychology', *Personality and Social Psychology Bulletin,* vol. 10, pp.31–42.

Morgan, H. and Thomas, K. (1996) 'A psychodynamic perspective on group processes' in Wetherell, M. (ed.).

Pepitone, A. (1981) 'Lessons from the history of social psychology', *American Psychologist,* vol. 36, pp.972–85.

Potter, J. (1996) 'Attitudes, social representations and discursive psychology' in Wetherell, M. (ed.).

Reich, J.W. (1933) *Mass Psychology of Fascism,* New York, Simon and Schuster.

Reich, J.W. (1981) 'An historical analysis of the field' in Bickerman, L. (ed.) *Applied Social Psychology Annual,* vol. 2, Beverley Hills, Sage.

Rogers, C. (1980) *A Way of Being,* New York, Houghton Mifflin.

Sarason, S.B. (1978) 'Nature of problem solving in social action' in Murphy, J., John, M. and Brown, H. (eds) (1984) *Dialogues and Debates in Social Psychology,* London, Lawrence Erlbaum in association with the Open University.

Schönpflug, W. (1992) 'Applied psychology: newcomer with a long tradition', *Applied Psychology: An International Review,* vol. 42, pp.5–30.

Sherif, M. (1977) 'Crisis in psychology: some remarks towards breaking through the crisis', *Personality and Social Psychology Bulletin,* vol. 3, pp.368–82.

Stevens, R. (ed.) (1996) *Understanding the Self,* London, Sage.

Stevens, R. (1996a) 'The reflexive self: an experiential perspective' in Stevens, R. (ed.)

Stevens, R. (1996b) 'A humanistic approach to relationships' in Miell, D. and Dallos, R. (eds).

Strickland, L., Aboud, F., and Gergen, K. (eds) (1976) *Social Psychology in Transition,* New York, Plenum Press.

Tajfel, H. (1972) 'Some developments in European social psychology', *European Journal of Social Psychology,* vol.2, pp.307–22.

Tajfel, H. (1984) *The Social Dimension: European Developments in Social Psychology,* Volumes 1 and 2, Cambridge, Cambridge University Press.

Tajfel, H. and Fraser, C. (eds) (1978) *Introducing Social Psychology,* Harmondsworth, Penguin.

Thomas, K. (1996a) 'The defensive self: a psychodynamic perspective' in Stevens, R. (ed.).

Thomas, K. (1996b) 'The psychodynamics of relating' in Miell, D. and Dallos, R. (eds).

Toates, F. (1996) 'The embodied self: a biological perspective' in Stevens, R. (ed.).

Vetere, A. (1996) 'A gender sensitive perspective on personal relationships' in Miell, D. and Dallos, R. (eds).

Wetherell, M. (ed.) (1996) *Identities, Groups and Social Issues*, London, Sage.

Wetherell, M. (1996a) 'Group conflict and the social psychology of racism' in Wetherell, M. (ed.).

Wetherell, M. (1996b) 'Life histories/social histories' in Wetherell, M. (ed.).

CHAPTER 11
RESISTING SOCIAL PSYCHOLOGY

By Roger Sapsford and Rudi Dallos

1 Introduction

> The essential ideological function of ... social psychology ... is to depoliticise ... and to present [itself] as a neutral domain of technical expertise ... applied to the benefit of the whole of society.
>
> *(Gross, 1974, pp. 42–3)*

It is probably fair to say that social and clinical psychology have become well entangled in modern life. For example, it is commonplace to hear elements of behaviourism/learning theory, psychological theories about groups and developmental psychology reflected in ordinary conversations. The language and concepts of psychoanalysis had become common cultural currency by the 1970s. (For the purpose of this chapter, psychodynamic ideas will be accredited to social rather than clinical psychology despite their therapeutic applications; clinical psychology tends to be more behaviourally-oriented.) As Jonathan Potter (1996) says: '...our common sense is indeed a sediment from past theorizing about psychology and the self'. There is evident interest in popular psychology – chat shows, countless articles on personality, sexuality and relationship problems in magazines, and so on – and academic psychology courses are also very popular. (At the time of writing, the Open University has more than 2,600 students a year studying the *Introduction to Psychology* course, and over 8,000 each year on the psychology programme as a whole.) At one time it could have been argued, with some justice, that the 'customers' of social psychology were not workers, children and delinquents, but industries, schools and control agencies. Now, in contrast, one might want to claim that this extensive popularity and popularization has the effect of 'giving away' social psychological knowledge to the public at large, rather than making it available 'on prescription only' to controlling groups such as managers, psychiatrists, senior educationalists and the government. It is available in book form, for 'self-medication', to parents bringing up children, to those who want to improve their work and social skills and to those who see themselves as having problems with relationships. 'Professional advice' is very freely available in magazines and on television and radio.

Nonetheless, the element of control remains. In this chapter we shall argue that social psychology still has a control function, exercised in five different ways.

1   At the level of applied work, social and clinical psychology are used in the 'people trades' – for example, in social work, education and nursing care – as a set of techniques for 'piecemeal social engineering'. They are used to change people, for their own good and that of others, so that they conform to the behaviour and performance expected of them and the circumstances in which they find themselves. Psychology's use in industry, commerce and education to select the 'right' people for positions and opportunities, to train them to perform at their best and to motivate them to optimum production is an equally clear example of psychology 'exercising control'. Further, social psychology still acts as the informing or validating 'corpus of knowledge' for a range of institutions and agencies whose function is, explicitly or implicitly, the maintenance of social order.

2   In taking on and exercising these functions, social psychology has fought for and acquired two kinds of authority: the authority of science and a 'professional' authority akin to that exercised by medical practitioners. Both in their different ways lend 'expert power' and influence to academic and applied psychologists (see Chapter 8, earlier in this volume.)

3   Particularly in the 'people trades' (but sometimes less so in industry and commerce) the practical effect of using psychological techniques is to 'de-politicize' and to 'individuate' – to pose problems and seek solutions at the level of individuals and groups and to propose 'technical' solutions to what might otherwise be seen as moral or political issues – and it teaches this approach to the professionals whom it helps to train and to legitimate.

4   At the level of social order the 'project' of academic social psychology has often been *utopian* social engineering – working for a better world by the application of (psychological) science. Such a project is 'obviously' to be applauded, but the world can be reshaped only if you have power; making its improvement a matter of the application of the 'correct technique' tends to mask underlying power transactions.

5   We shall also argue that social psychology constitutes the basis for an effective mode of social control by inculcating certain ways of thinking about the social world, setting out what is to count as evidence about it and shaping the language of personal and interpersonal relations.

Thus we think it fair to argue that social psychology has a function in social control at two levels. At one level it is directly applied to solve problems and optimize performance, or to train others to do so; at the other level it helps to create and maintain a set of 'models' of the nature of the person and the social world which shape and constrain our actions and our very understanding of ourselves and our needs, potentialities and obligations. However, the title of the chapter 'Resisting social psychology' was intended to point in two directions. On the one hand, the controlling force of social psychological thinking and practice may be worthy of being resisted. On the other hand, very often social psychology itself has pointed to the need for resistance and provided the tools with which to resist itself and its applications – in a straightforward way in the 1960s and 1970s, and through increasingly sophisticated and reflexive analysis of ideology and discourse in the 1980s and 1990s. A tradition of resistance forms part of the history of social psychology itself, and we shall be looking briefly in this chapter at some episodes in this history.

2 Clinical psychology and 'anti-psychiatry'

...taking what is an essentially political problem, removing it from the realm of political discourse and recasting it in the neutral language of science. Once this is accomplished the problems have become technical ones.

(Foucault, 1982, p. 196)

The most obvious form of control and manipulation occurs in clinical psychology and the psychotherapies, where changing people is the explicit purpose of the enterprise. Clinical psychology has traditionally been considered a separate field of endeavour from social psychology, and both have maintained a separation from psychiatry and psychoanalysis. However, there are important points of connection between all of them. Each has informed the 'body of knowledge' which is social psychology, and each has drawn on it. For example, the psychology of group dynamics has informed group therapy. Likewise, the notion of a dynamic unconscious and the relationship of 'symptoms' to interpersonal processes has informed theory and research in social psychology.

When clinical psychologists discuss clinical work they tend to do so as 'scientists' or 'professionals'. That is, they talk mainly about techniques and their outcomes, and seldom about the location of clinical work within a cultural and moral order. Within this world-view (shared by the therapists and their 'customers') patients or clients can be seen as being defined by others as deviants who need the help of social psychology to bring them into line and help them to conform and, not surprisingly, social psychology has quite a bit to say about the circumstances under which people do conform and the causes of 'deviation'. As an applied branch of a science it is concerned with mechanisms and manipulations, with doing a sound professional job based on sound scientific reasoning. Social psychology has rather less to say about how to encourage people *not* to conform, to resist pressure, to adopt creatively different lifestyles or modes of thought, etc. There is, indeed, a flourishing tradition within social psychology of research into group pressures and individual resistance to persuasion, but to the best of our knowledge this has had no influence on any form of therapy. Similarly, research and theory on prejudice and stereotyping has had little impact on therapeutic intervention, except to the extent that it may alert therapists to their own preconceptions. Indeed, the very presence of 'creative alternatism' has itself often been regarded as symptomatic of a mental illness or moral deviation and in need of cure or reshaping.

During the 1960s and 1970s there was a substantial reaction against 'scientific' approaches to social and clinical psychology and against contemporary applications of psychodynamics to therapy. (The psychodynamics of the time tended very strongly towards individualism and a medical model of 'mental illness', particularly in psychiatric hospital practice. For a more social interpretation see Thomas, 1996a, 1996b.) This reaction originated largely outside social psychology – from a group of radically critical psychiatrists and under the influence of the humanistic movement, which embraced ideas from Eastern philosophies and from existentialism – but it had a considerable impact on social psychologists. Four major objections to the 'scientific' approach emerged, to a greater or lesser extent in different people's work.

1 The experiences of individuals were 'dis-authenticated' – the views and experiences of people labelled as mentally ill, for example, were regarded as unimportant and as not reflecting 'what was really going on'.

2 The reductionism inherent in the scientific approach led to the investigation of behaviours and traits rather than people, so there was no way of understanding people *as* people within social psychology.

3 The stress on the characteristics and behaviour of individuals (or at best of ahistorical and context-free groups) favoured individualistic explanations over collectivist ones – in itself a political stance – and could be described all too often as 'blaming the victim'.

4 While people's actions and decisions belong essentially to the moral sphere, psychology was doing what is described in the Foucault quote above and reducing these actions to technical problems to be sorted out by experts.

These criticisms reach out further than social psychology, into the professional system of medicine and its focus on internal, organic causes of disorders. However, social psychology played its part in drawing attention to the narrow focus of the psychotherapies on the individual as the primary level of analysis. Talking of 'social causes', clinical psychology and the psychotherapies generally implied that problems were due to faulty learning and poor experiences. In other words, the individual was mis-programmed and needed a good 'systems analyst' to get the programming fixed, and/or to go 'off-line' for a while (perhaps with the help of medication) and then be plugged back 'on-line' again. The psychologist or psychotherapist as 'service engineer' carries out his or her professional function (see Sapsford, 1997, for a discussion of the 'service model' of therapy).

Some of the 'anti-psychiatry movement' made a radical attack on the whole concept of mental illness as something treatable by 'quasi-medicine'. Szasz (1962) for example, in *The Myth of Mental Illness,* attempts to present 'mental illness' as something more akin to a disarrangement of communication than to a bodily malaise. Others who accepted mental illness as a disorder tended to frame it as a disorder located in a different domain from that of personal or intrapersonal psychology – arguing, for instance, that relational processes within the family and the social order were key to an understanding of disorders. Laing, a psychiatrist and analyst, suggested in his book *The Divided Self* (1960) that forms of mental illness were linked to destructive interpersonal processes and formed 'intelligible responses to difficult social circumstances'. These included disorders of relationship in families in which people (especially women and children) would find themselves trapped. So the trouble was not inside individuals but in the transactions between members of the family. This still left therapy focused on failures of relationship in the family. Laing and others did attempt to extend this focus by looking at how these family processes were, in turn, a product of the contradictions, inequalities and abuses inherent in society and internalized into family life. (This was an early signalling of the feminist critiques and analysis of, for example, how women suffer in families because of the material and ideological oppression of patriarchy.) Interestingly, Hollingshead and Redlitch (1958) had offered a similar analysis of the correlation between serious mental illness and poverty/class inequality – that the poorest and most deprived have the worst mental as well as physical health.

Some of the radical offshoots of this movement, such as the cross-fertilization of therapy by humanistic psychology, showed interesting but perhaps predictable developments. Initially much concerned with political and social processes, humanistic therapy has tended to become more concerned with fitting individuals into an unchallenged social order, in the same way that Russell Jacoby (1975) accuses American developments of Freudian theory of backsliding from the political importance of Freud's insights. There is, of course, nothing wrong with, and much to be said for, helping people to achieve the most that they can in the way of contentment and attainment from the circumstances in which they find themselves, but doing so tends to mean that 'the way things are' is taken for granted as natural or inevitable. You can then finish up with a style of 'self-improvement' whose main aim may appear to be returning tired, stressed executives to their desks on a Monday morning bright, confident, competitive and ready to do business.

Therapy and self-improvement are 'obviously good things', so why would we want to criticize them? Spend a couple of minutes thinking what criticisms could be made while still holding on to the essentially beneficial purpose of these activities.

ACTIVITY 11.1

It would be a great error to suggest that therapy is not needed, or to deny that what it delivers is for the good of its clients. People do have confused experiences, they do suffer real and great distress and become trapped in untenable ways of experiencing and dealing with the social world. However, it may be an equal and opposite error to fail to acknowledge that these 'deviant states' may be, in part, a function of social processes – well understood processes of labelling and deviance amplification whereby normal but extreme behaviours and experiences can become marginalized, stigmatized and eventually pathologized in the service of social control (Boyle, 1990). It is also a valid criticism of the therapeutic endeavour to point out, while not denying its value, that its desired end-product is a human being fit for social circumstances, not social circumstances fit for human beings. In its practices, therefore, it tends to support the existing social order and to obscure its problems and inconsistencies. It is this, the social embeddedness of the therapeutic endeavour and its function as part of the network of social control, to which the 'anti-psychiatry movement' drew attention.

3 Social institutions and 'anti-psychology'

The fallacy involved in representing social norms as laws of nature is, of course, that the former can be altered if we so wish, but the latter cannot; and if this fallacy becomes incorporated into scientific orthodoxy, the latter becomes an obvious instrument for maintaining the status quo.

(Ingleby, 1974, p. 318)

Over the years, psychology has staked out a claim to expert knowledge in a range of fields and contributed to the shape of many public-sphere social institutions. Professions grounded in branches of social and individual psychology and regarding themselves as part of the discipline have acquired authority and been accepted as expert in a number of applied fields. In education it was tests of 'intelligence' – dividing the ineducable from the badly schooled – which first gave psychology a stake in the area and legitimated its claims to expertise in it at the beginning of the twentieth century. These tests quickly moved from a way of identifying 'the feeble-minded' (as children with special educational needs were then labelled) to a way of classifying the ability of all children. Even in periods when the actual tests became less fashionable, the overall notion of a school population being normally distributed with respect to an identifiable and, in principle, measurable level of ability remained, and our notions of schooling are fundamentally imbued with the idea of the innate ability of children needing to be brought out.

In the 1920s psychology captured the role of adviser to juvenile courts on the treatment and disposal of delinquents and children 'in need of control' (for example Burt, 1925) and as 'child guidance' advisers to schools and parents. Psychologists have since established a routine expert status in the assessment of criminals for sentencing by the courts, in the training of social workers and probation officers to handle criminals in the community and in their rehabilitative treatment within prison.

The period from the end of the nineteenth century to the middle of the twentieth also saw the growth of industrial psychology to advise on, select and regulate workers and working conditions: the 'aptitude test' industry; attempts to modify the physical and organizational environment of factory work to maximize output and minimize labour turnover; psychological management training in 'human relations'; 'job enrichment'; and 'human resource management'.

Within the private sphere, the role of psychological knowledge is so well entrenched that it seems natural and inevitable, but it is, in fact, of fairly recent origin. The private sphere as something separate from the more prestigious and financially rewarding 'world of work' is, itself, an invention of the nineteenth century (see Watson, 1996) and psychology's power to determine how mothers should bring up their children (and to rule on other 'related' issues such as whether mothers have the right to take full-time paid employment) is more recent still. These powers were increasingly conferred on *medicine* by the growth of home visiting – later health visiting – during the early years of the twentieth century and the role of doctors as experts advising on it and determining its form. While health visiting remains under medical/nursing control, soon after the Second World War much of the expert status passed to psychology and it is now psychologists who advise on the mental and intellectual welfare of children and devise tests of the normality of their development. In taking this role over from the medical professions, psychologists have acquired some of the authority of medicine – some of the same respect and right to intervene in people's everyday lives. (See also Miell and Croghan, 1996, for a discussion of the 'professional strangers' in health, psychology and social work whom we now take for granted as available to fulfil some of people's needs for care and support.)

Those who advise mothers would not see themselves as manipulative in any malign sense but as 'benevolent experts' doing their best for both mothers and children. Their expertise has sometimes been characterized, however, as using the mantle of 'neutral' science to give objective validity to essentially *moral* positions – that it is natural for women to want to mother, that mothers should give their undivided attention to their children and put them before every other consideration, that certain forms of mothering are superior to others, and so on.

So social, clinical and developmental psychologists hold positions of expert power in the current world. They are employed and are influential in education, in industry, in therapy and in the health services in general. They are called as witnesses in courts, assess the mental state of prisoners on remand, assess convicted prisoners for allocation and run rehabilitative treatment programmes in prison. In addition they train other professionals who have a 'care and control' or managerial role; psychology is an important part of the training of doctors, nurses and other health workers, prison officers, teachers, social workers and business managers, among many others. Three propositions underlie the formal content of this training, even if they are never articulated or even apprehended.

1   Problems may be detected and solutions attempted at the level of individuals – an obviously true proposition, but one which can serve to distract attention from wider and more politically sensitive areas.

2   People can and, under certain safeguards, *should* be manipulated for their own good – indeed, social psychology in its applied guise tends to avoid altogether any inspection of the notion that 'working on people' could have moral and political aspects.

3   More subtly, there is a range of ways of being, understanding the world and behaving in it that are functional, acceptable, average (or acceptably deviant from the average) and that achieving these is a proper goal of intervention and counselling.

The expert role would mostly be seen, by those who employ psychologists and by the psychologists themselves, as something used for good. Therapists, for example, are in the business not of controlling people but of helping them to be happy or at least to cope with the social world as it is. The same could rightly be said of other sorts of applied psychologists employed in education, industry or the criminal justice system. No kind of psychology is, in itself, 'radical' or 'progressive', and all branches of social psychology have been at odds with current social norms at one time or another. 'Scientific' social psychology has been much exercised, at many stages of its history, by how we should deal with major social problems. The experience of the Second World War, for example, spawned a number of now famous studies into the conditions under which ordinary people will torture others 'in obedience to orders' (Milgram, 1974) and the kinds of people most likely to do so (Adorno et al., 1950). Experimental psychologists such as Philip Zimbardo spent much of the 1960s and 1970s exploring violent behaviour and particularly the situations under which people will oppress and persecute others, stimulated by the phenomenon of lynch mobs on the one hand and the oppressive behaviour of American prison guards on the other (Zimbardo, 1969, 1976; Haney et al., 1973).

ACTIVITY 11.2   Can you think of other examples of this?

Examples include the study of 'bystander apathy' stimulated by a real-life murder which bystanders ignored (see Brown, 1996), and Margaret Wetherell's 1996a discussion of the motivation of some psychologists in studying 'race' and stereotypes. Social psychological research on prejudice and stereotyping is indeed one of the clearest examples of a line of work motivated to study a social problem *because* it is a social problem. (On the other hand, one should perhaps not over-emphasize or over-idealize the applied nature of this work, or Zimbardo's. Though it tackles social problems, it builds 'scientific' understanding more than it seeks immediate solutions and seeks to expand psychology's knowledge base more than it seeks to overcome prejudice or deindividuation. Most psychological researchers are academic psychologists first and concerned with practical applications only afterwards.)

Beyond this kind of study, however, social psychology has also been responsible for breeding resistance to its own social powers. The 'anti-psychiatry' movement had therapy as its main focus, but it was followed by a broader 'anti-psychology' movement. Social psychologists of the 1970s reacted very strongly against the implications of the scientific model of social and clinical work. They were not sure what social psychology *should* be – indeed, this is something we are still debating – but they were quite clear about what it should *not* be. Nigel Armistead's introduction to his *Reconstructing Social Psychology* (1974), a key work of the period, is a spirited attack on positivism and determinism. This develops into a 'radical humanism' in the writings of psychologists such as John Shotter, which opposes attempts to understand humanity through the metaphor of the 'generalized machine' (Gauld and Shotter, 1977) and tries to reassert social psychology as a *moral* science whose purpose is 'to increase not people's mastery over other people but their mastery over their own possible ways of life' (Shotter, 1974, p. 68). See also Shotter (1975) and Fransella (1975) for similar arguments.

A related attack on the 'human as machine' metaphor has been the attack in developmental psychology on the notion that the human infant is a passive recipient of learning and the popularization of the idea of 'the active child' (see Dallos, 1996). Inspired by the work of Bruner (1977), Trevarthen (1977), Brazelton and Main (1974) and others, this line of thought argues that what is missing from accounts of socialization is the realization that babies are *active* in seeking what they want and in initiating relationships; from the very beginning of their development they are biologically prepared to enter into social relationships. Thus socialization is not *only* a process in which the mother teaches her baby but is, rather, a two-sided interaction, with children teaching their mothers how to mother at the same time as they are learning from them; both parties to the interaction initiate as well as respond. In effect this turns social psychology upside down and questions its inherently individualistic stance; the question becomes not how children learn to engage in relationships (they do this, to some extent, from birth) but how they learn to become individual, isolated selves. It is then also apparent that this development of isolated individuality occurs in different ways *and to different degrees* in different countries, different subcultures or even different families.

4 Critical psychologies

> Scientists firmly believe that as long as they are not conscious of any bias or political agenda, they are neutral and objective, when in fact they are only unconscious.
>
> *(Namenwirth, 1989, p. 29)*

This kind of psychology, which stresses relatedness and interaction as more fundamental than individuation, might be seen as to some extent 'subversive'. Capitalism flourishes where the population (or at least the working-class population) takes for granted the value of individual advancement, competitiveness, self-sufficiency and self-discipline. (This was firmly believed by the Victorians, who promulgated these values in their tracts and in their schools.) To the extent that the 'individualistic lobby' is strong in social psychology, it is consonant with fundamental cultural themes and works to support and reproduce them. To the extent that psychology's attention turns to relationships, joint action and intersubjectivity, it may tend to undermine them.

Beyond this, and beyond the 'radical humanism' of writers such as Shotter and Fransella, the 1970s reached the realization among some authors that the same psychology which they were attacking as supportive of the existing unequal order could also be turned to subvert or change it. Thus the final chapter of Nick Heather's *Radical Perspectives in Psychology* (1976) is 'Psychology and the oppressed', suggesting that psychologists should actively be furthering the interests of women, black people and gay people and finishing with 'the idea that everybody is oppressed in our kind of society, even those we usually call the oppressors' (p. 126), advocating a Marxist psychology as one element in correcting the situation. Phil Brown (1974) calls even more strongly for psychology to take on board Marx's insights and work towards emancipation:

> Psychology, like the ruling-class forms of production/distribution it supports, believes in a pessimistic humanity for which 'original sin', 'instinct' or 'inappropriate response' dictate the need for social control. Marxism counters such an attitude with its own view of humanity ... transcending the past in the creation of newness ... Instead of passive pawns, we become active creators.
>
> *(Brown, 1974, pp. 165–6)*

To a large extent the politics is external to the psychology in this kind of work: social psychology is to *do* much what it has always done, but in different interests. Apart from specifically technical matters – e.g. harnessing techniques of persuasion – the goal is the development of human potential for collective sentiment and action beyond what a capitalist society regards as safe or convenient, and the emancipation of those in whose interests society is *not* currently organized. A recognition of the power of ideology – the presentation as natural, normal, right and in our own interest of ways of thinking and organizing the social world which, in fact, further the interests of one class or group over another – is present in the work of people like Heather and Brown. For the most part, however, they conceptualize it in a rather 'externalized' way, either as a deliberate conspiracy of the powerful to mislead or, more subtly, as 'false consciousness', a set of mistakenly accepted beliefs about the world which act to conceal real inequalities of power and privilege.

This tradition is still very live in social psychology, as witness a paper by Jost and Banaji (1994) on the concept of 'justification' – defined as 'an idea being used to provide legitimacy or support for another idea or for some form of behaviour'. They list social events, thoughts and feelings, aggressive or discriminatory behaviours, our own or other people's social status, in-group aggression or discrimination and the prevailing social conditions in general as matters which we find the need to justify. They distinguish ego-justification, group justification (in which stereotyping plays a major role) and what they call 'system justification':

> System justification is the psychological process by which existing social arrangements are legitimised, even at the expense of personal and group interest ... Central to this discussion is the concept of false consciousness, defined here as the holding of beliefs that are contrary to one's personal or group interest and which thereby contribute to the maintenance of the disadvantaged position of the self or the group ... Examples might include 'accommodation to material insecurity or deprivation' ... 'needs which perpetuate toil, misery and injustice' ... 'a kind of comfort in believing that one's sufferings are unavoidable or deserved' ... and thinking that 'whatever rank is held by individuals in the social order represents their intrinsic worth'.
>
> *(Jost and Banaji, 1994, pp. 1–2)*

Do you see any weakness in the way the concept 'ideology' is used by Jost and Banaji? Spend a couple of minutes thinking about this.   **ACTIVITY 11.3**

This way of looking at things entails a tendency to regard ideology and the social/societal world in general as some kind of constant environment, passively experienced, and to locate *action* at the level of individuals or groups. This separates the study of ideology from the empowerment of individuals. Ideology becomes a set of beliefs inherent in a society, experienced probably as self-evident truths, which come to regulate people's action and shape or constrain their choices. Most importantly, it is argued that these beliefs or 'self-evident truths' are supported by the evidence of existing inequalities – for example, the poor accepting that they must be less able or they would not be poor. This model can lead to a view of society as fragmented in terms of interests, with the capitalist class in a conscious and clever conspiracy to misrepresent the world in order to favour their own interests. Though such a conspiracy might exist in some instances, however, the force of what Jost and Banaji suggest is that the privileged groups may themselves be maintaining beliefs they have absorbed – in other words, that they too are 'cogs in the social machine'. Certainly one would not expect privileged groups to challenge the dominant ideologies which favour them, and there is substantial evidence that they rarely do so; the women's movement arises from women who have experienced oppression, for example, and challenges to racism come from under-privileged minority groups. However, in this view it is difficult to see how *anyone* ever manages to challenge the dominant ideology; it presents an 'over-determined' view of social relations.

Social psychology's reading of ideology became more sophisticated in the 1980s, as the theorization of the concept has developed outside the discipline. For example, Althusser's notion of ideology is not of a 'thing', a feature of the environment, but as the basis of any kind of social interaction; Althusser's ideology is not an aspect of environment – it *is* the environment.

> [Ideology is] not false consciousness or distorted perception [but] the organisation of material signifying practices that constitute subjectivities and produce the lived relations by which subjects are connected ... to the dominant relations of production and distribution of power ... in a specific social formation at a given historical moment.
>
> *(Ebert, 1988, p. 23)*

In other words, ideology creates both individuals and their social worlds: it is a framework of meanings within which we locate ourselves, discover what it means to be 'a person' and understand our (unequal) relationships with other such people and with social institutions. (See Wetherell, 1996a for a discussion of racism as part of the shifting construction of identity out of available ideological resources.) The force of talking about '*material* signifying practices' is to point out that we do not just learn from being told, but from living in a world ordered in a particular way. I learn how to be a factory worker or an academic or a student, for example, not by being told how to behave – or not *only* from being told – and not just by imitation, but by being cast in these roles, experiencing them and learning by living them.

Althusser's notion is that we are not socialized as such, but rather 'always/already social' – we are born into a world which consists of a framework of roles, meanings and expectations, concretized in social institutions, which pre-dates the birth of any given individual and into which the individual *must* fit if he or she is to have any social reality at all. (We are talking here not just of verbal statements about the social world, but also about the patterns inherent in how people act. See, for example, discussion of how boundaries are maintained and crossed on the factory floor and work discipline maintained or subverted in Collinson, 1992.) Children discover themselves as children, as sons or daughters, as school pupils and so on, by being recognized in these roles by other people (usually adults, who are *significant* and *powerful* other people, often charged as agents with the responsibility of socialization and behaving accordingly); in the process they are, quite unconsciously, adopting a social identity and defining themselves *to* themselves as persons. In other words, the roles exist before any given child comes to fill them; who the child shall be, and in what place within the network of social powers there, is a 'place' that was there before the child arrived to fill it.

A major impact of this kind of thinking on social psychology has been the realization that even the nature of 'the self' cannot be taken for granted as given but must be seen as something *produced* by continuing historical and structural processes, and as being constantly reproduced by them. In other words, the self is not fixed, any more than ideologies are fixed or, indeed, than social relations are fixed. Everything is subject to change; it is actively recreated by our acceptance of ideologies and therefore identity positions, and in the process of recreation it may subtly change (see also Wetherell, 1996b, particularly sections 1.3 and 1.4.) This line of thought was taken up by the editorial collective of the journal *Ideology and Consciousness* and used as the centre of a project to build an adequate theory of subjective experience in a socially deter-mined world (Adlam et al., 1977).

This is an improvement over the use of ideology earlier in the text, but it still has problems; spend a couple of minutes thinking what they might be. (Hint: think about the distinction between the hermeneutic and the emancipatory in Chapter 5 of this volume.)

ACTIVITY 11.4

This kind of analysis gives insight into why we are as we are, what we be-lieve and in whose interests we believe it; it makes a genuine link be-tween the personal and experiential and the structural and political. It still does not give a 'handle' for personal action, however – it is con-cerned with the production of selves by the socio-economic system. With the further development of Althusser's work on ideology by Michel Foucault, the notion of a 'grand theoretical explanation' in terms of generalized underlying causes began to dissolve into a more complex and fluid understanding of the importance of *particular* histories in the genesis of ways of mapping the social world ('discourses'). Previously Althusserian psychologists gratefully accepted this less deterministic and more fluid way of theorizing the insertion of the personal into the social (e.g. Henriques et al., 1984). One thing the language of discourses cer-tainly does is to help with the 'conspiracy' problem associated with the concept of 'false consciousness'. We can replace it with a notion more akin to 'complicity', which is more plausible. We do not have to say that the middle classes conspire to present a false picture of the world, whether consciously and explicitly (for which there is little or no evi-dence) or unwittingly but somehow in concert (which seems too large a set of coincidences to be believable). Instead we can posit a whole range of situations in which an idea or practice arises which is in the interests of middle-class people or groups who happen to be present and who, unremarkably, pick it up and use it or encourage it – to the detriment, say, of working-class people or black people whose interests are *not* served by it. Thus in place of a monolithic conspiracy to impose a single ideology we have a whole series of incidents, unrelated except that they involve people and groups of the same social standing. Thus we may see people as constituted by discourses in several important senses, but at the same time we can sensibly talk about them *using* discourses (and, of course, adapting them and changing them).

One consequence of the growth of critical theory into a concern with discourses and their historical provenance has been a renewed examination of the discipline of psychology itself. Perhaps the most influential work has been the detailed study of psychology's history and influence on particular institutions carried out by people such as Nikolas Rose (1985, 1989, 1990). One force of this kind of critique is to abolish absolutely the notion of the societal and the ideological as 'background' or 'constant environment' and expose it as something constantly changing – sometimes imperceptibly, sometimes with great rapidity – and as a *part* of individuals, not as something set *over* them. Attitudes and ways of seeing the world, this kind of thinking would argue, are not something fixed which we receive, but something we take up and reinforce or change by the way in which we use them. Thus it draws attention to the (witting or unwitting) active role of social psychologists in maintaining and shaping our collective creation, 'the world as we know it':

> Psychology is not merely a space in which outside forces have been played out, a tool to be used by pre-given classes or interest groups. To the extent that various of its theories have been more or less successful in enrolling allies ... in producing calculable transformations in the social world, in linking themselves into stable social networks, they have established new possibilities for action and control. In establishing and consolidating such networks, in forcing others to move along particular channels of thinking and acting, psychologists have participated in the fabrication of contemporary reality.
>
> *(Rose, 1990, p. 112)*

The effect of this tendency to analyse social psychology as a product and a producer of social histories and power-laden interactions between peoples and groups has been to raise a substantial problem for which there is as yet no consensus solution. What is to become of the discipline, if it can no longer see itself as the neutral and unbiased producer of truths about people but must recognize that it has been – like other disciplines – in the business of producing techniques for management? Some have argued that the realization of the discipline's role in answering political needs spells the end of social psychology: 'Social psychology – all of it – is a branch of the police; psychodynamic and humanistic psychologies are the secret police' (Richer, 1992, p. 118). Others have claimed that it should at least give up claims to overarching theory and concentrate on the insights that can be given by exploration of particular cases and applied psychological practice (Polkinghorne, 1992; Shotter, 1992).

Our feeling is that to announce the end of social psychology would be premature. Undoubtedly its insights and techniques will continue to be used for the purposes of social control in schools, hospitals, therapy, policing, industry and elsewhere, but to say this is not necessarily to attack the discipline's integrity: no society can exist without some form of social control, so the question is not *whether* social control but *what forms* of social control. Undoubtedly the theories of social psychology will continue to shape our way of seeing ourselves as selves and to inform 'common sense' about what it means to be human and to be social; it would be extraordinary if all the efforts of social psychologists did not have *some* impact on the world. Undoubtedly social psychologists will continue to think they could build a better world and, some of them, to act on this belief – and so they should, provided that other people monitor what they are doing. Social psychology itself has a good record of acting as its own critic and watchdog, as this chapter has demonstrated.

Perhaps most important, however, is that social psychology should continue to act as a body of *empowering* knowledge which can be used to *resist* social control – including the control which the discipline itself colludes in exerting:

> Psychology should seek the task of developing forms of inquiry by means of which people might arrive at a greater understanding of, and a greater degree of control over, their own behaviour and experience, their own relationships with others and their own place in the social order.
>
> *(Heather, 1976, p. 59)*

> ...the species-character of man, the human creativity which should be the end of existence, has become a mere means of survival. Man works to live rather than lives to work. As Marx said, 'The problem is to organise the empirical world in such a manner that man experiences in it the truly human, becomes accustomed to experience himself as man, to assert his true individuality'.
>
> *(p. 132)*

The techniques of social psychology have always been available to those who wish to rethink their lives and their relationships. Now, with the growth of social critique within social psychology, a more powerful tool of resistance is made available. Susan Gregory's 1996 article on 'disability' illustrates how this tool can be used: it unpicks an area of 'taken for granted' knowledge and shows that it is not necessarily true, that there are other ways of thinking about people who carry the label of 'handicap'. This kind of analysis of prevailing discourses, which social psychology shares with critical sociology, is probably the most emancipatory of all its techniques, and we hope that this volume has shown you how it may be used within your own lives.

We should note, however, that to emancipate people is still to manipulate them; we should be critical even of the critics when they recommend beliefs or courses of action as 'being in your best interest'. No branch of social psychology is emancipatory in all its applications, just as no branch is devoted solely to social control. To the extent that critical approaches become a new orthodoxy, a new resistance will doubtless by needed.

References

Adlam, D., Henriques, J., Rose, N., Salfield, A., Venn, C. and Walkerdine, V. (1977) 'Psychology, ideology and the human subject', *Ideology and Consciousness,* 1, pp.5–56.

Adorno, T.W., Frankel-Brunswick, E., Levinson, D.J. and Sanford, R.N. (1950) *The Authoritarian Personality,* New York, Harper.

Armistead, N. (ed.) (1974) *Reconstructing Social Psychology,* Harmondsworth, Penguin.

Boyle, M. (1990) *Schizophrenia: A Societal Delusion?,* London, Routledge.

Brazelton, T.B. and Main, M. (1974) 'The origins of reciprocity: the early mother-infant interaction' in Lewis, M. and Rosenblum, L.A. (eds) *The Effect of the Infant on its Care-Giver,* New York, Wiley.

Brown, H. (1996) 'Themes in experimental research on groups from the 1930s to the 1990's' in Wetherell, M. (ed.).

Brown, P. (1974) *Towards a Marxist Psychology,* New York, Harper.

Bruner, J. (1977) 'Early social interaction and language acquisition' in Schaffer, H.R. (ed.) *Studies in Mother-Infant Interaction,* London, Academic Press.

Burt, C. (1925) *The Young Delinquent,* London, University of London Press.

Collinson, D.L. (1992) *Managing the Shopfloor: Subjectivity, Masculinity and Workplace Culture,* Berlin, de Gruyter.

Dallos, R. (1996) 'Creating relationships' in Miell, D. and Dallos, R. (eds).

Ebert, T. (1988) 'The romance of patriarchy: ideology, subjectivity and postmodern feminist cultural theory', *Cultural Critique,* vol. 10, pp.19–57.

Foucault, M. (1982) 'The subject and power' in Dreyfus, H. and Rabinow, P. (eds) *Michel Foucault: Beyond Structuralism and Hermeneutics,* Brighton, Harvester.

Fransella, F. (1975) *Need to Change?,* London, Methuen.

Gauld, A. and Shotter, J. (1977) *Human Action and its Psychological Investigation,* London, Routledge and Kegan Paul.

Gregory, S. (1996) 'The disabled self' in Wetherell, M. (ed.).

Gross, G. (1974) 'Unnatural selection' in Armistead, N. (ed.).

Haney, C., Banks, C. and Zimbardo, P.G. (1973) 'Interpersonal dynamics in a simulated prison', *International Journal of Criminology and Penology,* vol. 1, pp.69–97.

Heather, N. (1976) *Radical Perspectives in Psychology,* London, Methuen.

Henriques, J., Hollway, W., Urwin, C., Venn, C. and Walkerdine, V. (1984) *Changing the Subject: Psychology, Social Regulation and Subjectivity,* London, Methuen.

Hollingshead, A.B. and Redlitch, F.C. (1958) *Social Class and Mental Illness: A Community Study,* New York, Wiley.

Ingleby, D. (1974) 'The job psychologists do' in Armistead, N. (ed.)

Jacoby, R. (1975) *Social Amnesia: A Critique of Conformist Psychology from Adler to Laing,* Boston, Beacon Press.

Jost, J.T. and Banaji, M.R. (1994) 'The role of stereotyping in system-justification and the production of false consciousness', *British Journal of Social Psychology,* vol. 33, pp.1–27.

Kvale, S. (ed.) (1992) *Psychology and Postmodernism,* London, Sage.

Laing, R.D. (1960) *The Divided Self,* London, Tavistock.

Miell, D. and Croghan, R. (1996) 'Examining the wider context of social relationships' in Miell, D. and Dallos, R. (eds).

Miell, D. and Dallos, R. (eds) (1996) *Social Interaction and Personal Relationships,* London, Sage.

Milgram, S. (1974) *Obedience to Authority,* New York, Harper and Row.

Namenwirth, M. (1989) 'Science through a feminist prism' in Bleir, R. (ed.) *Feminist Approaches to Science,* New York, Pergamon.

Polkinghorne, D.E. (1992) 'Postmodern epistemology of practice' in Kvale, S. (ed.).

Potter, J. (1996) 'Attitudes, social representations and discursive psychology' in Wetherell, M. (ed.).

Richer, P. (1992) 'An introduction to deconstructionist psychology' in Kvale, S. (ed.).

Rose, N. (1985) *The Psychological Complex: Psychology, Politics and Society in England 1869–1939,* London, Routledge and Kegan Paul.

Rose, N. (1989) *Governing the Soul: Technologies of Human Subjectivity,* London, Routledge.

Rose, N. (1990) 'Psychology as a "social" science' in Parker, I. and Shotter, J. (eds.) *Deconstructing Social Psychology,* London, Routledge.

Sapsford, R.J. (1997) 'The ethics of therapy in prison' in Cullen, E., Jones, I. and Woodward, R. (eds) *Therapeutic Communities in Prison,* Chichester, Wiley.

Shotter, J. (1974) 'What is it to be human?' in Armistead N. (ed.)

Shotter, J. (1975) *Images of Man in Psychological Research,* London, Methuen.

Shotter, J. (1992) '"Getting in touch": the meta-methodology of a postmodern science of mental life' in Kvale, S. (ed.)

Stevens, R. (ed.) (1996) *Understanding the Self,* London, Sage.

Szasz, T.S. (1962) *The Myth of Mental Illness,* London, Secker and Warburg.

Thomas, K. (1996a) 'The defensive self: a psychodynamic perspective' in Stevens, R. (ed.).

Thomas, K. (1996b) 'The psychodynamics of relating' in Miell, D. and Dallos, R. (eds).

Trevarthen, J. (1977) 'Descriptive analyses of infant communicative behaviour' in Shaffer, H.R. (ed.) *Studies in Mother-Infant Interaction*, London, Academic Press.

Watson, D. (1996) 'Individuals and institutions: the case of work and employment' in Wetherell, M. (ed.).

Wetherell, M. (ed.) (1996) *Identities, Groups and Social Issues*, London, Sage.

Wetherell, M. (1996a) 'Group conflict and the social psychology of racism' in Wetherell, M. (ed.).

Wetherell, M. (1996b) 'Life histories/social histories' in Wetherell, M. (ed.).

Zimbardo, P.G. (1969) 'The human choice: individuation, reason and order versus deindividuation, impulse and chaos', *Nebraska Symposium on Motivation,* vol. 17, pp.237–307.

Zimbardo, P.G. (1976) 'A social-psychological analysis of vandalism: making sense of senseless violence' in Hollander, E.P. and Hunt, R.G. (eds) *Current Perspectives on Social Psychology* (4th edn), New York, Oxford University Press.

Index